CONTEMPORARY YUGOSLAV LITERATURE

CONTEMPORARY YUGOSLAV LITERATURE

A SOCIOPOLITICAL APPROACH

by SVETA LUKIĆ

edited by GERTRUDE JOCH ROBINSON

translated by POLA TRIANDIS

UNIVERSITY OF ILLINOIS PRESS
Urbana, Chicago, London

First ten chapters, portions of the biographical notes, and
the chronology of literary events originally published
in Yugoslavia by Prosveta, Belgrade, in 1968 under the title
Savremena Jugoslavenska Literatura (1945–1965)

English translation, editor's notes, preface, and Chapter 11 © 1972
by The Board of Trustees of the University of Illinois

Manufactured in the United States of America

Library of Congress Catalog Card No. 77-166116

ISBN 0-252-00213-X

CONTENTS

A NOTE ON THE SPELLING AND PRONUNCIATION OF SERBO-CROAT WORDS

s = s as in single

ś = sh as in shell

c = ts as in hats

č = ch as in change

ć = similar to but lighter than
    č — as ch in march

ž = g as in mirage

z = z as in zoo

j = y as in yes

nj = ny as in canyon

g = g as in get

dž = j as in jump

dj = similar to but lighter than dž

lj = li as in billion

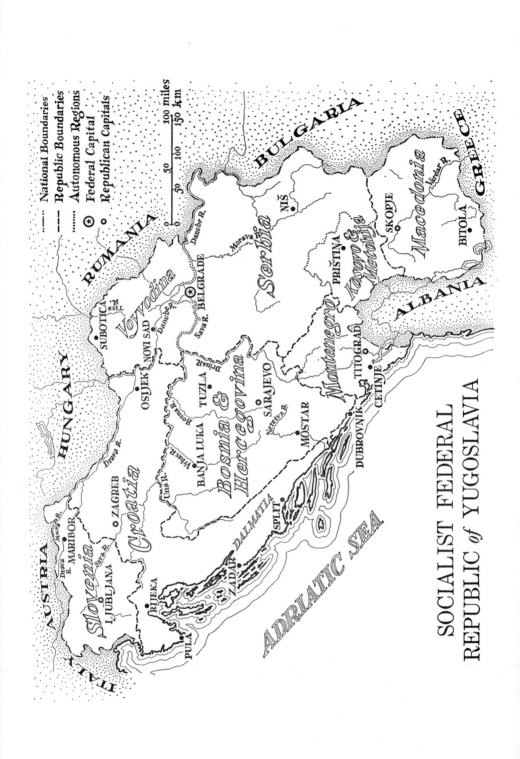

National Boundaries
Republic Boundaries
Autonomous Regions
⊗ Federal Capital
∘ Republican Capitals

100 miles
150 km
100
50
50
0

AUSTRIA

ITALY

HUNGARY

RUMANIA

BULGARIA

GREECE

ALBANIA

Slovenia

MARIBOR
Mura R.
Drava R.
Sava R.
LJUBLJANA

Croatia

Drava R.
∘ ZAGREB
Una R.
Krka R.

RIJEKA

PULA

Dalmatia

ZADAR

SPLIT

DUBROVNIK

Vojvodina

SUBOTICA
Tisa R.
NOVI SAD
Danube R.
Danube R.

OSIJEK

⊗ BELGRADE
Sava R.

Serbia

Morava R.

NIŠ

Bosnia & Hercegovina

BANJA LUKA
Vrbas R.
Bosna R.
TUZLA
Drina R.
SARAJEVO
Neretva R.
MOSTAR

Montenegro

TITOGRAD
CETINJE

Kosovo & Metohija

PRIŠTINA

Macedonia

SKOPJE
Vardar R.
BITOLA

ADRIATIC SEA

SOCIALIST FEDERAL
REPUBLIC *of* YUGOSLAVIA

EDITOR'S PREFACE

FOR MORE THAN two decades Yugoslavia has made headlines, first in the political arena and lately in the economic and cultural fields. Quite a number of books have been written about its political decentralization and experimentation with a mixed market economy. We have also heard about the transformation of the League of Communists into an "educator" and those novel organizational forms called workers' councils which run factories and publishing houses cooperatively. Much less is known, however, about Yugoslavia's unique and almost Western-style freedom in the cultural sphere.

When and how did de-Stalinization occur? What were the effects of the cultural thaw on literary style, subject matter and the production of books in general? Did the abrogation of the principles of socialist realism stimulate the emergence of new literary forms and a more variegated style of writing among Yugoslav authors? What is the party's role in literary organization today? And finally, how open is the country to European and American literary influences which have reshaped twentieth century thought and expression?

Sveta Lukić discusses all of these questions and many others. His book is unique in that it traces the interrelationship between literary style and factors such as party control, cultural expenditures, literary organization, and available audience. As such its goal is mainly theoretical, to utilize the complex phenomenon of "literary life" for the identification of aesthetic criteria. It is also the outspoken account of a literary critic who has himself been involved in many of the literary-political debates described. As such the book is both an intensely personal as well as a provisional document which affords us an intimate glimpse into the cultural struggle for freedom of expression in Yugoslavia.

Sveta Lukić, born in Belgrade in 1931, is one of the group of well-educated "new critics" who studied at Belgrade's faculty of pure philosophy. While still a student in the late fifties, he was one of the *Delo* editors when that journal spearheaded the fight for cultural liberalization. The impact of the "modernism-realism debate" is thus assessed from first-hand experience. Lukić is an essayist in the classical sense of this word. He publishes intellectual prose discussing contemporary literary problems and is interested in art as well. Among his books are: *Razlozi* (Reasons For) 1957; *Buna Protiv Reči* (Revolt Against Words) 1961; *Umetnost i Kriterijumi* (Art and Criteria) 1964, and *Estetička Čitanka* (A Reader in Aesthetics) 1964; as well as two volumes of poetry: *On Realism* (1969) and *Contemporary Serbian Poets* (1970).

In 1966, Lukić joined one of the largest Yugoslav publishing houses, Prosveta, in Belgrade, as editor of its essayistic and philosophical library *Karijatide*, which explores the theoretical foundations of twentieth-century thought. Like many of his colleagues, he is additionally active as a critic writing for various journals and newspapers, an author of a well-known radio series called "philosophical theater" about modern philosophy and a writer of provocative television plays. These explore the attempts of the Serbian petit bourgeoisie to fit into the new socialist society which is essentially alien to their customary way of life. He has been an adaptor of film scripts, and, finally, he is an unconventional denizen of the Belgrade literary milieu.

Since Sveta Lukić writes what he thinks, his books are always controversial. The present volume, too, has raised a stormy debate involving four main points. The first accusation contends that *Contemporary Yugoslav Literature* is not history but a personal account and evaluation of the author's Belgrade experiences and literary friends.

The critic points out that he never intended to write a history in the old-fashioned sense of the word, because there are as yet too few data for such an evaluation. Instead, he says the book analyzes "the relationship between literary life and literary standards, or the extent to which literary life influences the formation, the content, and the impact of literary standards. This question is theoretical and it is therefore most appropriate to consider my book as a sociologico-aesthetic treatise."

A second, frequently raised objection criticizes Lukić's use of the term "Yugoslav literature" as an undercover attempt at Pan-Serbian integration of otherwise diverse literary streams, such as the Croation, Slovenian, Serbian, Bosnian, Macedonian, Hungarian, and Albanian. Doubtlessly these streams have different historical origins, but the author points out "the sociological determinants of postwar Yugoslavia, and accordingly, the imperatives of postwar literary life are the same throughout the federal territory of Yugoslavia. . . . Therefore, this argumentation, or more precisely the lack of it, is primarily politically determined. . . . I insist and shall further insist on the necessity of overcoming this kind of regionalism and provincialism."

Third, there is his much debated assertion about the "mediocrity" of Yugoslav literature. Lukić feels that critics have misunderstood his use of the term which is not meant to be pejorative, but to indicate that the majority of literary productions hover around a "golden mean" as defined in the concluding chapter of his book. In addition, he points out that Yugoslav works share the historical fate of other small Balkan and Slavic literatures which are translated and published abroad primarily for their political or erotic aspects rather than for their intrinsic value. As to the final assertion, that he has not been complete in his chronology of literary events, Lukić notes that it is impossible for a single researcher to bring all the necessary material together. This will hopefully be the task of future historians who may want to build on this study.

The importance of Sveta Lukić's book is twofold: first, it introduces a new sociological concept, "literary life," which explains contemporary literary phenomena. Second, it discovers and clarifies a new stage, "socialist aestheticism," in the cultural development of communist societies. Even socialist aestheticism, which evolved out of a revolt against the dictates of socialist realism does not, however, permit complete freedom of expression in the arts. While socialist realism told an artist what to write, socialist aestheticism is a nega-

tive program telling the artist what not to write. As such it has encouraged a form of escapism in Yugoslav literature which manifests
itself in stylistic experimentation far removed from everyday reality.
Essayistic and fantastic prose as well as meditative poetry are new
trends fostered by socialist aestheticism in Yugoslavia.

The discovery of a literary phenomenon as pervasive as socialist
aestheticism is relevant not only for Slavophiles interested in Balkan
literature, but for sociologists and political scientists concerned with
understanding the democratization of Eastern European societies.
Lukić notes that socialist aestheticism in the arts is now on the wane
in Yugoslavia, where more modern trends are emerging. Yet other
socialist countries like Czechoslovakia and Hungary in the after-
math of their "thaws" are barely entering this stage. Once again
Yugoslavia's ideologists and writers have thus set the pace and become weathervanes anticipating directions of social and cultural
change which other Eastern European countries may traverse in
the not too distant future.

Sveta Lukić's book is the first in a projected series of University
of Illinois Press translations of modern Yugoslav thought in sociology, literature, politics, philosophy and history. These books aim
to acquaint American scholars with the intellectual ferment created
by debates between Marxist and other intellectuals in Yugoslavia
today. Three factors make this country particularly interesting to
the Western social scientist: its unique position as a bridge between
capitalist and socialist ideas and organization, the amount of experimentation with cultural, economic and political institutions encouraged by Tito's government, and the fact that developments here
have often been copied in other Eastern European societies.

Editing these pioneering works for an American audience presents
a number of technical problems which the reader of *Contemporary
Yugoslav Literature* must keep in mind. To begin with there is the
fact that this book was written for a well-informed internal audience which has personally experienced much of what Lukić talks
about. His commentary is therefore often elliptical, taking much
literary and political knowledge for granted. Where necessary the

editor has supplied background notes as well as commentaries for the orientation of the American reader.

Then, there is Lukić's sometimes Aesopian, sometimes conversational style which is difficult to render into English. While Lukić is outspoken in comparison with others writing about party influences and the lack of ideological programs in Yugoslav culture, an outsider must still occasionally make the effort to read between the lines. Finally, there is the problem of checking the adequacy of a translation. Here thanks must go to Dr. Petar Kokotović, a close friend of Lukic's, who gave unstintingly of his time and inspiration.

The author has written an *Epilogue* for this edition evaluating Yugoslav literary developments since 1965 to bring his foreign readers up to date.

GERTRUDE JOCH ROBINSON

AUTHOR'S INTRODUCTION

MANY READERS may be misled by the title of this book and thus expect a standard historical treatment of Yugoslav literary works produced in recent decades. My purpose, on the contrary, is primarily theoretical, to test the insights gained in two earlier works, *Estetička čitanka* and *Umetnost i kriterijumi.* These two books laid the theoretical aesthetic bases for a theory of literature which would have permitted a comparative aesthetic study on the one hand, or a broader sociocultural analysis on the other.

I decided in favor of the latter, which involves the task of analyzing the climate — literary, social, cultural, historical — in which literary standards are formulated and the ways in which they affect the work of art itself. This is most efficiently done by studying "average" literary output rather than masterpieces, because this is where aesthetic standards are most frequently molded by nonaesthetic considerations. It is therefore most appropriate to consider my book as a socioaesthetic treatise.

My own sociological approach differs from the classical in that it does not establish a clear, oversimplified relationship between the writer, the work and society. Such an approach never goes beyond interrelating the class struggle and ideology of an epoch with the content of the literary work. My investigation introduces the notion of "literary life" and views it as a complex phenomenon, including, however, such measurable factors as literary trends, politics, criticism, associations, journals, and the literary audience. Using contemporary Yugoslav literature as a testing ground, I have tried to prove that this sociological method can do more than point to "social equivalents." It can penetrate and illuminate the style and content of a work of art itself. In fact, it points up the existence of a new historical phenomenon: "socialist aestheticism." This socialist aestheticism becomes a stage in the development of the literatures of socialist countries when they liberate themselves from socialist realism. Socialist aestheticism has both positive and negative effects. On the positive side it emphasizes the autonomy of the literary work as literature, rejecting a utilitarian or propagandist role for art. Content, on the other hand, is negatively affected in that socialist aestheticism breeds a literature which fails to depict contemporary realities.

Four major conclusions emerge from the analysis:

1. Literary life in Yugoslavia has produced its own set of literary standards.

2. Taken together these standards make socialist aestheticism into an indirect program or negative program for literary creation in the postwar years.

3. This program has influenced the content of books, their style as well as their relationship to their audiences.

4. Socialist aestheticism, which need not influence a book's aesthetic quality, has introduced new literary trends into Yugoslav writing.

Since Yugoslavia lacks a history of contemporary literature my discussion will have to go into greater historical detail than would be necessary if previous studies were available. I will deal with this history, however, only from a very special angle selecting those factors which contribute to literary life. In addition, I want to assemble biblio-biographic material to be used in a history of literature yet to be written. The title of the current book, *Contemporary Yugoslav Literature,* and its subtitle more closely define the goals I have set myself in an attempt to provide a discussion of literary life and literary criteria in Yugoslavia.

S. L.

PART I. THE LITERARY SITUATION

1. LITERARY LIFE IN CONTEMPORARY YUGOSLAVIA

A DEFINITION OF LITERARY LIFE

TO DETERMINE the broader social and cultural context of a literature such as ours in Yugoslavia is impossible. We must therefore limit ourselves to a narrower field, not only for methodological reasons, since it is difficult to generalize generalities, but because there is a need for a framework which will encompass the entire complexity of literary creation and still permit rational inquiry. The complex of phenomena and relationships included in the concept "literary life" provides such a frame for the study of literature in any milieu. During the last 150 years literary life has had an immediate effect on literary creativity, just as it has been molded by the influences of literary creativity. Literary life combines literature with other human activities and within it literary standards themselves are formed.

How can we define literary life? Different definitions are possible. In most general terms, we can say that literary life includes all the determinants of literature, with the exception of the very nucleus itself, which is defined as the "creative literary moment." In other words, literary life is an ordered system of relationships between literature and society, between literature and an epoch. It expresses measurable and comprehensible realities, and for this reason it is most convenient and realistic to concern ourselves with it.

Literary life is made up of numerous components, such as literary directions, movements, groups, trends and currents, the connection between the state, the party, official ideology and literature, literary politics in general, literary criticism, and the audience. In addition there is literary organization itself, as well as the mass media, and such other factors as publishers, competitions and prizes; and finally, the social status of the writer and his understanding of his own responsibility and mission in society.

From this general definition it follows that literary life has been "part of the game" ever since a sociological orientation in aesthetics has existed. And truly the classical sociological school (Taine,[1] Guillot and Souriau) touches upon literary life, dealing with the relationships of reality and literature both broadly and in detail. The traditional biographical and psychological schools of criticism take at least some of the components of literary life into account. However, not even the most outspoken sociological aestheticians such as Georg Lukacs [2] emphasize the importance of literary life sufficiently. This is understandable since literary life disturbs their pattern of analysis.

The sociology of art — particularly after World War II — approaches literary life in a more precise and defined way.[3] Regardless of this, however, literary life was an object of research much earlier, but not in a sociological context. The first to deal with literary life were the Russian formalists: Viktor Shklovski, Boris Eichenbaum, Yuri Tinyanov, Roman Jakobson, Boris Tomasevski and others.[4] They were pioneers of modern theory and of the history of literature and to a certain extent, of instrumental literary criticism as well.

In a little more than a decade, they changed the traditional analysis of literary works. They corrected beliefs which, under the influence of romanticism, postulated that works of genius were isolated, exceptional phenomena which stood at the apex of their epochs. A belief, in short, which remained faithful to the old-fashioned static way of observing the manifold connections between art and reality.

---

[1] Cf. Hippolyte Taine, *Histoire de la littérature anglaise*, Paris, Hachette, 1899, xxii–xxxiv.

[2] Georg Lukacs, *Problemi realizma*, Sarajevo, Svetlost, 1957, pp. 152–61.

[3] Cf. Robert Escarpit, *Sociologie de la littérature*, Paris, Presses Universitaires, 1956, pp. 5–16.

[4] So far the most exhaustive reviews and evaluations of formalist teaching are in: *Russian Formalism*, by Victor Erlich (The Hague, Mouton and Co., 1955); *Vybor z formalnej metody*, Trnava, 1941; Flaker-Skreb's *Stilovi i razdoblja* (Naprijed, Zagreb, 1964); and Branimir Donat's essay "Tzv ruski formalizm" (*Delo*, 1964, no. 8–9).

Because they had understood and reinterpreted the interrelationship between form and style, the formalists abandoned the isolated treatment of individual literary works. They also parted with the tradition of concentrating only on outstanding literary creations, turning their attention to the second-rate works, periodicals, literary circles and popular literature. Tinyanov and Eichenbaum have written about this in their introduction to *Russian Prose*[5] and Tinyanov has discussed it separately and more precisely in his article on literary evolution.[6] Historical and theoretical considerations thus led the formalists to be interested in literary life and realize its significance. Marxist sociological criticism after 1925 forced men like Boris Arvatov[7] to bring about a synthesis between the sociological and formal methods.

The formalists, however, were strenuously opposed by such a liberal as Lunacarski, and by the more serious Marxist critics, Kohan and Polanski. They were also thoughtlessly attacked by the dogmatic literary group led by Averbakh and Bobrov, who wanted to uproot formalism altogether.[8] Their concentration on the problems of literary life may therefore be considered a concession which the formalists were able to make without greatly undermining their critical concepts, since their sociological outlook included only a superficial layer of social equivalents of literature. Literary life, as we have said, is made up of a number of nonliterary factors, such as the distribution of power in society, or the means and conditions of production.

Viktor Zirmunski reproaches the formalists for this seeming revision of their "literary order" of phenomena.[9] On the other hand,

---

[5] *Russkaya proza* (in the edition of B. M. Eichenbaum and J. I. Tinyanov.) Leningrad, Academia, 1926.

[6] Tjnyanov, Yuri, "Vopros o literaturno evoluciji," *Na literaturnom postu*, 1927, no. 10.

[7] Boris Arvatov, "O formal'no-sociologiceskom metode," *Pečat i revoluciya*, 1927, no. 3.

[8] Discussion, "Uz rasprave o formalistickoj metodi — K sporam o formal'nom metode." Participants: Boris Eichenbaum, Lev Sakulin, Sergei Bobrov, Anatoli Lunacharski, Pierre Cohen, and Valeriy Polyanski, *Pečat i revoluciya*, 1924, no. 5.

[9] Viktor Zirmunski, "Voprosy teorii literatury," *Academia*, Leningrad, 1928.

Shklovski humorously pointed out that the greatest fault of the formalists was that they had failed to draw up socio-literary equivalents, and had gone to extremes in their terminology. In other words, he felt that the formalists were inconsistent.

Eichenbaum formulated the best definition of "literary life" in his article "About Literary Life," published in 1927 in the periodical, *Na postu,* which was the organ of the angriest antiformalists.[10] But in spite of this an objective study of literary life did not really develop. On the contrary, the formalistic school was quickly banned together with other literary groups formed in the first decade after the October Revolution. It is a pity that this task was interrupted at the very stage when the formalistic and sociological approaches to literature were drawing closer together. As a result of this failure, the sociological orientation in literature is abstract and rigid at present, and historicism without sociology is meager, academic, and, to a large extent sterile.

SPECIFIC FEATURES AND PERIODS
OF CONTEMPORARY YUGOSLAV LITERATURE

From the theoretical point of view, our central question is: How are criteria for evaluating literature developed within the climate of literary life and what do they have in common? To this we must add a second question: Do the criteria become norms and programs of literary creativity, and if so, to what extent? I do not think that these problems have previously been stated and investigated in this way. We must therefore analyze those main elements of literary life which have just been enumerated. This kind of primarily theoretical investigation is commonsensical and does not pretend to be as exact as the natural or the more established of the social sciences. Combining this theoretical approach with the historic, I wish to investigate the newest period of Yugoslav literature, which is a significant part of her contemporary history. I think the field is well chosen. It is narrow, relatively defined, and yet suitable for extract-

[10] Boris Eichenbaum, "Literatura i literaturnyi byt," *Na literaturnom postu,* 1927, no. 9.

ing general conclusions on the basis of observable phenomena. A sociological accent will dominate because of the nature of the subject.

It is difficult to study phenomena which are still current and which cannot be judged definitively in literary-historical terms. However, this does not mean that one must go to the other extreme, such as one segment of postwar Yugoslav literary criticism, which almost completely abandoned the literary treatment of poetry and literature. If nothing else, the study of "living history" has the allure of authenticity to discover the rhythm of literary life as well as the evolutionary process of a literature. In approaching our living history, we will first have to clear up some existing questions which are frequently interpreted in different and even opposite ways.

First of all, we are faced with the question of the basic and specific characteristics of Yugoslav literature. Miroslav Krleža has written on several occasions about this, and it seems to me that this is one of the central themes of his rich, temperamental, and lucid aesthetic theory. Svetozar Petrović formulated these general characteristics in a single sentence, found in his account at a symposium on Yugoslav literature in Sarajevo 1964: "The methodological questions which are specific to the study of our literatures have grown out of the particular historic conditions in which these literatures developed here at the outskirts of a civilization to which they belong today, but as the literatures of a small, underdeveloped and multi-national country." [11]

While the history of our contemporary literature is not particularly complex, the term "contemporary" itself is not very precise. What are its historical limits, and more exactly when does that period begin? In 1941 or in 1945? It is possible to push the beginning even further back. The period 1930–41 also is of questionable use because it is split up into a number of segments. Modernism, which developed as a movement before the end of World War I, had already run its course by that time. Surrealism appeared and then "social literature" — two movements which are still with us. This is a fact which we must bear in mind if we wish to construct a history of

[11] Svetozar Petrović, "Metodološka pitanja specifična za proučavanje naših nacionalnih književnosti," *Putevi*, 1965, no. 3.

literature. And yet most critics stubbornly insist on periods which are delimited by wars, possibly to show even in the history of literature that we are a warriorlike nation.

For the sake of convenience let us take 1941 or 1945 as the beginning of the contemporary period, because it suggests the outlines of a more realistic division into literary periods. It is a good beginning point since it indicates that our literature has gone through the same developmental phases as other parts of postwar social life, including all branches of art, science, philosophy, political practice, and as a matter of fact Yugoslav society as a whole.

One more thing needs to be taken into account: the history of literature should be divided into periods according to dominant directions, styles, artistic works and well-known personalities. Yet this is difficult because we are dealing with a historic process which is still going on. Consequently, our chronology needs to be based on certain fixed points of literary life itself. Such an approach would at the same time be most objective. According to this criterion, and according to the dominant characteristics of literary life, four phases of postwar Yugoslav literature stand out:

From 1945 to 1950. The initial period of unification divided into two parts, with the second literary period after 1947 grayer and less fertile.

From 1950 to 1955. The period of polemics in the struggle against socialist realism and dogmatism, representing a search for cultural and general social liberation.

From 1955 to 1960. The period of flowering in which domestic literary discussions dominate, in particular the clash between modernism and realism — a period also characterized by the development of varied literary trends and by notable creative achievements.

From 1960 onward. A quiet period during which passions were calmed and new results and analytical approaches were produced.

If we look more narrowly at the last twenty years of Yugoslav literature we can basically distinguish two periods:

From 1945 to 1950. The phase of unification when the attempt

was made to create national realism as a more moderate variation of socialist realism.

Since 1950. The phase of liberation and domination of socialist
aestheticism.

In this discussion we will however follow the first, more detailed,
division in order better to emphasize the most important lines of
development in postwar Yugoslav literature.[12] The second part of
the book will deal with each element of Yugoslav literary life separately, as well as with their interdependence. We will also explain
there in greater detail certain aspects of our newest literary history in order to complete the picture. Now, within the framework
of this chronology, we have to take a quick look at some of the turning points of literary life in postwar Yugoslavia.[13]

LITERARY LIFE 1945 TO 1950

In the first two years after the liberation and the revolution there
was artistic liveliness both in Belgrade and in some other Yugoslav
centers. Ilya Ehrenburg notes a similar thaw in the Soviet Union in
which a promising normalization had set in. There the period covers
the end of the war until the Zhdanov report on the periodicals *Zvezda*
and *Leningrad.* It is enough to mention the prose of Alexander Bek
and Victor Nekrasov, the articles of Ehrenburg, the wartime poems
of Constantin Simonov and Alex Surkov, the verses of David Simonov,
Boris Sluchko, Mikhail Lukonin and Yevgeny Dolmatovski. The publication of such works would have been unthinkable either previously
or subsequently, at least not until the appearance of Alexander Sol-
zhenitsyn, a phenomenon which is perhaps isolated.[14]

In Yugoslav literature at the same time some very creative works
appeared. Older writers were publishing texts begun earlier under

---

[12] Cf. *Mala enciklopedija,* Belgrade, Prosveta, 1968 (2nd edition, in press)
section on contemporary literature in Yugoslavia, which uses the more limited
division into two phases.

[13] From now on those essays and articles which are mentioned in the Appendix in the Chronology of Literary Events will be cited only where necessary for
clarity.

[14] Ilya Ehrenburg, *Ljudi, godine, život,* translation, Belgrade, Kultura, 1967.

the occupation; among these Ivo Andrić, Isadora Sekulić, Veljko Petrović, and Jus Kozak are most important. Then there were the prewar Slovenian expressionists, like Anton Vodnik and Jože Udović, and in Croatia, Petar Šegedin, Vladan Desnica and Ranko Marinković, who produced works which were either a continuation, or in some cases, a crowning achievement in realistic writing. Finally, writers like Goran Kovačić, Radovan Zogović, Skender Kulenović, Mirko Banjević, Milan Dedinac, Oskar Davičo, Matej Bor, and Venko Markovski were already adding new poetic accents growing out of the national liberation war.

At that time, too, traditional lyric poets who were touchingly, but unsuccessfully, trying to capture the theme of the building of socialism received considerable praise. They included Desanka Maksimović, Gustav Krklec, and Gvido Tartalja, as well as such former members of the socialist literature movement as Jovan Popović, Čedomir Minderović, Tanasije Mladenović, Dušan Kostić and Marin Franičević. Finally, a young generation appeared on the scene, the "prugaši" * who were inspired by the building of a new society but were semitalented and illiterate. Exceptions among this group were Vesna Parun and Jure Kastelan, who were already outstanding poets, while others such as Stevan Raičković, Branko Radičević and Radomir Konstantinović matured later and freed themselves from this poetry and its mold.

Publishing activity was renewed under strong and direct Soviet influence, which was evident in the organization of publishing houses, in the contents of publishing programs, and in the style of editing. A string of journals began to appear in all regional centers, some of them similar in format to the "fat" Russian ones. Belgrade's review *Književnost*, for instance, was fascinatingly reminiscent of Russia's *Novi Svyat*.

The development of Macedonian literature is also very characteristic of this period. Blaže Koneski says:

> For the first time since the liberation it (Macedonian literature) can develop fully. Poetry has the greatest flowering and is the leading form

---

* Young people who volunteered for youth brigades to build railroads and streets. — *Ed.*

of literature. At the end of the Second World War and immediately following, a new generation of poets appears: Slavko Janevski, Blaže Koneski,
Aco Šopov, Gogo Ivanovski. They liberated Macedonian poetry from its
folk stimulus and discovered new possibilities for Macedonian poetic language. Prose, too, appears for the first time in this period, searching for
mature artistic expression. The first prose writers are Vlado Maleski,
Jovan Boškovski, Kole Časule, Georgi Abadžijev. The struggle for national
liberation and the affirmation of a new life are the main literary themes
in the first postwar years; romantic in spirit this writing is often exclama-
tory and its greatest weakness is its schematism. Regardless of this, however, the period did produce some good prose and poetry.[15]

The critic Hasan Mekuli gives us details about Yugoslav literature
in the Albanian tongue (Shiptar) which also first appeared in the
period after 1945:

The beginnings of this literature are relatively old, but have not been
studied sufficiently. They are tied to the tradition of folk literature, as
well as to a number of individuals who wrote illegally in the 19th century
either in their native Albanian using Arabic characters or in Arabic. The
most noted writers of that period are Tahir Efendi Luka (Djakovica),
Tahir Efendi Popova (Uroševac), Redzep Voka (Tetovo), Haili Malići
(Orahovač), Imer Lufti Pečarizi and Lazer Ljumezi (Prizren), Saip
Žurnadžiju and others.* In the period since World War II with its new
conditions of social-political economic and cultural life, an Albanian literature has originated which is in many ways new. It has developed both
under the influence of native Albanian literature as well as the literatures of other Yugoslav peoples. All kinds of literary forms are represented and various trends manifested and a new constellation of writers
has emerged.

The dean of this literature is the poet Esad Mekuli, an active partici-
pant in the revolutionary ferment of the interwar period, editor of the
literary journal *Jeta e re*, translator, author of articles and two collections
of poems. Others who belong to the older generation are Hivzi Sulejmani,
a prose-writer (collection of stories *Vetar i kolona*), the chronicle *Ljudi*,
the comedy *Miš u džepu*; Mark Krasnići, writer and scholar; Tajar Hatipi,
story-teller and children's writer; the dramatist Josip V. Relja (*Nita*); the

---

[15] Blaže Koneski, "Makedonska književnost," article written for *Mala enciklopedija*, Belgrade, Prosveta, 2nd edition, in press.
* The names in parentheses are towns in the regions near Albania. — *Trans.*

novelist Sinan Hasani; the story-teller and dramatist Murteza Peza and
the critic Vehap Sita.

Albanian literature developed more intensively after the founding of
the periodical *Jeta e re* which gathered around it some 200 creative writers
from all Albanian regions of Yugoslavia including Serbia, Macedonia,
Montenegro and Croatia. Its pages publicized works by the middle generation such as: Enver Derčeku, the poet; Ramiz Kelmendi, the story-
teller; Hasan Mekuli, the critic; Murat Isaku, the poet and prose writer;
Fahredin Gunga, the poet, and others.[16]

After a brief flowering, the situation suddenly deteriorated between 1947 and 1950. It brought literary silence for the significant
writers on the one hand and a unification of the less fertile minds
who remained in the literary "arena" on the other. A partial explanation for this is given by existing circumstances: the specific political
position of Yugoslavia, in the East-West struggle, a position which
was further complicated by the Cominform expulsion, and the very
real social-political difficulties of the country in its transition from
a monarchy to a socialist republic.

In the Soviet Union, the first country of socialism, socialist realism
was already in control through omnipotent formulas about art and
monolithic artistic practices. Its influence did not bypass Yugoslavia
entirely, although it is a historic fact that that particular line did
not catch on too well even before 1948. The writings of the poet,
critic, and politician Radovan Zogović also reflect this. He was one
of the most influential men of literary politics in the first years after
the liberation and was later considered one of the most fantastic
literary Informbureauists in Yugoslavia.

At that time a new trend appeared which stressed the need for
a critical approach to the contemporary world. Krleža's text "Književnost danas," published in 1946 in the first number of *Republika*
suggested this, though this line of thought was not adopted at the
time. In Yugoslavia socialist realism manifested itself more strongly
in the fine arts than in literature, although there were certain examples, such as some of Ivo Andrić's shorter and weaker pieces
which were written in its spirit. Though the Yugoslav writers' po-

---

[16] Hasan Mekuli, "Književnost na albanskom jeziku u Jugoslaviji," *op. cit.*

lemic against Stalin called for the abandonment of the principles of socialist realism, dogmatism and rigidity continued to exist and in some instances increased. Contemporary books and periodicals confirm this assessment, particularly two anthologies of poetry and prose by young Yugoslav writers. The same picture is painted in miniature by Risto Tošović.

In criticism, a division into realism and nonrealism, or rather realism and formalism, which covered all aesthetic problems further corroborates this particular phase. Realism was declared to be the very essence of art. That which could not be included in this category was called formalism and judged to be worthless, damaging, and reactionary, and, in a last line of attack, as the work of the enemy.

LITERARY LIFE IN THE FIFTIES

In the initial period, approximately up to 1950, there was pressure to unify and homogenize writers along ideological-aesthetic lines. Instead of lively debates a relatively unified chorus dominated the scene, especially between 1947 and 1950. Although the basic tone remained dogmatic, socialist realism did not take over completely.

After 1950 there was a rallying of writers or more precisely, a new kind of unification. It was in many ways the very opposite of what had gone before, progressive, and antidogmatic. It grew out of the battle against Stalin and against our domestic dogmatism in art and aesthetics. Its real nature was political and literary-political. It was often a disorganized, affective, meaningless, unpersuasive, and declaratory polemic which was however guided by a just cause for revolt. It took the form of a long collective monologue directed against socialist realism.

Parallel and integral to this debate was the desire to publish and freely use the insights of modern literature — both international and native — to liberate current cultural and artistic creativity. This struggle anticipated and then accompanied an ever stronger and more exuberant upturn of modern Yugoslav art.

The new era in Belgrade began with the publication of Oskar Davičo's essay "Poezija i otpori" which was read without repercussions in 1949 at the Serbian Writers Association, but was not published until 1951 in *Mladost*. The text played an extremely important role in the liberation and de-dogmatization of our literature. It pointed the way for new developments in Yugoslav literature. The same was accomplished by Dobrica Ćosić's novel *Daleko je sunce*.

In Croatia Petar Šegedin's report at the Congress in Zagreb in 1949 played a simlar role.[17] Since the other republics also had cultural awakenings it is obvious that general conditions for the liberation of Yugoslav literature were ripe. During the years of debates, criticisms were often carried to extremes, suddenly demanding that art should serve no one and nothing. Dogmatic Marxist aesthetics were discredited with the argument that there are neither Marxist physics nor Marxist lunches or the like. This is the period during which our aestheticism was created — a specific and characteristic phenomenon in the art of socialist countries, and world art as a whole.

In the years after 1950, literary life became stronger, richer and more freely flowing. Our first real modern works of art have their beginnings at this point. Literature spread and there was increasing variety. Take for example avant-garde prose, touched off by Oskar Davičo's novel, *Pesma*. Original new works by Ranko Marinković, Vladan Desnica, Edvard Kocbek, Dobrica Ćosić, and Antonije Isaković, provided variations on the more classical writers like Ivo Andrić (who at that time was completing *Prokleta avlija*), Mihailo Lalić, Mirko Božić, Vjekoslav Kaleb, and Ciril Kosmač. Heading the new, modern Belgrade school of poetry were Ciril Zlobec, Zvonimir Golob, Mak Dizdar, Mateja Matevski, Gane Todorovski, and others. In this period too the essays of Dušan Matić and Marko Ristić were influential, as were the ideas of the critic Borislav Mihajlović Mihiz.[18]

In the field of literary criticism, the debate between Zoran Mišić and Milan Bogdanović on the meaningfulness and meaninglessness of poetry pinpoints the moment when freer internal dialogue began. In Belgrade a controversy flared up between the young fighting group

---

[17] V. Vlatko Pavletić, "Književnost prelomnih desetlječa," *Borba*, December 4, 1966.

[18] Cf. Dušan Matić, *Anina Balska Haljina* SKZ, 1956; Marko Ristić, *Od istog pisca*, Novi Sad, Matica Srpska, 1957; Borislav Mihajlović, *Od istog čitaoca*, Belgrade, Nolit, 1956.

rallied around the periodical *Mladost* and the conservative *Književne novine*. It culminated in 1952, a year marked by constant skirmishes between the newly founded paper *Svedočanstva* and the leaders of *Književne novine*. Both of these groups were fluid and provisional and by the end of 1952 their publications were already banned.

The following year there was a premature and fruitless attempt in Belgrade to gather the elite of both journals, as well as writers from other republics, around a new publication *Nova misao*.[19] This periodical was, however, short-lived, and publication was stopped after the fall of Djilas. In fact, the entire Djilas affair affected the men and atmosphere of *Nova misao*.

After the stormy events of January, the year 1954 was quiet. Only Voja Rehar continued the crusade against dogmatism bravely and alone in the reconstituted *Književne novine*. This crusade began the previous year with a polemic against Boris Ziherl, who questioned the value of French existentialism. The same year the cultural student newspaper, *Vidici*, introduced a new literary generation including Peter Džadžić, Jovan Hristić, Borislav Radović, Svetlana Velmar-Janković and Bora Ćosić. But passions still dominated reasoned analysis as shown by the article by Puniša Perović, published in *Nova stvarnost*, in which he roundly attacked this new generation as well as Eli Finci, the critic who supported modern literature.

By the beginning of 1955 the realism-modernism polarization however became quite clear. This polarization, which had germinated in the shelter of our affective and undifferentiated aestheticism, soon went beyond this phase both in a good and a bad sense. It was meaningful insofar as it defined two opposing approaches in art; emphasis on reality on the one hand and stylistic experimentation on the other. This conflict clarified the real content of the earlier polemics. Many critics and writers joined the debate, particularly in Belgrade where they formed two camps, each centered around one of the new periodicals, *Savremenik* and *Delo*. The two groups opposed each other in bitter polemics about transpositions, such as that between

[19] Cf. the discussion at the Plenum of the Communist Party of Yugoslavia, *Politika*, January 21, 1954.

Petar Džadžić, the actively critical editor of *Delo*, and Ivan Lerik, the rising star of *Savremenik*.

In the fifties literary life in Skopje was mainly organized around the periodicals *Sovremenost* and *Razgledi*. Here too, however, a similar controversy flared up in literary theory and practice between the realists Dimitar Mitrec, Dimitar Solev, and Gorgi Stardelov and the modernists Aleksandar Spasov and Milan Djurčinov. The theoretical discussions of Mita Hadži Vasilev on reflection and expression were mainly related to Macedonian literature.

In Sarajevo, the controversy between modernism and realism was no less sharp, though it did not include written polemics. Fighting on the side of modern tendencies were Slavko Leovac, Husein Tahmiščić and Vuk Krnjević. In Zagreb, the main exponents of antidogmatism were the editors and collaborators of the periodical *Krugovi* among them Josip Barković, Vlatko Pavletić, Nikola Milićević, Milivoj Slaviček, Zvonimir Golob, and others. Literary life in Ljubljana finally had its own more marked characteristics, since the struggle was broader and more open. Here the progressive younger writers, Janko Kos, Taras Kermauner, Primož Kozak, Dominik Smole, and Dane Zajc, rallied around the periodical *Beseda*.

It is interesting to note that in this struggle which began in 1950, poetry and painting, both abstract forms, were the greatest centers of controversy. Historically the victory was won by the modernist trend, which espoused the cause of free creativity, the search for new forms of expression, and the equality of various kinds of literary style and currents, from popular to avant-garde.

Among the young and the middle generation few artists resisted the temptation to modernize their means of expression. The transformation of certain former socialist writers such as Tanasije Mladenović, Čedomir Minderović, and Risto Tošović, who belonged to the first postwar generation, is characteristic. They became the first "modernists."[20] Their transformation was a result of a number of innovative books, contact with modern world art, and also the general atmosphere of democratization in society and the Communist

---

[20] Predrag Palavestra, "Srpska poezija," *Savremenik*, 1967, no. 6, pp. 510–12 and 515–21.

party. Meanwhile, literary and art criticism continued to be disorganized, even though they were not completely secondary in this movement.

In evaluating this period it is extremely important to underline the following: the modernism-realism debate was the battle cry in the fight for normal cultural relations between Yugoslavia and the world, and for stylistic and critical freedom, as well as the broader question of political democratization in socialism. In a certain sense, the art, and especially, the literature of this period represented one of the most important ideological battlegrounds, considering the reverberations caused throughout the country and abroad, and especially in the Soviet Union, by the battles fought in Belgrade.[21]

From the vantage point of today these discussions turn out to have been above all broadly cultural in nature and not limited to literature, art or aesthetics. Debates were carried on by "fronts." And yet, those who were in the motley camps must have already been aware at that time of their differences and even of their discords. On the modernist side, this was brought to light in 1955 in the December issue of *Delo*, and in a journal of many opinions entitled *Prilike*. But unfortunately participants did not go much beyond this initial realization.

In the following years there was greater tolerance often achieved, however, by force and through party penalties. In the beginning, opposing camps would recognize a writer and his work for tactical reasons. Subsequently, literary works came to be valued more and more for their own intrinsic worth and for the cause which they represented. Literary fredom grew with each work and modern artistic tendencies became recognized, at least to the extent that they were guaranteed the right to exist, to receive prizes, and so forth.

The processes by which the modernism-realism camps became more flexible was not simple. Some convincing examples are given

[21] R. Volodina, "V bor'be za realizm," *Inostrannava literatura*, 1958, no. 6 (reply: Ervin Šinko, "O borbi za realizam R. Volodine," *Delo*, 1959, no. 2); Z. Gerškovîć, "Krah revizionisteskih pseudoprorokov," *Zvezda*, 1958, no. 11 (reply: Mila Stojnić, "Ni utuk na utuk ni odgovor," *Delo*, 1959, no. 4); also A. Maliska and K. Zelinski at the 3rd Congress of Writers of the USSR, "III vsesojuznyi s'ezd pisatelej SSSR," *Sovetskyi pisatel*, Moscow, 1959, p. 65.

by the editors of *Delo*. If not from the very beginning, then certainly from 1957 onward, some of the editors and most active collaborators were in favor of finally beginning discussions of "sensitive" literary questions with their counterparts. First of all, they wanted to raise the topic of differences, literary, aesthetic and other, among the writers of the "modernistic" camp, and second they wished to introduce critical evaluations of new works. Until that time all editors, and in particular Oskar Davičo, had prohibited their periodicals from reviewing their own and friends' books. Those who were in agreement with the new strategy did not care whether this would spell doom to existing groups or whether the dialogues took place within the existing framework. It was essential, in their minds, to overcome the restrictiveness of existing groupings and to encourage basic criticism in order to make further differentiation in our literary life possible.

Other editors felt that this would be interpreted as a weakness by the opposing camp. And yet the editorial board of *Delo* fell apart in 1958 precisely because it was unable to solve this and similar questions. In other words, the writers who had gathered around that periodical had not been able to find a framework for something which was already at that time an essential need of our literary life. A more objective differentiation of our literature was not sanctioned, nor was a purely literary analysis accepted as a critical approach.

Consequently there followed a new, almost apathetic period which continues up to the present. In this last quiet decade from 1960 to 1970, the following, at least, had to become evident: that previous discussions which were too polemical and emotional had an immediate and many sided effect on our literary life, and indeed on our creativity. Not only were these discussions justified historically, but they had a definite and doubtlessly positive significance. Despite all exaggerations, especially in 1952 and 1955, these polemics opened the way for greater creativity. They made many literary works possible, sometimes, in fact, provoking them. This applied not merely to isolated works, but rather to entire currents of new Yugoslav literature. At least at that time significant ideas were being discussed. Finally, since all that was negative was brought to light, we were able to overcome the clearly defined limits and limitations of our postwar literary atmosphere.

LITERARY LIFE IN THE SIXTIES

The period after 1960 led to the further flowering of Yugoslav literature. During this time notable poetic works were created by Dušan Matić, Desanka Maksimović, Ivan V. Lalić, Borislav Radović, Branko Miljković, Slavko Mihalić, Vlado Gotovac, Irena Vrkljan, Edvard Kocbek, Cene Vitopnik, Jože Dudović, Dane Zajc, Mateja Matevski, Vuk Krnjević, Mak Dizdar, and others. In addition, Andrej Hing, Primož Kozak and Dominik Smole (drama), Slobodan Novak, Antun Šoljan, Mihailo Lalić, Antonije Isaković, and Dimitar Solev distinguished themselves with their new prose writing.

The work of a few young critics seeking a deeper interpretation and reevaluation of our traditional national values is perhaps most characteristic of this period. They emerged after the majority of critics ceased their ever sharper, emptier and more meaningless polemics. In this field, where literary criticism and literary history meet, serious works were produced in Belgrade by Miodrag Pavlović, Petar Džadžić, Zoran Mišić, Zoran Gavrilović, and Zoran Gluščević. In Zagreb, almost all the younger critics turned toward the instrumental interpretation of literary works. The Slovenes, especially Janko Kos and Taras Kermauner, successfully interpreted Slovene literary history and contemporary art in sociological terms. The Macedonian critics, Aleksandar Spasov, Milan Djurčinov, and Gane Todorovski, increased the Macedonian sense of identity by illuminating the personalities and works of the past. On the whole our criticism became informed, more literate, and more objective.[22]

The younger generation which got its start at the close of the first polemic against Stalin, around 1954, was, however, unable to penetrate the attention of professional circles. The tragic suicide of Branko Miljković, poet, essayist, translator, Bohemian, and lover of life symbolizes their neglect. In Belgrade this generation included

[22] On the formation of currents in Yugoslav literary criticism, see "Simpozij o kritici," *Razlog*, 1964, no. 4.

the group around *Vidik*, in Zagreb they were the former members of the periodical *Krugovi*; in Macedonia this same generation was tied to the periodical *Razgledi*. In Bosnia they were the lonely "warriors" Slavko Leovac, Husein Tahmiščić and Vuk Krnjević. The Slovenian segment of this group traveled the rocky path from *Beseda* to *Perspektiva* while the younger Montenegrins briefly rallied around the review *Susreti*; and the Hungarians from Voyvodina were attracted to their traditional literary organ *Hid*.

I have often spoken of this generation as a generation "in the shadows" or in "reserve."[23] This same term can also be applied to their contemporaries in the Soviet Union: Yevgeni Yevtushenko, Vassili Aksionov, Bela Akhmadulin, Andrej Vosnesenski, and others. The situation was similar in other socialist countries, especially in Poland. After 1960 another talented new wave appeared, with its own critics, problems, and difficulties.

The growth of the literature of the Hungarians of Voyvodina during this period must be separately mentioned. Although it had begun to develop after World War I, it can not be taken seriously until after 1945. An especially positive role was played by those writers who were most active in the fifties and who contributed to a greater integration of this literature into the literature of Yugoslavia. They were Laslo Gal, Ferenc Ferer, Karolj Ač, Nandor Major and others. Their earlier attempts were followed by a full flowering especially in poetry:

Contemporary Yugoslav Hungarian poetry has experienced a veritable renaissance in the past years thanks to a new and numerous generation of young poets who have gathered around the journal *Iffusag*, and later around the periodical *Uj simpozion*. Many new names and new poems support this claim and indicate that this poetry was receiving new impulses and moving along new, as yet untrodden paths. . . .

The effect of these young poets is manifold. They have brought a new, fresher, poetic expression. They have started to write new, more modern poetry, seeking inspirations from contemporary life, and other poetries of the Yugoslav peoples as well as the poetry of Hungary.[24]

[23] I spoke in detail about this in an interview with Feliks Pašic which was reprinted in his book *Savremenici*, Novi Sad, Matica srpska, 1966.

[24] Jožef Varga, "Poezija jugoslovenskih Madjara," *Borba*, February 18, 1968.

But even during this very quiet period, particularly in Belgrade, writers did not regroup themselves realistically or according to their literary affinities. Old groupings were, unfortunately, not abandoned entirely. In recent years, instead of groups forming openly, a wait-and-see tactic has been adopted along with false, superficial conciliations, pact-makings, and connivings all of which ignore the solution of debatable questions.

A quasi-theory was promulgated that our recent literary past was the result of equal "guilt" on the part of modernist and realist factions which had developed for no special reason and which was now forgotten in order to set things right. It is interesting to note that former conservatives, the very ones who were so opposed to free creativity, were the ones promoting this theory. This kind of an atmosphere hides a great number of problems left over from previous periods, which now appear in a new light and raises entirely new ones.

But the new discussions were again of the same nature — head-on, emotional, and narrow. Considering the context in which they were taking place, it must be pointed out that these discussions were primarily detrimental and contained dogmatic elements not present in the disputes after 1950. There is so much bad blood in them that even attractive ideas are lost and the author disqualifies himself. Defenses too are dubiously aggressive. In a word, our current squabbles are prewar, old-fashioned, and traditionally Balkan. They reached their peak in the reverberations caused by Miodrag Pavlović's *Antologija srpskog pesništva* published in 1964.[25]

THE LITERATURES OF YUGOSLAVIA
AND YUGOSLAV LITERATURE

In this text, and in general, I use the term "Yugoslav literature" loosely. Obviously, the picture which I draw of "our literature," of "our" literary life and standards, should apply to Yugoslavia as a geographic entity. Without doubt, however, I most often have in mind the literary situation in Belgrade. This leads some critics to believe that I am only concerned with the literature of other Yugo-

---

[25] Marko Ristić, "O jednoj antologiji, opet," *Forum*, 1965, no. 3. Compare with the writer's text, "Naše književne raspre" (III), *Borba*, July 11, 1965.

slav peoples to the extent that they fit in with my more narrowly drawn picture. Thus, Miloš Bandić asks in a discussion published in the November 1965 issue of *Delo*, "O Tokovima i strujama u našoj savremenoj literaturi," whether I have not presented the development of the entire postwar literature in the way I have, because I narrowed it down to the development of Belgrade modernism, a movement to which I myself actively belonged at one time.[26]

But the most frequent objection is that in this type of text the partial experience of a national literature is unjustifiably generalized in order to represent the entire Yugoslav scene. Vlatko Pavletić accuses Zoran Gulščević, Zoran Mišić, and me of this in an article published at the beginning of 1967.[27] Earlier, in internal discussions about the Yugoslav outlook of Yugoslav literature, the Slovenian critics from the *Perspektive* circle emphasized that centrism and pan-Serbian expansionism have generally been hidden beneath this cloak of Yugoslavism. In 1965, Josip Vidmar, an opponent of *Perspektive* reproached Dobrica Ćosić with the same criticisms made by the *Perspektive* group about those who did not agree with Ćosić's views of Yugoslav art and literature.[28] It is interesting to speculate on the origins of this sudden Slovenian unanimity. Possibly it is based on a common fear for the basic cultural interests of the Slovenian people.

Three important questions were raised in the past: the Yugoslav question in literature, Yugoslav literary standards, and the relationships between the literatures of the Yugoslav people. The first was discussed in 1956 when Zoran Mišić's article "Za jedinstveni jugoslovenski kriterijum" appeared. To this the literary conservatives reacted especially strongly in Belgrade, and it also evoked responses from both the conservatives and the modernists in Slovenia. The second was a topic of conversation in 1962 between Dobrica Ćosić and Dušan Pirjevac, following the publication of Pirjevac's text "Slovenstvo, jugoslvenstvo i socijalizam." The dialogue between Antun

[26] *Op. cit.*, p. 186.

[27] Vlatko Pavletić, "Jugoslovenska književnost ili književnost Jugoslavije," *Vjesnik*, January 22, 1967.

[28] Dobrica Ćosić, "Zajedno i drugačije, ili aktuelnosti naše savremene kulture," *Praxis*, 1965, no. 4–5, pp. 525–26.

Šoljan and Nandor Major questioning the existence of a Yugoslav literature signalled the beginning of a third argument.[29] The situation is not much clearer today than it was ten years ago. The only thing that is clear is the necessity for frank questions and the need to work seriously on finding answers. The unsolved question of the status of our national literatures makes sterile our work in many areas, and also influences literary life and creativity itself. To illustrate this point, it is sufficient to mention the lack to this day of a history of our literature. After the war the only surveys of Yugoslav literature were written by foreigners such as the Hungarian Zoltan Csuka, the Italian Giovanni Maver and others.[30]

Certain critics and writers are particularly angered by the concept "Belgrade literature." Why "Belgrade" and not Serbian? They consider this to be a most perfidious attempt at disguising nationalistic localism. What is at stake here is simply the precise use of a term. The concept "Serbian literature" has not been well defined and threatens to create great confusion. For example, it is not clear whether it refers to the entire literature which has been created in the territory of the Socialist Republic of Serbia, or to the literature which has been created by writers of Serbian nationality, regardless of where they live. To establish a definition is not unimportant since problems are constantly arising in the planning of anthologies like *Srpska književnost u sto knjiga,* and corresponding volumes in other republics.

Postwar Belgrade has become the home of writers from Montenegro, Croatia and Bosnia, not to mention Jews from all over. No one knows whether these writers consent to being included in Serbian literature, especially if this inclusion has greater national pretensions or carries with it actual literary or social obligations. It is a fact that they are surrounded and greatly influenced by events where they live and work. But does this uniquely characterize each one

[29] Nandor Major, "Postoji li jugoslovenska književnost," *Telegram,* January 13, 1967 (letter to A. Šoljan).
[30] Zoltan Czuka, *Istorija književnosti jugoslovenskih naroda (A Jugoslav nepek irodalmanak fortenete),* Budapest, Gondolat, 1963; Giovanni Maver, *Letteratura serbo-croata* and *Letteratura slovena,* Milan, 1960.

of them? There is also a group of writers in Novi Sad, mainly Serbs, who are not developing in the Belgrade literary milieu. Finally, one must not lose sight of the Hungarians, Rumanians, and Shiptars. Their younger generations are no more closely tied to what is happening in our literature than they are tied to their own national centers.

We must conclude then that Belgrade is the diversely dynamic and centrifugal cultural center of Yugoslavia and when we speak of Serbian literature we often primarily think of the literature of Belgrade which is frequently better known than that of other areas. For this reason not only is it more convenient but also more honest to use the term "Belgrade literature," rather than to refer to these products as Serbian.

In addition we are justified in speaking of a Belgrade literary circle, in the same way as we use the term "Paris school," because there is a real cooperative creative effort based on historical, social, and literary affinities in Belgrade. The Belgrade formula finally saves us from chauvinism and narrow nationalism and avoids centrism and reliance on certain privileges which the center of the country provides. Anyone who studies in detail the conditions under which writers live in Belgrade — as distinguished from their colleagues in the other republics — will easily be convinced of this.[31]

To summarize: every attempt to rise above the city or national-republic framework in discussing postwar Yugoslav literature will meet with great resistance. The main question is whether there is any justification for discussing Yugoslav literature as an organic whole.[32] The vast majority of writers, cultural workers and ideologues throughout Yugoslavia would reply in the negative if we were to make an inquiry or even hold a plebiscite. However, it is not easy to fathom their argument. If we examine the existing discussions we will discover the following main points. Practically the entire

---

[31] Cf. my introduction to *Savremena poezija*, Belgrade, Nolit, 1965, pp. 9–10.

[32] I have published my view on these questions as well as my reply to Vlatko Pavletić in *Vjesnik*, January 29, 1967, in an article entitled "Jugoslovenska perspektiva jugoslovenske književnosti;" and in greater detail in "Književni život i savremena jugoslovenska književnost," *Izraz*, 1967, no. 10.

problem which should really be of a literary or literary-historical nature is turned into a national question. The equality and independence of the various Yugoslav nationalities is always underlined. Each of our peoples has a different cultural history and each relies on this particular history. Generally considered, it is argued that culture, and therefore literature, is significantly independent of socio-political events. Finally, it is assumed that each national republic is a narrow, autonomous, feudal literary principality.[33]

From this standpoint it is easy to declare that a more united Yugoslav literature is only an export formula. It turns out that the only ones who notice its unity are those who superficially observe our products from abroad. This autonomous concept of culture, biology, and superficial history combines to form a mixture which is reminiscent of a national mystique which has been recently affirmed in each of our republics from Slovenia to Macedonia. For this reason it is even more imperative to look at things with a sociological eye and in a sociological context.

Above all, it must be remembered that real foundations for a new Yugoslav society do exist and have consequences — just as the uprising (1941) and the socialist revolution (1945) and the equal rights of nations and the principle of self-rule are reciprocally influential on one another. No particularities of the different states, whether positive or negative, have eradicated their existence and their influence.

In this respect Shiptar literature is very interesting. Hasan Mekuli writes:

About a hundred literary works originating in Yugoslavia in the Albanian tongue since 1945 are proof of the successful start, the serious artistic level and the uninterrupted advancement of a young literature; of its desire for new, modern expression and humanism. Because of its ties to the language, and to the traditions, because of its local color, this literature is Albanian, but it is Yugoslav in content because it is created in a new socialist community and carries the seal of the new era.[34]

[33] Muhamed Filipović's article "Bosanski duh u književnosti — šta je to," *Život*, 1967, no. 3, is especially absurd.
[34] Hasan Mekuli, *op. cit.*

LITERARY LIFE IN THE SIX REPUBLICS

As far as literary life itself is concerned, it seems to me that there is no basic difference between Belgrade and the other regional centers. I have already mentioned that Zagreb was initially more quiet. But the agitation around the periodical *Krugovi* corresponds roughly to the fight between modernism and realism in Belgrade after 1950. In addition, after 1962 there was a fleeting attempt to bring about a more committed grouping of young writers.

Perhaps the most specific example of young writers getting together occurred when nine thirty-year olds, led by Croatia's Anton Šoljan, put together an issue of the review *Književnik*. They demanded of literature a more immediate critical approach to reality, they pleaded for a broader commitment on the part of writers and announced the revision of many inconsistent literary values. Other things were mentioned in this issue with which the majority of young writers throughout Yugoslavia would have been in agreement. And yet the reaction in Zagreb was vehement. The conservatives, it turned out, were numerous and stronger than expected. Thus the first voice of the group formed around *Književnik* was also its last. They were administratively liquidated when appropriations were withheld from the magazine, and penalties imposed by the party.

The Slovenians emphasize to the point of absurdity their own particular postwar development, not permitting the introduction of any broader frameworks. But the question remains open, whether this development was really so specific, and if it was, how it influenced the "rest" of Yugoslavia. To clarify this point it is worth looking at the development of the group of Slovenian writers and intellectuals who began their literary work in the magazine *Beseda*.

This magazine became doubly committed in 1951, struggling both against bureaucracy and for a more European outlook. Examples of the first were Janko Kos's criticism of Boris Ziherl, and Taras Kermauner's attacks on Josip Vidmar and Roman Albrecht. The broader outlook was represented by Filip Kumbatović Kalan's discussion of Igor Torkar's merits. With certain exceptions, the situation at that time was similar to the one in Belgrade.

In 1955 *Beseda* again struggles against the middle generation which is closer to the bureaucrats and Boris Ziherl. This situation too is similar to that in Belgrade. *Beseda* later becomes *Revija 57*, a journal with an unclear history, beset by drastic incidents such as had not occurred in any of the other national literatures. This stands out as a significant difference, and one which merits attention.

It seems however, that Slovene literature had to endure more direct political repercussions than that of other centers. Consider the restrictions on Vladimir Kralj, and Edvard Kocbek and Matej Bor. There isn't a significant Slovene writer who has not been during the past twenty years warned many times, in fact even forced, to abstain from raising sensitive questions in his literature and public declarations. Not a single text avoided political difficulties of some sort. Edvard Kocbek, a former federal minister of culture, was unable to publish for ten years because of his book of stories *Strah i srčanost*.

The group from *Beseda*, rejuvenated by new members, regrouped in 1960 around the periodical *Perspektive*. This magazine was very agile, daring, and serious, featuring many problematical ideas. Its primary intent was, according to Kermauner, to discover new cultural possibilities and perspectives by criticizing prevalent cultural views which see everything in economic terms. *Perspektive* inexplicably ceased publication in 1965.[35]

Various other characteristics make the group from *Perspektive* even more similar to their contemporaries in Zagreb and in Belgrade: for instance, their general culture, their rejection of native folk traditions, and their more direct involvement with modern world literature. Of course, certain other differences continue to exist — in theory, in approach to reality, and above all in literary politics. Unfortunately the dynamic impact of the *Perspektive* group remained largely within Slovenia, and failed to have a wider influence in Yugoslavia.

I have purposely chosen to consider the development of the most extreme postwar Slovenian group, because even this development does not convince us of a perfect, autonomous Slovene literary path.

[35] This review of Slovene literature, for which I am indebted to Taras Kermauner, was first presented in a discussion entitled "Tokovi i struje u jugoslovenskoj savremenoj literaturi," *Delo*, 1965, no. 11.

I don't know whether the literature created "here and now" is more Yugoslav than it was previously. Perhaps one should not go so far as to claim this. This would only be oversimplified sociology as opposed to a similarly oversimplified theory of national mystiques. But at least, each national literature represents one aspect of the literature of Yugoslavia, or rather, of Yugoslav literature.

In conclusion, I feel one element is even more important and perhaps more decisive. It is absolutely essential for all of us writers and intellectuals in Yugoslavia to shed our regionalism, our deadly particularism and our provincialism. The common interest in broader horizons and greater syntheses in literature is an important means of doing this. Our national literatures and cultures must first pass the test of being relevant to the Yugoslav consciousness before they embark on the often overambitious efforts of attaining worldwide validity. For this reason, in spite of all reservations, I consider Yugoslav literature as the literature of the Yugoslav people, at least in a general discussion such as this one.[36]

[36] My text in *Vjesnik* was followed by Vlatko Pavletić's polemical reply "Zakoni krvi nisu presudni," *Vjesnik*, February 5, 1967 and "Organičenja umjetnika u njemu samom," *Vjesnik*, February 6. The subject of our dialogue was touched upon more directly by Miroslav Vaupotić in "Sablast Pavla Popovića kruži Jugoslavijom," *Telegram*, February 10, and by Mirko Bošnjak in "Nesporazumi naši nasušni," *Telegram*, March 3. This discusison was terminated by "Deklaracija o nazivu i položaju hrvatskog književnog jezika" and "Predlog za razmišljanje."

2. THE CHARACTER OF
CONTEMPORARY YUGOSLAV
LITERATURE

POSTWAR LITERARY RESULTS

CONTEMPORARY Yugoslav literature is relatively rich, and, even more important, very varied, which shows that art in a socialist milieu need not be reduced to a fixed number of moulds. In Yugoslavia it branches out exuberantly and in many directions. Although there are no particular schools or movements, certain distinct tendencies can nevertheless be identified — from the realist tradition to the contemporary avant-garde. Different formal approaches are being used and behind each of these stand differing views of the world of life and of meaning. It is not at all simple to determine which of these versions is the most socialist, and whether, in principle, there can be just one. They exist simultaneously and not one of them is jeopardized by censorship. Andrić's Nobel Prize and the emergence of contemporary Yugoslav literature on the world stage were achieved without sensation and political scandals, as a result of the literary quality of these works. In addition, our writers have become more professionally sophisticated in the course of the past twenty-five years.

The Chronology of Literary Events in Yugoslavia 1945–65 offers among other things, a list of the most interesting literary works published during more than two decades of development of contemporary Yugoslav literature. From this list it is not difficult to single out outstanding works and personalities. But for this discussion, general developmental tendencies are more important.[1]

During this period, poetry made notable gains, breaking as a whole with primitive folklorism, with naïve patriotic pedagogy, and with rhetoric. The general level of culture of poets and the number of cultural-historical associations found in their works grew significantly. Parallel with this we find an effort to perfect the mastery of poetic forms. A more objective, less emotional, more refined and deeply intellectual lyric evolved, which did not become stilted. In the past few years a new generation of communicative and theatrical lyricists appeared.

Prose too grew after World War II with the greatest and most obvious expansion in the novel. This most popular and remunerative literary form has been developing both in the younger and the more established Yugoslav literatures. There has also been a growth in the short story, which has traditionally been a Yugoslav strong point.

Looking at the themes of our new prose writers we find a relatively wide range of topics. In addition, the majority of writers have introduced a series of innovations in the classical canons of prose technique. Even in the works of the "moderates," composition has been modernized and there is a thirst for greater and more immediate psychological authenticity. Poetic elements are combined with prose and the fable and narrative are less absolute. One can even speak of the appearance of new prose trends.

For the first time in the history of our literature a new form of poetic fantasy in prose has developed during the last ten to fifteen years; it deals with the village or with solitude. Even intellectual or philosophical prose has turned to these themes. Such a prose scarcely existed before the war except perhaps in the works of Miroslav Krleža and Rastko Petrović. The two themes have even influenced

---

[1] General summaries of the development of postwar Yugoslav literature have been provided by Ravbar and Janež in "Pregled jugoslovanskih književnosti," *Obzorja*, Maribor, 1960; Zoran Mišić in his introduction to the French edition of the anthology of Yugoslav poetry (Paris, Pierre Seghers, 1959), Dragan Jeremić in his article "Filozovske koncepcije savremene jugoslovenske književnosti," *Život*, 1964, no. 2, and by the author in "Jedna varijanta estetizma" (excerpt from *Umetnost i kriterijumi*).

realistic prose, which also became modernized and is now producing worthwhile works, both numerically and qualitatively. With the growth of analytical ability and the greater education of our critics there is a larger number of essayists in the field of literary commentary, who, studying a particular work or literary phenomenon, shed new light on key questions in literature and life.

THE PROJECTION OF REALITY
IN CONTEMPORARY LITERATURE

Contemporary Yugoslav literature, including realistic prose, lacks contemporary subject matter, by which I mean an established socio-political national theme. In addition, our literature has no original, expressive, and contemporary approach to its subject matter. We are still groping for a way of seeing the world befitting the modern intellectual who lives in the second half of the twentieth century.[2]

To elucidate this fact let us use the concept of "contemporary reality" in very broad terms. Reality can quite simply be the material used for literary transformation. Reality is also a means by which we can conquer authenticity, and express the immediacy and vibrancy of life. Finally, by its logic and meaning, reality can determine the very essence of a literary work. Whichever significance we give to reality, or whether we bestow all meanings at once, we come to the same conclusion: the contemporary life of Yugoslav society portrayed in contemporary Yugoslav literature is pale and transposed; sometimes it is completely left out. We discover in it nothing but remnants of life, traces of its atmosphere, or some very ephemeral details — as though contemporary life were a stage set! Those striking, inherent, and unique phenomena of life which are reflected in our literature do not constitute its main charm. Without exaggeration, we must conclude that postwar Yugoslav literature is a neutral reflector of its epoch.

Until recently, the main preoccupation of our prose writers was man at war and in the revolution. As early as 1950 writers demonstrated considerable freedom of thought in the treatment of this

[2] Petar Džadžić, "Poezija i novi svet," *NIN*, November 29, 1966.

theme, especially in comparison with their colleagues in other socialist countries. This does not mean however that a genuine revolutionary literature had been created as for instance in the Soviet Union
during the twenties. Possibly Oskar Davičo accomplished the most
in this direction with his novels *Pesma* and *Čovekov čovek*. Antonije
Isaković has captured some of the essence of this revolutionary period, especially the moment when "the revolution devours its children." The human price of the revolution was also treated freely in
Dobrica Ćosić's first novel, *Daleko je sunce* as well as in his wartime
epic *Deobe*. Similar thoughts are also expressed in the work of Vjekoslav Kaleb as well as in the prose of some of the Slovenian writers
such as Beno Župančić, Lojze Kovaćić, Miško Kranjec, Ivan Potrč,
and Primož Kozak.

Serious prose writers have dealt with the problem of war in terms
of contemporary reality. Their hero is part of history and society,
although this relationship is incidental. This type of prose elaborates
on man losing his foothold and becoming decadent and degenerate
while his society is changing and falling. This is especially true of
the Dalmatian eccentrics in Ranko Marinković's stories and in his
novel *Kiklop*. The same considerations apply to the Proustian and
Mannian contemplations of the bourgeois heroes of Vladan Desnica
and Vučo. Both of them are weighted down by their own past and
cross over to the "other side" with many reservations. It is even true
of the lyrically meditative socialist fighter in the prose of Ciril
Kosmač.

Such talented postwar writers as Radomir Konstantinović, Andrej
Hing, Petar Božić, Momčilo Milankov, Bora Ćosić, Dimitar Solev,
Slobodan Novak, Antun Šoljan, Sead Fetahagić, and to a certain
extent Miodrag Bulatović (in his first book *Djavoli dolaze*) deal
with even more general problems. They are concerned with man's
isolation in the world today, the passage of empty time, the vegeta-
tion of the little citizen in an atmosphere of soulless urbanization,
in a world dominated by insensitive technology and indifferent
people.

In other works of some writers, particularly in the plays of Dominik Smole, Marijan Matković, Jovan Hristić, and Velimir Lukić, classical mythology becomes the historic setting. Or more exactly, some

of the great myths of antiquity are adapted to picture today's reality often with a farcical twist. Another type of Yugoslav prose goes back to the more recent historical past, to our small towns and villages. Ivo Andrić, for instance, has not recreated the past with his portrayal of Bosnia as much as the critics make us believe; he rather projects a vision of a new world with its inherent and silently gnawing problems. Next to Andrić, Meša Selimović has most consistently evoked Moslem Bosnia with his novel *Derviš i smrt.*

In his book *Korena,* Dobrica Ćosić tried to make the old Serbian village a symbol of the past, and of our backwardness. But instead of presenting a negative picture he overexalts the virtues of the village. Other writers too are seeking refuge in fictions about the village. Mihailo Lalić sighs over the fate that his village cannot escape and over which its inhabitants can only torment themselves. Ćopić's peasants, on the other hand, are able to turn all armies, powers and regimes upside down. No one can best them, or destroy them, and with their peasant wiliness, they manage to remain ostensibly independent. Even so, it turns out that they are quite satisfied to remain in historic misery and primitiveness.[3]

This means that present day reality is absent from the entire spectrum of Yugoslav literature and does not even exist in the works mentioned above or in any postwar writing. Some older critics have drawn attention to this lack, calling it occultism and evasiveness.[4] I would not go so far, because in the first place, it is not always a question of a conscious or prearranged reaction on the part of the writers. And in the second place, our young literature, in the postwar period and especially after 1950, encountered many technical and formal problems discovered and solved by the avant-garde, and by Western art, and it thus legitimately entered a phase of experimentation. Third, and most essential, the literature produced in the 1950's is far from being without value. On the contrary, its results are solid and interesting in many ways.

Since the beginning of classical realism, concrete prose which deals with contemporary reality has always been the trunk support-

[3] See *Umetnost i kriterijumi,* pp. 199–201, on the subject of themes in contemporary Yugoslav literature.

[4] Borislav Mihajlović, "Okultizam," *Politika,* November 17, 1957.

ing the literary tree. This is so because this type of prose describes reality in familiar terms. It helps contemporaries to recognize themselves. It can moreover also be used for nonartistic purposes, ideological, or political. When reality, which is the main preoccupation of this prose, is defined, all other literary streams can more easily find their place in the total literary spectrum. Without this concrete prose no avant-garde trends can develop. In short, it is a question of establishing proportions. Once this is done, fantastic and intellectual prose need not be accepted or rejected on the basis of "realism" or a lack thereof as has happened in the past.

The more "abstract" type of literature poses two complex problems for writers: to preserve some contact with reality and not to reduce it to a mere game of forms. This was one of the biggest temptations safely resolved by Yugoslav artists because our strongest historical tradition is realistic. By insisting on transposition, sublimation and a high degree of stylization, our prose writers in fact have created a highly abstract literature which captures the more lasting elements of man's destiny. In an old-fashioned way one would say that it deals with "general and eternal motives." It is obsessed with man stripped bare, and his basic existence, unencumbered by ephemera such as local color, ideology, political involvement, and so on. A considerable number of talented authors have used this approach. Even love, which is one of the most conspicuous "general and eternal" motives has seemed to be too temporal, conditional and unauthentic, so that since the liberation in 1945 probably not more than twenty pages have been written on this subject, or as much space as was devoted to love by Davičo in *Pesma*. The message of our immediate postwar prose is stylized truths about man, truths which often became a game, or black humor.

Strangely enough, the exaggeratedly serious, heavy and slow-moving wartime prose of Mihailo Lalić is similar to the obsessive dream of Bulatović's beggar from the Book *Vuk i zvono* and later works. What is even more paradoxical, this book also resembles the constructed humorous situations of the first novels of Bora Ćosić, *Kuća lopova, Svi smrtni* and *Andjeo je došao po svoje*, and Milankov's drawn out tale about the ironies of life of petty people. Just this kind of prose has provided postwar literature with the most original works.

However it cannot be denied that these kinds of literary works are strained and artificially contemplative and not always authentic or profound. In short we sense that they are constructed. In spite of the relativity of present day life the language of prose should be light and regular" according to Shklovski's "dea prorsa" in *Socialist Aestheticism: Yugoslavia's New Literary Trend.*[5]

Yugoslav postwar literature contains certain manifestations of aestheticism. One of its variations did indeed grow out of the newest experience of Yugoslav art and culture. But, before we go on, let us clarify the term and its meaning.[6] On the whole, aestheticism differs from, and is at times opposed to, sociological, pedagogical, rational, and any other kind of instrumental aesthetic. It denies utilitarian values, and going to the other extreme, emphasizes the uniqueness and self-sufficiency of art and its internal structure.

Sensual aesthetics and the traditional hedonistic interpretation of art as an audible pleasure are closely intertwined with aestheticism. However, its roots go back to Kant's "four moments," or four definitions of art: "That is beautiful which pleases without interest"; "that is beautiful which pleases without concept"; "that is beautiful which does not display its purpose"; and finally, "that is beautiful which is generally liked."[7] Schiller's theory of play as well as a great number of romantic works of art fall under these definitions. In more recent times, "art for art's sake" or symbolism has been inclining towards aestheticism. Today almost all abstract art whose theorists and defenders emphasize the importance of portraying the inner reality of the soul is stamped with aestheticism.[8] The first phase of surrealism is also marked by aestheticism, as well as the opinions of the "Serapion Brothers" (a Russian postrevolutionary group), the French anti-novel, and the "new wave" in films.

The above concepts of art are not difficult to criticize from a theoretical standpoint. It is more important here to investigate to what extent they can be synthesized. It is claimed that what is common

[5] Viktor Shklovski, *Teoria prozi*, Moscow, Goslitizdat, 1929, p. 25.

[6] A more detailed discussion of aestheticism can be found in *Umetnost i kriterijumi*, pp. 150–56.

[7] Immanuel Kant, *Kritika rasudne snage* (translation), Zagreb, Kultura, 1957.

[8] Michel Seuphor, *Abstraktna umetnost* (translation), Zagreb, Mladost, 1959.

in all of these concepts is that they emphasize form over content, and that they therefore must culminate in formalism. Though such a view would clarify the situation, it is in fact not true. If we use the terms strictly, then aestheticism at best can lead to old-fashioned formalism and to the theory of "embellished form" dealing with exterior appearances of works of art. In our time serious formalism is quite different.

Formalism is a word which has been used and abused, as well as misrepresented by vulgar criticism. The formalists themselves are to blame for this, for they make art absolutely autonomous and also make form absolute. But formalism is not really speculative, or without content. It is rather a theoretical framework full of concrete substance. Contemporary investigations of artistic forms have become scientific. Formalism as an aesthetic can give answers to certain questions, as well as serve as a framework for future research. In essence, formalism goes beyond speculative aesthetic doctrines and criteria. And today, when theoretical-aesthetic fallacies are criticized, formalism need not be involved.

Perhaps formalism historically grew out of aestheticism, or vice versa. In any event, although the two are not identical, they are interrelated. Stalinist socialist realism must be blamed for creating the greatest confusion because it labeled every aesthetic trend as formalism and then disqualified formalism with arguments possibly applicable to the old-fashioned formalistic school, not to aestheticism. Meanwhile, serious modern formalism attempts to be scientific, while aestheticism continues to grope in uncertainty. It is a series of slogans rather than a well-reasoned theory of art. It occupies a diffuse space between stressing the autonomy of art and the study of its structure. It struggles for aesthetic self-sufficiency without ever developing a more complex framework for the study of works of art. Perhaps its greatest merit is that it opposes instrumentalism and the subjection of art to some other purpose.

Our own particular brand of aestheticism originated somewhere between 1950 and 1956 during the struggle against official Stalinist social realism and against dogmatism in general. Its appearance marks the first indigenous opposition to socialist realism. A constant, open polemic was characteristic of this beginning phase in which many points of view crystallized. It is difficult to talk about this or that individual — theoretician, critic, politician — as the originator of this aestheticism. It grew in our art, in our aesthetic, in our ideology, and in our journalism. Its authors are anonymous, a collectivity. The already-mentioned extraordinary Belgrade Plenum of the Yugoslav Writers Union in November of 1954 bears proof of this point. Here we find writers who differ significantly in terms of their aesthetic concepts converging to a common point of view. Among them were Miroslav Krleža and Josip Vidmar, Marko Ristić and Ervin Šinko, and Oto Bihalji-Merin and Janko Kos.[9]

What was at stake was neither polemic for polemic's sake nor theory for theory's sake. Aestheticism is, first of all, the expression of a certain climate in literary life, in which the "literary" side of literature is emphasized, in which literature becomes its own theme and its own purpose. In it, worldwide modern experiences are assimilated and unpleasant questions of communication with the reader are avoided. In the beginning of the fifties we notice a similarity between literary life and the character of literary works created in the period. In short, many of our new works and their accompanying critiques are stamped by the new aestheticism.

THE NEWEST PROSE WORKS NOT INFLUENCED BY AESTHETICISM

During the last fifteen years, only a relatively small number of works were uninfluenced by aestheticism. To prove this point, I will analyze some new prose works, limiting myself to Belgrade and to Serbian writing, because it was here after all that aestheticism was the most blatant during this period.

I will start with a collection of stories by Živojin Pavlović, *Dve večeri u jesen.*[10] Pavlović is a versatile, inquisitive, dynamic and creative personality. Besides his work as a film producer, he is also noted for his essays and perceptive film critiques. Pavlović's first story was printed in 1957. His first book *Krivudava reka* was published by Nolit

[9] Cf. Izvanredni plenum saveza književnika Jugoslavije, published by the Yugoslav Writers' Union, Belgrade, 1955.
[10] Živojin Pavlović, *Dve večeri u jesen*, Novi Sad, Matica Srpska, 1967.

towards the end of 1963, but was immediately banned. His films, too, were shown only after great difficulties. The first, *Povratak,* remained in the vaults of Avala-film for several years; while *Grad,* one of whose authors is Pavlović, was subjected to a pogromlike trial in Sarajevo.

Krivudava reka is set during the early years after liberation — somewhere on the eastern periphery of our country. The militia and the Ozna [secret police] are chasing the last remaining traitors and bandits who are trying desperately to cross the frontier. Their long and difficult chase, their ramblings through the woods, through the snow, and the frost offer more than just an exciting spectacle. Concrete action is most frequently used by the author to show the fate of the pursuers and their psychology, their intimate world, their bravery and cruelty, their fear, their self-sacrifice and the hazards of everyday life. These stories reveal life unsparingly and nakedly. At times the pursuers are similar to the pursued, behaving like them and eventually becoming one and the same as a result of their bitter destiny. For a moment, the entire world is turned upside down in this dramatic vision.

Not only does *Krivudava reka* have a unique theme, but one which is the product of an authentic and consistent view of life. Out of these stories there grows almost unobtrusively a serious symbol: life is an uninterrupted race, gloomy rather than bright, in which even the winners bear traumas, suffering and unhappiness, below the zero-mark of mankind.

Pavlović uses a small, precocious child, from the story "Plakat," to observe the happenings and the heroes of his novel. The boy listens to stories about them in overcrowded local trains immediately after the liberation, in the winter twilight of villages, in the house of some wartime fighter. The childlike fantasy adds its share to those legends which are born among the people and in the locale in which they occurred, and which quickly spread to the surroundings.

Beginning with his first prose work Pavlović was striving to create a more concrete, a more normal realistic prose. Such an attempt was rare in Belgrade and only the newest generation of writers has been returning to this language and approach. Pavlović writes in a simple, almost stingy style, combining interior monologues with objective description, concentrating on offering a precise vivid picture full of atmosphere and potential significance. In several stories Pavlović has achieved striking effects, above all in "Plakat," "Legenda," and in *Krivudava reka*.

Pavlović published three more books after *Krivudava reka* demonstrating a development toward tight, realistic writing. *Dnevnik Nepoznatog* (1965), which received the Otokar Keršovani publishing house award, was written earlier. As a youthful work it does not deserve much attention. In the novel *Lutke* published by Prosveta in 1965, Pavlović comes temporally and thematically closer to our days, choosing a more objective approach and creating a more disciplined whole. This development of his style could already be anticipated in his first book.

The prose of *Dve večeri u jesen* is more similar to *Krivudava reka* than to *Lutke*. In terms of composition this work has been treated in a more probing, ramified, and free way. The theme before us is the wartime diary of the same young boy from the Serbian provinces through whom Pavlović experiences the world in *Krivudava reka*. In this war all kinds of armies are jumbled together, along with children's war games, love, and sexual adventures. War is the fatal determinant of the future life of the boy and his friends, and it is also the fatal determinant of everything else in existence.

What is best in Pavlović's prose is the intermixing of wartime and puberty. Long-legged, pimply boys drag themselves through dusty village streets, experiencing war in the guns and bombs they find, the killings they see, their encounters with fear and death. At the same time they watch soldiers and resistance fighters with all kinds of women and have their own first sexual experiences. Personifications, symbols of war and maturation, bombs and sex are all mixed together.

The force of these individualized spectacles is quite extraordinary. Unfortunately, Pavlović does not always manage successfully to extract the symbolic meaning of an event. This is particularly evident in the ending of the story *Todor Piper* in which Todor Piper's ghost returns to his home town. Nor is the use of the symbolic snake in the story about the bloated cow justified. Human suffering and vivid portrayal are the two strongest qualities of Pavlović's prose. Also, in this book the author has attained a clearer, more immediate simplicity than in his stories in *Krivudava reka.*

Dve večeri u jesen could have been more uniform, but that is not a big imperfection. Pavlović's real flaw as a writer is his overdone naturalism, which is almost a kind of literary exhibitionism. He seems to have a desire to say something coarse, raw and brutal at any cost, almost out of spite, and to demolish sacred objects and strike indiscriminately at taboos and prohibitions. What is frequently in question is Pavlović's erroneous belief that what he is attacking is actually forbidden and that it is worth striking down.

Once he starts out in this direction, Pavlović knows no limits. The following is a small example of this: the mother of the main hero, a young boy, "is rocking the baby which some guerilla fathered the same night that they slaughtered the father." Carried away by his exhibitionism, Pavlović crams into one sentence several facts which are of prime importance to the story and which should be divulged more gradually.

In literature such crude naturalism cannot be functional. But in addition to psychological reasons and despite a certain literary mannerism, the traces of the "shock" concept, which has a completely different meaning in films, are also evident in Pavlović's writing. In the far distance one can also notice Pavlović's forceful reaction to aestheticism, which for so long dominated, not to say ravaged, the prose of Belgrade. His reaction to it is so strong that he is at times carried to opposite extremes.

No one has developed constructivist literature with such consistency as Radomir Smiljanić in his prose works which include the collection of short stories *Alkarski dan* (1964), his novels *Martinov izlazak* (1965) and *Vojnikov put* (1966), and his new novel *Mirno doba.*[11] His approach is that of a musician or a mathematician. He establishes certain set rules of the game, defines basic positions, while everything else is inferred from these and tied in with them. Such an approach in which everything must be explicitly demonstrated is very complex. For this reason it seems to be used most often and most successfully in dealing with more neutral themes such as antiquity

[11] Radomir Smiljanić, *Mirno Doba*, Belgrade, Prosveta, 1969.

or the problems of man in the era of technological civilization. Here the writer works with a limited number of elements which he can handle more easily and which he can more efficiently combine into a whole. Those who take a more striking contemporary theme, whether social or political are exposed to the dangers of not proving certain important historic assumptions, and falling into reportage. Abstract and constructionist works have additional dangers. Their defects are more easily discovered and less easily forgiven.

In his novel *Mirno doba*, Smiljanić has demonstrated the maturity of his constructionist style. He carries it through to the end, without compromise, unconcerned with his audience. Although his prose is not always attractive, it is not anti-audience, nor is it uncommunicative. In certain portions of his work there is dullness and satiety. However this is the only and not very high price Smiljanić pays for the consistency of his approach. The milieu which Smiljanić presents consists of unspecified events which occur almost in a vacuum. The setting of his novel is on the banks of a big river. An army comes and encamps, and prepares to fight another army on the opposite bank. Everything else in the novel is seen through the eyes of a military stenographer whose quiescence and discretion border on anonymity. In the end it is discovered that he is not all that naïve, for the quiet stenographer turns out to be an informer working for the army on the opposite bank.

Smiljanić constructs his entire world from scratch, stone by stone. He treats his material objectively, like Kafka, recording with restraint, functionally using strict prose. But out of this seeming frigidity there emerges a tempestuous and bloody irony which underlines the main point of the novel. If *Mirno doba* is a farce, it is a tragic one. In the end a flood carries off both armies, and covers every living thing. Such an end does not carry in it the message of moral relativism but rather the committed, frightening verdict of the anonymous brutality of war. Far from being abstract, what looms before us is a recreation of the difficult history of our country during World War II, the occupation and resistance, the occupiers and the insurgents.

The virtuosity of Smiljanić's writing is impressive, encompassing deft variations on one theme, the role of repetition in creating effects and the play of a few main leitmotivs. Smiljanić holds all the threads in his hand and always keeps in mind the whole. His novel is like a symphony. It is this quality that should be particularly emphasized, for no one else can approach him in this. Smiljanić is a writer who has remained, unjustly, unrecognized.

In 1967 Miodrag Bulatović's novel, *Heroj na magarcu* was published by Otokar Keršovani in Rijeka. After a long hiatus, the new book of one of those Yugoslav writers whose greatest success, publicity and renown had been gained abroad, finally appeared in our language. Unfortunately, Bulatović's novel passed without notice. The limited reviews and critiques were quite restrained, although *Heroj na magarcu*, because of its literary merit, deserved a much better fate.

Starting with overemphasized and hyperbolic anecdotal assertions about Montenegrins and Italians, Bulatović succeeded in creating his own vision of a crazy but unhappy world, a witches' dance which winds through Montenegro during the course of World War II. This vision is best portrayed by numerous vivid and forceful scenes, such as the drinking bout between the occupying Italian officers and the Montenegrin girls in the cafe of Gruban Malić, one of the main protagonists. Bulatović's rather loose writing and his obsession with eroticism, which quite often and quite easily carry him into pornography, raise minor questions. Precisely for these reasons we should devote more attention to this book.

In his novel *Rat je bio bolji* (1968–1969) [12] Bulatović continues the themes and the same approach of *Heroj na magarcu*. After the holocaust of the war in Montenegro and the shipwreck of Italy and Germany, the heroes of *Heroj na magarcu*, Gruban Malić and the former occupiers, set out through Europe, from Italy, through Switzerland and France to Scandinavia and Holland.

The same destiny of Europe during World War II also obsessed Curcio Malaparte, the only writer with an overall vision of the war in Europe. He recreated this vision in his books *La pelle* and *Kaputt!* Although his literary expression is not on par with his horrifying vision, the vision exists. According to Malaparte, good, old Europe,

---

[12] Miodrag Bulatović, *Rat je bio bolji* (serialized), Savremenik, 1968, nos. 1–12. Der Krieg War Besser, German translation published by Karl Hanser Verlag, Munich, 1968.

which was already sick and angry, disintegrates during World War II. Ostensibly, to save Europe from itself, it is destroyed by the Germans only to be rescued by the Americans who are the new barbarians.

The ties between Bulatović and Malaparte are more than Bulatović's dedication of *Heroj na magarcu* to him. *Rat je bio bolji* is in fact the direct connection between these two authors. Bulatović also portrays Europe at the end of the war and as a whole. But he stresses a different point, and perhaps even sees things from a different angle. Bulatović's Europe is overrun and conquered by different barbarians, the Slavs, who are communists on top of everything else.

The second difference is even more important. Bulatović's Europe is not nightmarish and crazy as a result of the war situation, nor because of the relationships between nations and men. Each man is displaced and crazy. The nightmarish laughter does not come from the picture but rather, the picture is the point of departure. Bulatović constructs his farce on the cleverest displacement of every man and of all relationships.

The foundation of *Rat je bio bolji* is an anecdote which is even more risqué than *Heroj na magarcu*. The primitive pansexual Slavs through Gruban Malić, a Montenegrin from Bijelo Polje, a clown and communist, a crazy Don Quixote, fertilize and impregnate an old, tired, worn out Europe. Everything is sprinkled with eroticism, politics, and reflection. Bulatović presents erotic metaphors as the primary reality itself. Bulatović's novel is filled with current historic associations. And yet it is obvious from everything that has been said that it cannot be assessed as a realistic work. This is a work of black humor and fantasy, and one cannot make the same demands on it as one would on a realistic novel which accepts, at least on one level, a direct interplay with history and a comparison with reality.

What is best in Bulatović's novel is the vision of an unhappy world. Here one of Bulatović's old qualities finds expression again in a new form. This quality is Slav compassion, or "the opening up of the literary work toward life." It was already present in his first novel *Djavoli dolaze,* and is perhaps most developed in his second book *Vuk i zvono.* To understand this point we should remember Oscar

Wilde's comment to André Gide about *Madame Bovary*, which he considered a superb work, but found introverted and cold and repellent in its objectivity. The advantage of the Russian writers is that their books are open toward life. This "openness" of Wilde's is in fact the surge of pity toward man.

In recent times, Bulatović has been "opening up" too much and is slipping into exhibitionism. In his new book as in *Heroj na margacu*, eroticism becomes pornography for its own sake. The confessions of Bulatović's heroes have become increasingly garrulous. When Bulatović tries to be humorous he keeps harping on a joke until it loses all meaning. For this reason his text seems thin. But this is not the main flaw of this novel. A much greater drawback is the fact that Bulatović does not complete his vision in Italy where the theme came full circle. The book's final two sections are added mechanically and merely repeat what was said more convincingly, earlier. His epilogue is most disappointing of all, since it includes an unrelated episode. This interjection does not leave him sufficient time to return to his hero Gruban Malić who was left tilting at windmills in Holland. The reader is tempted to ask Bulatović to omit the last two sections and to rewrite the epilogue.

Aleksandar Popović's *Čarapa od sto petlji*[13] is a collection of dramatic texts by the most productive and popular stage writer in Belgrade. A serious analysis of Popović's current drama must study certain problems in his texts. Critics were especially confused after the premiere of *Jelena Cvetković*, a play which is not and could not be included in the collection. How could one of our avant-garde writers produce a work which "smells" so much of socialist realism? The contrived comedies *Krmeći kas, Ljubinko i Desanka, Sablja dimiskija* and others (grotesques, burlesques and farces) all had two basic drawbacks. First of all Popović's dramatic dynamism stems mainly from his language. Fortunately that language is amusing, lively, colloquial, a well-conceived mixture of folk talk and Belgrade slang, which has not been heard on our stage since Nušić.* The language's

---

[13] Aleksander Popović, *Čarapa od sto petlji*, Belgrade, Prosveta, 1967.

* Popular Serbian playwright, 1864–1938 — *Ed.*

music alone frequently indicates the point of the text. Yet without a doubt, this is not sufficient to make a good play.

In the second place, the structure of Popović's comedies is illusory. Their content offers us that which is beyond the real and the surrealistic in life. His plays are fragments of life situations and of relationships between people, transcribed notes on tapes which record life in our streets and houses, cut and spliced at random by the author. Popović has tried to put together this stream of life, and to construct forms, with too great and too naïve a belief that events will knit themselves together within the framework of this slice of life. Although he has abandoned "theatrical truths," he does not succeed in achieving a more serious dramaturgy. These comedies lack a realistic dynamic, whether on an emotional or intellectual plane. We are affected only by their logical spontaneity and their lifelike authenticity.

It is difficult to evaluate Popović's writing, because in determining what to leave out of a work, the author seems to be guided by strictly technical considerations. He would in other words determine the volume of words in relation to the size of the book. In evaluating the dramas of Aleksandar Popović, our public, which is desirous of contemporary content, contemporary themes and the critics' interpretation of reality, must be content with morsels of reality. It enjoys plays provided they have at least scratched the surface of contemporary life. Popović's text is filled with such details: verbal craft, swear words, juicy expressions. Finally, we must add that he is popular because it is easy to insert, or to impute, political and ideological allusions into the scattered structure of Popović's comedies. Such is the case with similar texts in all socialist countries. They are surrogates for social satire and easy criticism of "everything that exists."

In conclusion, let us draw together the common factors working toward aestheticism in the most recent Belgrade and Serbian prose produced by writers of many different orientations. Weaker writers are led into a blind alley by this theory, but many authors continue to create worthwhile works in the name of aestheticism. Efforts to go beyond aestheticism are perhaps more intense than in earlier years. To break out of this vicious circle, writers oscillate between naturalism and the grotesque. In spite of these extreme reactions, escape is very difficult.[14]

Serbian prose offers two books by Dragoslav Mihailović* which have passed this difficult test. Though he was born in 1930, his first book, a collection of short stories entitled *Frede, laku noć*, did not appear until 1967. It was immediately acclaimed and even received the Belgrade October Prize. This was not important in itself, since any intelligent, sensitive, literate man can write a book today. In Yugoslavia there is an unwritten law that the second book determines whether someone has the capacity to become a real writer. Only a year after his first publication, Mihailović's second book, *Kad su cvetale tikve*[15] came out as absolute proof that a new prose writer was born. *Kad su cvetale tikve* is more than just good prose. It came at a time when critics and the public alike lamented the lack of books about our postwar reality.

Mihailović's novel is that kind of prose. It is a critique of reality and depicts life in a complex way, woven with black and white threads. The book marks an important juncture in the rejuvenation of our contemporary literature. Because of these qualities it was welcomed in circles other than professional, literary, and artistic. It is rare that a typesetter will stop in the middle of his work and gather his coworkers around him to read them a text. But this is what happened when an installment of Mihailović's book was being prepared for the holiday issue of a newspaper. And for weeks people were looking all over Belgrade for the two numbers of *Letopis Matice srpske* which printed the first installments of Mihailović's work.

What kind of a story is it? It is a contemporary story about a man who is forced into exile in Sweden, why he went there and why he refused to return to his native Belgrade. It is a history of the outskirts of Belgrade. Dusanovac is a world with its own, specific, and rigid rules of the game. Because of them and with them Dusanovac suffers during unsettled times. The main point of the book focuses on

---

[14] "Umjetnosti 'o sebi' ili 'posebi', ili 'zbog sebe' nikada nije bilo," conversation with M. Krleža, *Borba*, November 28, 29 and 30, 1966.

* The author uses this Anglicized spelling of Dragoslav Mihailović's last name throughout the book. — *Trans.*

[15] Dragoslav Mihailović, *Kad su cvetale tikve*, Novi Sad, Matica Srpska, 1968.

relationships among people, their rules of the game and the times in which they live. The period is strange and dangerous, and the rules of the game are war. In part the rules are traditional, Balkan, patriarchal, in part they are based on modernization, urbanization, and the cult of force. This is a paradoxical mixture, just as the suburb is a mixture of village and city, both of which hang on tenaciously.

More specifically, all the participants of the game abide by the rules and react automatically. There is no question that the hero's sister's death will be avenged, and there is no obstacle which will keep the hero from carrying out his duty. The criticism of the peripheral world and of its morality discreetly breaks through the brutal story, carrying with it the moral message that man cannot isolate himself, that he cannot go to extremes, and that a life need not be paid for with another life.

The beginning of the story is artless. The main hero is a young man of the slums, a rising boxer, Ljuba Vrapče [the Little Sparrow] called "Champion," who has stolen another young man's girl right out from under his nose. In doing this he ignores the threats of his rival, Stole Apache, and his circle of friends. Somehow at the same time his brother and father are imprisoned because of the Inform Bureau. Supported by his mother, he asks the president of the club, a retired colonel, to let them go. In the ensuing argument he insults the colonel and is forced into the army, where his boxing improves. But tragedy occurs at home when his sister hangs herself after she is raped, his father returns from prison ruined, and his mother dies. He discovers the rapist's identity and finds Stole Apache, who has contracted tuberculosis in the meantime in a sanatorium. Stole will pay for everything in a final gruesome scene, but "Champion" will also have to pay. He is cursed by Stole's mother and pursued by the police; his only recourse is to escape to Sweden.

It is essential to state that Mihailović does not present this reality in the raw. Serious modern prose writers of the most varied orientations are increasingly becoming rationalists. They have a common working hypothesis which is essentially constructivist. A prose work is considered to be an enclosed homogenous system which has to be created from beginning to end. It is not a reproduction or a picture nor is it the substitution of one reality for another. In the first place, there are now new ideas about the completed, coherent structure of a literary work. On a higher plane of abstraction, this is again naturally an image, but it has been transformed into an independently constructed variation of man's fate.

Such an approach is particularly difficult when dealing with a contemporary theme. But Mihailović adapts it quite successfully. The story has two parallel themes. The first is boxing and the career of Ljuba Vrapče, and seems to be most important. The second is the private life of the protagonist and his family. We catch glimpses of it from time to time. Otherwise, only an occasional, discreet sentence maintains the continuity and suggests a deeper sense of the course of events. After the death of Ljuba's sister a young man from Dušanovac, who was in love with her, tells Ljuba what happened and also that Stole Apache has disappeared. After the mother's death there is a hint as to what Stole is thinking about. When his father dies, Champion mentions, almost incidentally, that his "friend" Stole is still in the sanatorium, but there is no further mention of revenge. His desire for vengeance is only indicated indirectly in Champion's conversation with his trainer who refuses to continue his training on the grounds that his boxing will serve another purpose. Only the final scene discloses everything.

We have here a constructed work which is psychologically authentic and told in terse, objective prose. It is not local. The Belgrade periphery, which most of the readers of the book have not even seen, is only conditional, as is the city of Belgrade itself which is presented as a godless, hellish city full of atheistic people. Finally, even boxing is conditional. More than just the "noble art" it is a "trick" the author uses in his composition and a way of expressing the morality and life philosophy of Champion's milieu, and the means for Champion's final accounting with Apache.

Mihailović's case makes clear the difficulties which face a contemporary writer who is a rationalist and constructionist, when he wishes to deal more directly with contemporary life. The first danger in such a text is that the key historical assumptions will remain unproven, and that they will be taken for granted in the same way they are taken for granted in life itself: on the basis of foreknowlege. If the reader is not thus equipped, he will be unable to understand

and accept the text. The other danger is that the actual facts will remain raw and outside of the literary context. To say the least, the literary game of contemporaneity is a very risky one. But this risk is worthwhile, as Dragoslav Mihailović has shown.

Mihailović's book was quickly followed by the appearance of Slobodan Selenić's novel *Memoari Pere Bogalja* and Vidosav Stevanović's stories *Refuz mrtvak*. Borislav Pekić is currently publishing a novel about the Belgrade bourgeois intelligentsia and their socialist sons. Bora Ćosić abandoned his aestheticism in a collection of short stories *Priče o zanatima* and his novel *Uloga moje porodice u svetskoj revoluciji*, in which he portrays the first days following the liberation of Belgrade. Parallel with this, certain earlier struggles in Serbian prose to permit literature to criticize the present are now beginning to surface and are belatedly being given new meaning. All of these are good omens for overcoming aestheticism and for the creation of a truly normal pluralistic literary situation.

In the other Yugoslav cultural centers aestheticism was less prevalent and therefore the reaction against it was not as strong. Our previous discussion elucidates however that aestheticism, or the climate which it expresses, is an important, perhaps key point in the newest period of Yugoslav literature. The second part of this book will therefore analyze the main components of literary life, as well as the way in which literary life affected and created the literary standards which make up Yugoslav socialist aestheticism.

PART II. THE ELEMENTS OF
LITERARY LIFE

3. MAIN LITERARY CURRENTS

CONTEMPORARY Yugoslav literature can be classified in various ways. If we do not restrict our attention to literary form alone, but also consider differences in the way in which literary subject matter is organized, three basic tendencies emerge. These differences affect not only the logic of the content, but the artistic message itself. The three literary trends are *traditionalism,* in the broader sense, modified by modern experience, both in pure lyric and in so-called realistic prose; *a poetico-fantastic current,* which gained momentum after the liberation and especially during the fifties; and *intellectualism and "essayism,"* a novelty in our literature, with significant results in prose and poetry.

In practice, however, a different kind of classification has been used which is in fact more detailed as well as chronological. In it traces of former currents, which were preserved in one form or another, mingle with the newest orientations originating after World War II. This typology can be represented as follows: traditionalism, in the narrower sense, the classical current; early modernism, which was formed towards the end of World War I; the first postwar generation of "prugaši" and "kubikaši;* the "liberators of the spirit" of the early fifties; the younger or "reserve" generation, emerging around 1954; the youngest, who first appear after 1960.

* "Prugaši" and "kubikaši" are made-up words referring to those students who went on summer work brigades constructing railroads and roads. "Prugaši" are those students who wrote poetry glorifying these exploits. Both terms have a derogatory ring. — *Ed.*

Though this typology may seem confusing, we must pay close attention to it because it serves as a guide to critics, journalists and others active in literary life.

TRADITIONAL LITERATURE

Starting with the representatives of classical traditional literature, we find a lyric of "pure feeling." It would not be precise to call it simply romanticism, because it includes the entire poetry of feeling and reflection which covers "man's first ties with things and with himself," as viewed by classical common sense. It is poetry which we all recognize as poetry, almost by reflex, and which we accept as real, because we have basically been nurtured in its spirit. We can freely say about its authors, "they are real poets!" Among them are Oton Župančić, Alojs Gradnik, Pavel Golija, Desanka Maksimović, Desimir Blagojević, Dobriša Cesarić, Dragutin Tadijanović, Gustav Krklec, and Blaže Koneski.

The prose writers of this group, Ivo Andrić, Veljko Petrović, Isidora Sekulić, Hamza Humo, Isak Samokovlija, Frančišek Finžgar, France Bevk, Ciril Kosmač, and to some extent Vladan Desnica, deal with external themes and truths using local color and ornamentation. This classical prose is for the most part indulgently turned toward the past. It respects the established rules of narration and composition. Its innovations are mainly in theme and temperament rather than in treatment. There is nothing revolutionary, it is all solid and sure. The philosophy underlying this prose is usually a classical philosophy of life which views men following fate blindly. Sometimes it is even more openly religious. The work speaks for itself, while the author remains discreetly in the background.

It is obvious that this group consists of the oldest living or most recently deceased writers, who began their literary work immediately after World War I. Through the decades their literary concepts did not undergo very significant changes. They remained even when their authors tried to subject themselves to the dictates of socialist realism. Although it seemed that this trend would have no worthy successors emerging in the years from 1955 to 1960, the situation has changed in the past few years. Along with Stevan Raičković, a segment of younger Serbian poets is following this classical path. And there are also representatives of the new generation of prose writers who are reviving some qualities of traditional prose writing.

The works of these authors are more or less read like classical literature. Naturally, the degree of veneration is somewhat diminished since contemporaries and "domestic" problems are the subject matter. The general public believes that this is literature, and that literature should have this form. Even critics have agreed and praised the value of this literature in spite of discovering a conservative ideological basis in some of its works, as did Djordje Jovanović just before the war.[1]

EARLY MODERNISM

The next group which follows the traditionalists consists of the first modernists: Stanislav Vinaver, Miloš Crnjanski, Rastko Petrović, Momčilo Nastasijević, Dušan Vasiljev, Rade Drainac, Dragiša Vasić, Augustin Tin Ujević, Miroslav Krleža, Antun Branko Simić, Anton Vodnik, Anton Podbevšek, and others. These writers span both expressionism and surrealism. They are led by an individual intellectual revolt against bourgeois values. This revolt was not, however, directed against aesthetic questions, to which bourgeois society added many innovations.[2]

In addition to their striking simultaneous appearance before and immediately after the end of World War I, the members of this group are also united by a passionate pursuit of more modern views about contemporary man. In their works, man is in search of security. Sometimes the authors portray him as an intellectual seeking spontaneity, at other times they see him as a bitter, tired hero, disgusted by the great world slaughter. Sometimes he is an unstable member of the intelligentsia. Man strives to avoid the relativity of life through

[1] Djordje Jovanović, *Studije i kritike*, Belgrade, Prosveta, 1949 (see "Prividni realizam Ive Andrića," pp. 187–91 and *passim*).

[2] Stanislav Vinaver, "Manifest ekspresionističke škole," in *Gromobran svemira*, Belgrade, 1921, pp. 3–28.

a Christian or Slavic myth of Eros, which helps him find relevance within himself and towards his environment.

Prose writers as well react lyrically, subjectively, affectively, and passionately. It is interesting that with the exception of perhaps Krleža, not one of them has created a genuine social novel. Krleža himself, in the introduction to his play *Aretej*, interprets this lack in sociological terms. According to him the absence of social organization in the newly created Kingdom of the Serbs, Croats, and Slovenes (Yugoslavia) made a work of this sort impossible.[3]

Taken as a whole, this generation of writers is, in the real sense of the word, a European generation. I am here thinking not so much of their high degree of education, culture and refinement, or of the value of the works they produced. What is even more important is that their literary concerns were European. Sometimes they even anticipated results which Europe attained only later.

Although these were mainly microcosmic writers, many notable and significant individuals belonged to this movement. They developed important expressive innovations such as ironic narration, elliptical metaphor, free verse, and combined composition. This means that they knew how to combine historic themes with present-day meaning, and some were successful in developing satire to criticize life.

Unfortunately, this youthful movement, which was blurred and unpersevering, fell apart towards the end of the twenties for reasons which critics have discussed at length. In part these were social and political. The critics are also correct in emphasizing the negative social impact of these post–World War I modernists.[4] Marko Ristić, who had already stressed this back in 1932, however, is wrong when he extends this criticism to the literary work of these writers as well.[5] Modernistic works written at the beginning of the thirties, it must be emphasized, played an important, even historic, role in our own times. They were singled out as examples by the most progressive of our writers in the fight against socialist realism, as well

[3] Miroslav Krleža, "Pogovor *Areteju*," Zagreb, Zora, 1963.
[4] Milan Bogdanović, "Slom posleratnog modernizma" (1933), in *Stari i novi*, VI, Belgrade, Prosveta, 1961.
[5] Marko Ristić, *Tri mrtva pesnika*, Zagreb, JAZU, 1954.

as against our own dogmatism and conservatism.[6] The impact of Ristić's *Dead Poets*, for instance, lives on today. Its influence is not limited to the circle of professional writers, but extends to the general public in works like Miloš Crnjanski's *Seobe, Dnevnik o Čarnojevcu*, and *Lirika Itake*, Rastko Petrović's prose *Ljudi govore* and Tin's and Simiće's poems.

Krleža's work must be treated separately from the other modernists. The studies by Šime Vučetić and Ervin Šinko as well as the Anthology of the Yugoslav Academy of Science and Art in Zagreb dedicated to Krleža on the occasion of the fiftieth anniversary of his literary work[7] are too vague and full of veneration. In general it may be said that Krleža's influence was incomparably greater during the thirties than today. At that time the best young intellectuals were swept up by his texts which represented the only honest and superior voice in the "gloom" of Karageorgević Yugoslavia.[8] It was in fact through Krleža that they matured.

THE SURREALIST MOVEMENT

Surrealism in Yugoslavia is almost exclusively tied to Belgrade where many of its experiments and games, as well as good and bad examples are still alive. We encounter it in Zagreb only after the end of World War II, and there are some traces of it in Sarajevo and Skopje. Božo Vodušek, one of the greatest of Slovenian poets, was in his own way a surrealist. But here our enumeration ends.

In inception and significance, Belgrade surrealism follows the first modernist period. It is, in a certain sense, an extension of it.[9] Among domestic literary models contributing to the "liberation of the spirit," the surrealists recognize only Miloš Crnjanski and Rastko Petrović,

[6] Zoran Mišić, *Reč i vreme*, Belgrade, Nopok, 1953.
[7] This is also true of the articles in the Krleža anthology published by the Institute for Literary Theory in Belgrade.
[8] Petar Džadžić, "The 'man in revolt' in Krleža's novels," *NIN*, September 5, 1954. I have tried to explain this change in attitude towards Krleža which began after the war in a discussion of the play "Agonija" (see *Estetička čitanka*, Belgrade, Nolit, 1964, pp. 155–60). ["Karageorgević" refers to a Serbian dynasty founded in 1804; a Yugoslav monarchy from 1918 to 1944. — *Ed.*]
[9] Rastko Petrović, "O pojavi nadrealizma," *Delo*, 1963, no. 3.

plus Dis, while in the very beginning there was great respect for the poetic-Bohemian fate of Augustin Tin Ujević.[10] But what is more essential is that Marko Ristić, Dušan Matić, Milan Dedinac, Aleksander Vučo, Oskar Davičo, Djordje Jovanović, and others tried to import the truly amusing, creative and fruitful adventure of French surrealism to Yugoslavia and to our poetry and our language.[11]

In the begnnning, Belgrade surrealism did not have a very striking, decisive literary and cultural impact. Its declared intention — an uprising against nouveau-riche society and petit-bourgeois literature was neither wide nor deep. It was a modest, cramped, and at best lucid deduction derived from Parisian premises. The pamphlets, for example, of the Belgrade surrealists are not concrete and sharp. They are not aimed at a worthy enemy. Many are petty, such as Dušan Matić's open letter in response to an anonymous attack against Milan Dedinac's *Javna ptica*, his polemic with Dušan Nedeljković[12] and the famous slap given Rade Drainac.[13]

Our surrealism also adheres to the original theoretical assumptions about the automatic text. As a consequence, our folk literature, with its irrationality, humor, and fantasy remains insufficiently explored. Lyric and epic poems, tales, proverbs, riddles, and superstitions still wait to be used. How much could have and remains to be done is evidenced by the postwar writings of Vasko Popa, a belated surrealist. Examples can be found in his poetry and anthologies *Od zlata jabuka, Urnebesnik* and *Ponoćno sunce*. Zoran Mišić, another follower, on the other hand tried to re-evaluate Serbian poetry from the avant-garde surrealist point of view in his *Anthology of Serbian Poetry* as late as 1956.

Our surrealists have neglected to explore dreams and the subconscious in their works. Unfortunately they also paid no attention to the islands of primitive mentality which abound in our country in

---

[10] See *Svedočanstva*, first series, Belgrade, 1924, no. 1.

[11] Marko Ristić wrote on the formation of the Paris surrealist movement in "O nadrealizmu," *Svedočanstva*, 1924, no. 1.

[12] Dušan Matić, "Otvoreno pismo," 1927, reprinted in *Bagdala*, Belgrade, Prosveta, 1954; Marko Ristić and Koča Popović, *Koje su pobude i kakvi su uspesi školske filozofije*, Belgrade, Nadrealistička izdanja, 1932.

[13] Marko Ristić, *Književna politika*, Belgrade, Prosveta, 1952, p. 254.

regions such as Bosnia, Goč, Sansig, and Kosmet and which provided
so many examples for the Yugoslav edition of Fraser's *Golden Bough*.
Only Rastko Petrović knew and studied the Middle Ages, another
source for indigenous surrealist material.[14] Finally, instead of Artaud-
inspired experiments, we discover in the personal experiences of the
Belgrade surrealists an unexpected, solid temperateness, a bourgeois
outlook which runs counter to the real surrealist adventure. Some
men outside the movement, such as Ljubiša Jočić, were consequently
much more influential than the leaders of surrealism themselves.

In its original form, Belgrade surrealism represents a fashionable
literary revolt of the "literati." As such it is a pale version of the
original Parisian movement. Its effect is academic and dry, and
sometimes even a "contradictio in adjecto."[15] Since the group was
not coherent, it was ill-equipped for greater feats in surrealistic
waters. Most of its members as a matter of fact made their first
literary impact after the death of surrealism proper. We are thinking here especially of Dušan Matić, Aleksander Vučo, and Oskar
Davičo.

After the demise of the Cracow writers' group in 1930, which was
provoked by French surrealism, Belgrade surrealists included socialism in their abstract Freudian-Bretonian dreams. They added
rational meaning to baroque and verbal metaphorisation, and, thus,
imbued the purely formal preoccupations of earlier surrealists with
some social content.[16] The group also disagreed on the complex
question of the involvement of artists and intellectuals in the preparation of the socialist revolution. All that was left of Belgrade surrealism after 1933, therefore, were a number of former surrealists.
Today these men have more in common by virtue of their youthful
alliance and their "cultural *niveau*" than they have with other Yugoslav writers. In practice, the participants in the surrealist movement

[14] His book on the contribution of the Slavs to Renaissance art has unfortunately remained in manuscript.
[15] Marko Ristić and Vane Bor, *Anti-zid*, Belgrade, Nadrealistička izdanja,
1932.
[16] *Pozicija nadrealizma*, Nadrealistička izdanja, Belgrade, 1931; Davičo, Kostić, Matić, *Položaj nadrealizma u društvenom procesu*, Belgrade, Nadrealistička
izdanja, 1932; Marko Ristić, *Predgovor za nekoliko nenapisanih romana* . . .
(1935), reissued by Prosveta, Belgrade, 1953.

gave up the surrealist technique of writing with their initial attempts at the "socialization" or rationalization of content.[17]

What happened to them later is relatively well known. Dušan Matić, Aleksandar Vučo, Djordje Jovanović, and Oskar Davičo, who cannot really be considered a "group," joined the movement of social literature. Their voice was the magazine *Naša stvarnost*, edited by Aleksandar Vučo but essentially influenced by the Yugoslav Communist party. Marko Ristić with Miroslav Krleža and Milan Bogdanović, on the other hand, started the journal *Danas*. Shortly, though, there was another reshuffling of the surrealist camp. Ristić, Krleža, and Dedinac started publishing in *Pečat*, while Davičo was joined by some younger Krleža followers like Petar Šegedin, Ranko Marinković, and Marijan Matković, as well as left-wing intellectuals such as Zvonimir Richtman and Vaso Bogdanov. From this time onward men like Koča Popović and other former surrealists who had grouped around *Naša stvarnost* became Ristić's irreconcilable enemies. This split made the *Pečat* surrealists politically suspect throughout the thirties.

In fact, Belgrade surrealism did not accomplish its most important social and aesthetic function until the years 1952–56, during the period beginning with the founding of the periodical *Svedočanstva* and ending with the publication of *Delo*. Naturally the influence I have in mind was not a direct one. It consisted of the talented former members of an earlier movement, many of whom were already acomplished writers and intellectuals, meeting young writers in a new social and cultural context. Among these were Velibor Gligorić, Eli Finci, Oto Bihalji-Merin, and such young modernists as Vasko Popa, Miodrag Pavlović, Zoran Mišić, Radomir Konstantinović, and Risto Tošović. All of these were vitally interested in enlarging artistic freedom of creativity, and were experimenting with new subject matter and modern stylistic forms of expression. In this they needed mentors.

Oskar Davičo, the only one in the dogmatic period who wrote successful lyric poetry about the heroes of the revolution (*Zrenjanin*) was one of these. He published two novel poetical works at

[17] Milan Bogdanović, "Socijalizacija nadrealizma" (1933), reprinted in *Stari i novi, III*, Belgrade, Prosveta, 1961.

the time, *Hana* and *Višnja za zidom*. In addition, in 1952 he rejected socialist realism in *Pesma*, our first innovative novel about Communist youth in occupied Belgrade. A year later his long poem *Čovekov čovek* about the conflict between the prewar revolutionary dream and everyday socialism appeared.*

The intellectual lyric of another old surrealist, Dušan Matić, also contributed to preparing the ground for a genuinely diversified Yugoslav literature such as we have today. His work included among other things such lucid essays as "Poezija kao večita svežina sveta" and "Kad god se povede razgovor o književnosti" which clarified literary aims. Aleksandar Vučo's metaphoric confession of a déclassé intellectual in the novels *Raspust* and *Mrtve javke* developed new subject matter, while the essays of Marko Ristić reprinted in *Književna politika* and *Prostor — vreme* and his new commentaries of 1955 "O modernom i modernizmu" clarified modernist trends. Other elements of this new current will be discussed later.

Looking back, our surrealists were the only liberal political and literary light in Belgrade's intellectual wilderness during King Alexander's dictatorship. Since they were less vociferous than the Parisians they were also less open to attack. In general their writings were either mocked or ignored because theirs was at times a romantic revolt against all established orders. Unfortunately they became so isolated that they did not permit or acknowledge any criticism about themselves or their work. Later in the immediate prewar years when the surrealist movement as such had already fallen apart, came the difficult time in which sides had to be chosen in everything: in politics, in active revolutionary participation, in moral values. Because they were basically individualists, the surrealists were attacked both from the Left and from the Right. Even when they tried to repent, they came under fire as members of a movement or as individuals who had not outgrown the pernicious influence of surrealism. After the liberation they were therefore lumped with those who were writers of decadent, counterrevolutionary, godless, Trotskyite, immoral literature.

It is no wonder that the most distinguished representatives of this

* This book was taken out of circulation shortly after publication. — *Ed.*

62   CONTEMPORARY YUGOSLAV LITERATURE

movement, the former surrealists Marko Ristić, Dušan Matić, and
Milan Dedinac increasingly called on the experiences of their youth
to explain literary phenomena. In their autobiographical essays, they
overrate the importance of their coming together, which gave birth
to the Belgrade version of surrealism.[18] Hanifa Kapidžić, in his dis-
sertation about Marko Ristić, follows this lead and gives a very one-
sided, uncritical and untenable evaluation of our surrealism. Though
his *Srpski nadrealizam* otherwise contains all the essential materials
for studying this movement,[19] we must, as dispassionate critics,
take a new look at the movement. Surrealism, as we have noted
above, was clearly a forerunner of modern literary currents, and
practically all of the most talented Belgrade writers, from Vasko
Popa and Zoran Mišić to the youngest poets, representing several
literary generations, learned from and experimented with it. However, during the past few years, some of the most distinguished former surrealists, in particular Dušan Matić, who have been working
for a return of our literature to the subject matter of twentieth century reality, are in fact contributing to a new form of isolation. I am
not sure to what extent they are aware of their influence over younger
writers, but they bear their share of responsibility for the development of stylistic purism, conformism and aestheticism.

SOCIAL LITERATURE

Social literature is first of all a literary-political movement. This
means that it is a school with a certain set of stylistic norms. Social
literature, because of these set goals, was also the rallying point for
committed writers and intellectuals of democratic and antifascist
leanings in the period before World War II. These two aspects of
social literature coincide with two of its developmental phases.

The first phase from 1928 to 1932 represents the "Sturm und
Drang" of social literature. Its position at that time is laid out in

[18] Cf. Marko Ristić, *O poeziji Milana Dedinca i o našoj mladosti*, introduction
to Milan Dedinac's book *Poziv na putovanje*, Belgrade, Prosveta, 1965; interview
"Ja modernist nigda nisam bio," *Delo*, 1950, no. 8–9; also Milan Dedinac's introduction to *Od nemila do nedraga*, Belgrade, Nolit, 1957.
[19] Hanifa Kapidžić, *Srpski nadrealizam*, Sarajevo, Svjetlost, 1964.

such programmatic writings as "Beleška o omladini" by Otokar Keršovani; "Smisao književnosti i dužnosti piscaca" by Steven Galo-
gaza, "Pseudosociajlne tendencije naše književnosti" by Milan Dur-
man and "O Socialnoj literaturi" by Jovan Popović.[20] Its basic task
was to go beyond the modernism of the 1920's and classical realism.
The duty of literature was to commit itself directly to the proletarian fight for a new society. In a practical way, as expressed by
Keršovani, "our first priority was the demand for new content."[21]
Ljubica Djordjević the only serious writer of social literature
after the war, evaluated the first phase of socialist literature this
way: "Many pedestrian texts about artistically interesting themes
were written in the beginning period." [22]

In the second phase, the basic concepts of social literature were significantly changed. Above all, certain early exaggerations were largely
corrected. The classics were no longer rejected, nor were artistic problems and the artistic side of a literary work. More talented writers and more serious works began to appear. What is
probably most important is that certain former surrealists, as well
as Krleža and his younger followers, joined the National Front.

Ljubica Djordjević writes: "In the second period, social literature
was determinedly against coarse propagandizing and sloganeering,
against a social but banal content, against mechanically analyzing
reality through antinomies like: reactionary-revolutionary, individ-
ual-social, subjective-collective, and against the denial of worldwide artistic traditions.[23] In short, one could say that the aesthetic
base of social literature had become broader and deeper. Yet in spite
of this the second period of social literature did not solve all literary questions, least of all did it provide a unified and all-inclusive
point of view.

Some dogmatically disposed literary historians oppose social literature to bourgeois literature and particularly to surrealism in the

[20] All these texts have been reprinted in the anthology *Književnost izmedju
dva rata* (Volume II), Belgrade, Nolit, 1965.
[21] *Op. cit.*, p. 391.
[22] Ljubica Djordjević, "O poetici jugoslovenske socijalne literature," *op. cit.*,
p. 393.
[23] *Op. cit.*, p. 395.

thirties. This is incorrect because surrealism as a movement had been formed earlier and had already expired. This opposition is further oversimplified and misleading because some former surrealists participated in the second developmental phase of social literature. In fact, the main literary conflict in the thirties occurred within the framework of social literature rather than between social literature and surrealism, and precisely over the questions which Ljubica Djordjević considered to be settled by the "broadened" aesthetic base of the second phase. First of all, the surrealists approached this new movement with many of their old "habits." Even when they made direct compromises in their declarations and propagandistic literary works (like Dušan Matić and Aleksandar Vučo) they met great resistance from others with whom they were writing and collaborating in this movement.[24]

Immediately before the war this conflict became most overt. Ognjen Prica, Radovan Zogović, Milovan Djilas and Edvard Kardelj, helped by Todor Pavlov in Sofia, at that time settled their accounts with the group of "fellow-travelers" of the revolution gathered around Krleža and the progressively liberal magazine, Pečat. The main evidence of this internal conflict is provided by Miroslav Krleza's factious Dijalektički Antibarbarus, which fills a double issue of Pečat, and by the replies of its enemies contained in Književne sveske.[25] In this controversy, some surrealists sided with one faction and some with the other. Of the Pečat group, Marko Ristić was the one, along with Krleža, who was the most attacked, because of his essay "San i istina Don Kihota"[26] which caused the quarrel. Krleža's Antibarbarus was, in fact, written in direct response to criticisms that were published in Naša stvarnost. The Naša stvarnost surrealists Dušan Matić, Aleksandar Vučo, and Djordje Jovanović never participated in this discussion. Only Koča Popović, who had temporarily returned to literature from politics and the Spanish Civil War, sniped

[24]Radovan Zogović, Jovan Popović and Velibor Gligorić carried this trend over into postwar criticism as well.

[25]Miroslav Krleža, "Dijalektički Antibarbarus," Pečat, 1939, no. 8–9; Književne sveske, Zagreb, 1940, no. 1.

[26]Marko Ristić, "San i istina Don Kihota," Pečat, 1939, no. 1.

at Ristić and Krleža, but more in fun than in serious argument.[27] The subject of the dispute was the role of literature in society, and the problems of engaged literature. This fight went beyond literary questions. It was in many ways a political quarrel about the need for unity in the movement when class conflict was heightened and a pitiless world war was about to break out. The members of the Politburo of the Communist party participated in the fight because they too saw its political implications.

The case of *Pečat* marks a very important and sensitive point in the complex relationship between the party and culture, between the party and the intelligentsia. Up to now, this story has not been completely cleared up, nor solved. I believe that the state of our literary conditions and predicaments, and our literary strengths and weaknesses to this very day, go back to the inability to face these problems.

A new regrouping and differentiation occurred once more after 1948, toward the end of the period when wartime writers and those engaged in building socialism "rallied for the fight" and were united although they previously held conflicting views. After that the motley group of socialist-realist literati finally dispersed. As we have already mentioned, in 1952 some of its adherents joined the ex-surrealists, who had themselves, to a large degree, abandoned their former positions. In short, social literature became historically displaced. In subsequent quarrels, from 1955 onwards, the shadows of old conflicts were increasingly felt in terms of personal intolerance, traumas and human deformations found in some writers of this generation.

It follows from everything we have said that if there are basic principles of social literature, they are more similar to the ideas expressed in the first phase of this movement than in the later period of divergent ideas. Fundamentally, social literature asserts that literature must serve political and propaganda purposes. Combining Maxim Gorky, German expressionism and Janko Veselinović* into

---

[27] Koča Popović, "Ratni ciljevi, 'Dijalektičkog Antibarbarusa,'" *Književne sveske*, pp. 195–215.

* Nineteenth-century romantic peasant-realist — *Ed.*

a suspicious mixture of styles and ideologies, social literature portrayed the plight of villagers and workers with the aim of bringing
about change through social revolution. Their work is not to be
compared with Branko Ćopić, Ivan Goran Kovačić, Skender Kulenović, Karel Destovnik Kajuh, or Radovan Zogović who had during
the war written more talentedly about the country's struggles, suffer-
ings and hardships and the bright perspective for the future. After
its liberation from the Germans, the majority of writers extolled
this renewal, the building of socialism, and the transformation of
peasants and workers in a style laid down by Soviet socialist literature.

A number of Yugoslav writers active in war literature and postwar
socialist realism failed to understand a dangerous consequence of
political aesthetics: namely, that their artistic merit may not tran-
scend the moment. When we evaluate these writers and their literature, two questions arise. First, could things have been different in
the period after 1937,* when national and party forces had to co-
alesce? Did not *Pečat*'s different, apolitical position ultimately have
awkward consequences for this unity? It may, in fact, have influenced some intellectuals not to join the uprising in 1941. Second,
perhaps the dogmatic way with which the *Pečat*ites were criticized
was far too harsh for such a delicate institution as art. This is especially true if we are evaluating average writers, who require a great
many concessions and much freedom in order to flourish.

When the social and political situation changed, the most talented
writers of social literature, for example, Branko Ćopić and Mihailo
Lalić, Erih Koš, Vjekoslav Kaleb, Mirko Božić, Miško Kranjec, Bratko
Ureff, and Vlado Maleski were able to write better works than before. Most of the other writers, however, regardless of these changes,
remained semi-anonymous and mediocre. This fate, as a matter of
fact, befell those in particular who were the loudest singers in the
choir of social literature during its heyday before and right after the
war. It is also a fact that many of these mediocrities are modernistic
faddists today writing uninteresting books lacking in creative
originality.

* In 1937 Tito returned from the USSR and became First Secretary of the
Yugoslav Communist party. — *Ed.*

Perhaps the social realists were sacrificed to the political needs of the moment. I also do not know whether the group's propaganda effects were as important and historically decisive as they thought. They committed many well-intentioned, unavoidable errors, revolutionary and otherwise. While these writers were responsible for engaging literature to further the cause of social revolution, national uprising and socialism, they were also responsible for many of the negative aspects of our present-day literary scene. The social realists were unable to point the way to a new art dealing with twentieth-century man, nor did they further literary creativity. This was particularly true right after the war when they uncritically adopted verbal dogmatism, sectarian engagement, and political provocation to decide who had the right to speak about the new society, why and how.[28] Speaking from a strictly aesthetic point of view, it turns out that socialist literature is anonymous, and generally valueless. Everything worthwhile flowing from the pens of its members originated either before or after the introduction of social literature, and despite or beyond its influence.

THE FIRST POSTWAR GENERATION

With this evaluation in mind, it is perhaps unnecessary to discuss the first postwar generation of writers whose significance has already been explained by Predrag Palavestra.[29] They are interesting only insofar as they perpetuate the influence of social literature and Soviet socialist realism. This group is made up of authors included in Napok's anthologies *Poezija mladih* and *Proza mladih*, and of some of the first postwar writers who were also collaborators in the literary journal *Mladost*, published shortly after the liberation. They entered literature with the revolution, ostensibly as its equals, but were in general immature, uneducated and superficial, albeit very sincere. Their lyrical texts made us believe in the beauty of a biased,

---

[28] This is borne out by *Književne novine* in the periods 1951–52 and 1954–60; by *Savremenik*, 1955–58; in Zagreb by the attacks on the new series of *Književnik* 1961–62; in Ljubljana by the polemics between the dogmatists and bureaucrats and the groups around *Beseda*, *Revija 57* and *Perspektive*.

[29] Predrag Palavestra, *op. cit.*, pp. 517–24.

ideological reality, but despite all their words and gestures, they were really unable to create anything of value with their meager, poetic prose.

Around 1950, they turned, as a group, with resignation bordering on despair, to writing about "petty things" just as in their private lives they adopted a certain bohemian style typified by Raka Drainac.[30] Although this new Weltschmertz was as fake from a literary point of view as the earlier cosmic-communist optimism, it was difficult to take their change seriously. As a matter of fact, the reasons for this conversion are difficult to grasp. It seems, however, that the 1948 break with the Soviet Union, which hit this generation of "believers" the hardest, created a completely new social and cultural situation. These writers were apparently unable to enlarge their horizons, to become more educated and to develop a more complex perception of the world. Later, the fashion of modernism swept some of them up, mostly in the wrong way, and they are still struggling with it insofar as they have not abandoned literature altogether. Incapable of meeting these new challenges, many of them turned to bohemianism accompanied by alcoholism. This has been well described by Rehar.[31]

On the other hand, writers such as Jure Kaštelan, Vesna Parun, Radomir Konstantinović, Steven Raičković, Branko V. Radičević, Slobodan Marković, Ivan Minati, Lojze Krakar, Slavko Janevski and Aco Šopov justify this literary constellation which we have called the postwar generation. It involved many writers, but was wavering and inconsistent as a literary phenomenon. To tell the truth, the writers just mentioned were not its most noted participants and it is doubtful whether they would have even been part of it had administrative socialism offered them another alternative. This group of writers was not organized on the basis of particularly close affinities, but rather represented a collection of all "young writers" who, after the liberation, were a part of the Writers Union or candidates

[30] The manifesto of this "return" is Risto Tošović's poem of the same name which Palavestra discusses and quotes in his article "Vreme romana" (see *Savremena poezija*, pp. 255–56).
[31] Voja Rehar's article on Bohemianism in *NIN*, 1954.

for membership in it. Those who wanted and were able to, gradually extricated themselves from this grouping.

Radomir Konstantinović is probably the writer who changed most in the past fifteen years. He not only outgrew his early Dis*-type poems collected in *Kuća bez krova*, but Yugoslav literature has in him today one of the most hermetic, avant-garde, difficult (but readable), generally excellent writer, essayist and commentator. Vesna Parun and Stevan Raičković also reached a very high level of writing, though they continue to employ a melodious lyricism — but in a moderate intellectual way. For years Raičković has been masterfully asking the basic questions: "What is the purpose of a poem? What do I want to achieve with it?"

Along with Konstantinović and Raičković one must also mention their contemporary, Miodrag Pavlović, who first published several poems in 1951 in *Mladost*, and in *Književne novine*, which were then followed by a collection of poems. Pavlović is an intellectual who appeared unexpectedly as a serious and mature poet, freed of the burden of "enthusiastic literature," while others were still struggling to liberate themselves from the fallacies of the earlier period. He is a much better example of twentieth-century man than Vasko Popa. The latter was for the first time attracting attention at the time, though he had been writing and "clerking" in the Writers' Union previously.

Early in his career Pavlović published mature essays on the problems of modern art, on metaphors, on Lautréamon.† These were followed by other prose works, plays and a new collection of poems, *Stub sećanja*. His writings explain why Pavlović should become one of the leading and significant symbols of modern art in Yugoslavia. He has perhaps had an even greater effect on the struggle for spiritual liberation than the older writers, who had made many compromises in earlier periods. No wonder his objective, cerebral, even academic writing provoked such strong reverberations a decade ago in the stale atmosphere of that time. His works were considered

* A Yugoslav surrealist poet of the thirties — *Ed.*
† Nineteenth-century French poet, considered a precursor of surrealism. — *Ed.*

a scandal and political provocation on the one hand and aroused frenetic applause on the other.[32]

"LIBERATORS OF THE SPIRIT"

Literary-political reasons rather than aesthetic ones caused Yugoslav modernism, which bore the main burden of "spiritual liberation" in the fifties. The fact that modernism is neither a literary direction nor a school of writing was tedious and difficult to clarify in Yugoslavia. The misinterpretation has now crossed to other socialist countries and is particularly tenacious in the Soviet Union.[33] Modern-ernism was above all a characteristic of literary life in 1950. In speaking about modernism and spiritual liberation we will therefore elaborate on statements previously made concerning the development of literary life during that period. Let us illustrate with concrete examples.

In 1952 and 1953, both Belgrade's *Svedočanstva* and *Nova misao*, the latter a journal publishing distinguished Marxists from all fields, made no distinctions between realist and modernist writers who would be bitter opponents in the future. After 1954, however, a freer struggle of ideas in literature drew more clearly defined battle lines between realism and modernism.

Originally the circle of Yugoslav modernists was limited to those collaborating on the journal *Delo* in 1955–56. Among them were former surrealists such as Oskar Davičo, Marko Ristić, Aleksandar Vučo, and Dušan Matic, who were joined by their students Zoran Mišić and Vasko Popa. The latter were in turn supplemented by writers who grew up in the revolution such as Antonije Isaković and Dobrica Ćosić, and to a lesser extent Miodrag Pavlović and Radomir Konstantinović, while Borislav Mihajlović Mihiz is, for special reasons, not among this group. In addition, other young

[32] The impact of Miodrag Pavlović's writing has best been explained by Svetlana Velmar-Janković in her introduction to Pavlović's *87 Pesama*, Belgrade, Nolit, 1962 (2nd edition).

[33] Cf. "Aktual'nye problemy socialisticeskogo realizma," *Voprosy literatury*, 1967, no. 5 (summary of a conference held at the Institute of World Literature in Moscow).

writers joined *Delo* who had earlier (1953–54) published in the student paper *Vidici*. Headed by Petar Džadžić, they are Borislav Radović, Jovan Hristić, Bora Ćosić, Svetlana Velmar-Janković, Velimir Lukić, and Milovan Danojlić. Momčilo Milankov and Miodrag Bulatović, too, collaborated with them. On the periphery of this modernist circle were writers outside of Belgrade, who contributed from time to time, like Vladan Desnica, Petar Šegedin, Zvonimir Golob, and Irena Vrkljan, and from Macedonia Dimitar Solev, Mateja Matevski, and Gane Todorovski. The only Slovene appearing in *Delo* in 1955 is Josip Vidmar. Yet in 1956 the journal for the first time translates some Slovenian works, especially poetry by Jože Udović, Cene Vipotnik, Ciril Zlobec, and Dane Zajc, who write in a similar vein.

Literary life in *Delo* itself was fast changing during this period. After the first stormy year characterized by Davičo's and Džadžić's polemics against *Savremenik*, a quieter period of Zoran Mišić, Vasko Popa, and Miodrag Pavlović followed. Until 1958, objective and more neutral exchanges about art by contributors from all regions dominated. Serious, general essays are the predominant writings found in *Delo* and there is greater cooperation between all literary centers.

What held together this very heterogenous group which was united for six years but which afterwards disintegrated into as many parts as there were members? A satisfactory answer to this question is difficult to find, even in the previously mentioned inquiry entitled *Prilike*, published at the end of 1955, which was compiled by the editors and main collaborators of the journal. Not even a review of books written by group members in subsequent years sheds further light. Nothing more definite can be said than that the struggle for modern expression and for a modern literary hero was the cementing force.

Members of the *Delo* group certainly deserve credit for the most amusing, original and creatively risky postwar literature. In addition, while other groups remained without successors, with the exception of the prewar modernists, most of whom are now dead, the "Delaši," particularly Oskar Davičo and Vasko Popa, exerted con-

siderable influence on other writers, opening their horizons, stimulating their idiom and creativity. This sometimes goes as far as bor-
rowing and "copying" Davičo's contagious metaphorization.
Not even the "peasant" writers escaped this influence or failed
to modernize their writing. The *Delo* group awakened an interest
in modern literature in general, first in poetry and then in prose and
essays. Members of the group were the first to write about the moral
problems raised by the new revolution. They also drew attention to
the results of the first phase of the liberation from socialism and
dogmatism, namely, the expanded boundaries of creativity, of cultural politics, and of culture itself.[34]

To my mind the personality and activity of Dobrica Ćosić exem-
plify the real nature of our modernism and the process of "spiritual
liberation" which took place in the literature of the fifties. Dobrica
Ćosić appeared, alone and original, in the silent period following
the Cominform expulsion. He was the first to speak about man's fate
with greater insight because of experiencing the Yugoslav revolution. The significance of his novel *Daleko je sunce* has been emphasized by all of us. Ćosić furthered modernism by stressing the unity
of form and content, by subordinating purely local problems and
by espousing worldwide trends. But as early as 1952, and especially
after the publication of *Delo* he remained somewhat aloof from the
main battle and from the activism of the "camp" to which he actually
belonged and in which his literary friends and enemies placed him.

Ćosić prefers to campaign alone, and not just in a limited literary
way. I would like to call attention to his activities and pronouncements on behalf of culture as a whole, his interest in the creation of
a cultural base for Yugoslavia and his stress on the need for cultural contacts with the rest of the world. In this way he supported
the development of a new, unique socialist Yugoslav culture. De-

[34] See Chronology of Yugoslav Literary Events, 1945–65, books, discussions,
articles and polemics of the members of this group, especially during the period
1955–58; see *Delo*, 1957, no. 11, an entire issue devoted to the October Revolution; an inquiry by *Delo* (1956–57) on the question of Yugoslav artistic creativity
in general; plus such discussions as "O jugoslovenskom filmu," 1961, no. 3 and
1964, no. 6; "Naše književne teme," 1961, no. 12; "O našoj savremenoj književnosti," 1962, no. 1 and 3, and "Razgovor o nastavi književnosti," 1962, no. 5.

spite his positive contributions, Dobrica Ćosić's attitudes and pronouncements are flawed by impermissible descents, and superfluous compromises.[35]

In speaking about Belgrade modernism and the magazine *Delo* we have indirectly described the group around *Savremenik*. They too were heterogenous, and composed of members of social literature, representatives of the already-mentioned first postwar generation as well as some newer conservatives and traditionalists.

In conclusion, it is interesting to mention a phenomenon applying to these two groups as well as to similar ones in Skopje, Sarajevo, and other state capitals. After the sharpest polemics ceased and when the "camps" scattered, the impression remains until 1964 that their members continue to act in concert. Thus, where critical new literary situations arose, the same people seemed to band together. In fact, however, groupings of writers based on literary affinities have not existed in Yugoslavia since world War II.

THE "RESERVE" GENERATION

The "reserve" generation however was different. Its representatives shared the same view of literature, literary procedure, and predilection for modern literary tendencies. But in spite of these similarities, this group was less of an entity than previous generations, and from the beginning its members never really assembled. The reasons for this lie in certain social factors which affected the literary scene between 1952 and 1955. Four stand out most clearly. First of all it must be kept in mind that this is the period of general "de-dogmatization" and liberation in our society, and that an extremely strong and merciless polemic against socialist realism was instituted. To fill the void left by cultural Stalinism a new aesthetic was adopted which may be called socialist aestheticism. The development of our modern art as well as the development of our "modernism" owe much to this concept and the majority of our young writers of the period went through this school.

[35] This is best seen in his book of articles and interviews *Akcija*, Belgrade, Prosveta, 1965.

Second, it turns out that a crisis developed in criticism and in art theory. What were the determining criteria for literary values, it was asked, after classical aesthetic viewpoints were supplanted by cultural relativism? Third, it appears that the period from 1952 to 1955 brought a proliferation of the mass media forcing serious art to compete with entertainment and sports. The public began to take an interest and to choose sides freely according to its own affinities.

Finally, it turns out this generation was the first to have opportunities for professionalization. In spite of this there is a glaring paradox. While they are the first professional generation in our literature, they are published in limited editions and only for a small public! Though this group is the product of regular, happier, more open — in short freer — cultural conditions in postwar Yugoslavia, they are still primarily a "reserve" generation. This means that they have not freed themselves from the impact of the political and cultural battles fought earlier. While this generation did not fight these battles, its members bore the consequences. The group was also hampered by shifting modern and modernistic, real and inflated aesthetic criteria.

The "reserve" generation threw itself precociously into the fray, joining groups already in existence, such as the one centered around *Delo*. As a result, these young men at first lacked the possibility, and then lost the desire to introduce their own literary line or one that was characteristic for their generation. Although some of them did not have very well developed literary attitudes, they frankly exposed their own deformations, and rebelled against prevailing postulates and against old quarrels which essentially did not interest them in the least.

Private or even entrepreneurial individualism and a lack of cohesive feeling are not accidental characteristics of this generation. They were created by an immature, emotional reaction against certain phenomena existing in our literary life after 1950. Older generations of writers were tied together by a need for mutual support and assistance in the fight for modern ideas. For the young, anonymous responsibility quickly turned into personal irresponsibility. Everywhere there were compromises which began with ideology and ended with money. Naturally as a result the revolt of this new generation was not consistent. Born in the middle of the century, it is neither fish nor fowl.[36]

In poetry, some of the younger writers pushed the already overused Yugoslav aestheticism to the extreme. Two logical approaches illustrate this point. The young generation took Mallarmé's aesthetic postulate, which states that reality exists in order to result in a book, and turned it into an obsession with the book itself. The book becomes the symbol of serious effort in literature and the only literary result worth mentioning. For this reason the majority of these writers feverishly published more books than they should have or that they really had in them. A certain number, again, with opposite neurotic exaggeration, delayed the act of publishing and made their literary debut only after reaching the age of thirty. In Belgrade there are about ten such exceptionally talented writers: Vladimir Bulatović Vib, Nikola Milošević, Dušan Makavejev, Dragoslav Mihailović, Živojin Pavlović, Borislav Pekić, and Vasko Ivanović.

The other fact which emerges is a noticeable avoidance of public responsibilities and public functions, and an ensuing convenient commitment which is never in the wrong, publicly or culturally. Thus solitary artistic creativity and "splendid isolation" are superficially and incorrectly equated by this generation. This generation was trapped by preexisting conditions, and thus failed to develop independent literary aims.

One common characteristic of the members of this generation is the fact that they break with literary conventions and widen horizons. All of them also have a high level of general culture. They are self-assured professionals who are able to translate or to write about world literature as well as their own specialty. When I refer to their culture I also include the culture of their expressive apparatus.

[36] The problems of the "reserve generation" have been discussed by the following: Svetlana Velmar-Janković, "Subjektivne varijacije o generaciji i vremenu," *Delo*, no. 12, 1957; Dušan Makavejev, *Poljubac za drugaricu parolu,* Belgrade, Nolit, 1965; articles in *Književnik*, 1962, no. 1. Also see Janko Kos and Taras Kermauner in *Perspektive*; Mateja Matevski, "Bogata pesnička geografija," *Delo*, 1963, no. 3.

These writers have a rare feeling for and mastery of stylistic means, which at times, however, is premature and exaggerated. This preoccupation with formal characteristics has another important implication. The "reserve" generation is the first to abandon traditional lyrics and to break with established forms. The majority can write in various idioms simultaneously and with equal success. But more than that, in most of their texts they combine or discard classical types and styles. Their poetry is in large measure intellectual, cerebral, or at least more objective than the classical and romantic verse. Their prose is often either fantastic or essayistic.

The critics distinguish two groups in the "reserve" generation. One, is the essayistic and intellectual group, which includes Ivan V. Lalić, Jovan Hristić, Borislav Radović, Branko Miljković, Svetlana Velmar-Janković Dimitar Solev, Vlada Urošević, Vlado Gotovac, Antun Šoljan, Ivan Slamnig, Primož Kozak, Andrej Hing, Dane Zajc. These artists have also furthered our poetry. Their essayistic prose, in its freedom and subjectivity, has remained a consistent, rational commentary on life, divested of the classical fable and hero. In short, their work progresses normally, in line with certain basic assumptions, and without exterior upheavals, bohemianism or personal revolutions. On the whole this is a united, solid, cultured and perhaps the first totally urban literary group in the history of Yugoslav literature. Its lineage continues successfully among the youngest writers.

The second or fantastic group includes Miodrag Bulatović, Aleksandar Obrenović and Djordje Lebović, Gordana Todorović, Milovan Danojlić, Vojislav Kuzmanović, Čedo Prica, Zlatko Tomičić, Irena Vrkljan, Josip Pupačić, Duško Trifunović, Blažo Sćepanović, Sreten Asanović, Gojko Janjušević, Srbo Ivanovski, Ante Popovski, Simon Drakul, Blagoja Ivanov, Kajetan Ković, Smiljan Rozman, and others. At first glance it seems as though they follow classical literary canons and standards. In fact, the difference between them and the first group is quite radical, and is accentuated by those writers who are actually in the middle: Slavko Mihalić, Zvonimir Golob, Miroslav Madjer, Danijel Dragojević, Vuk Krnjević, Husein Tahmiščic, Dominik Smole, Veno Taufer, Mateja Matevski, Gane Todorovski, Bora Ćosić, Momčilo Milankov, Velimir Lukić, Ljubomir Simović, Božidar Timotijević, Aleksandar Ristović, and Andjelko Vuletič. The latter are all concrete realists and emotionalists, but their texts have a definite intellectual quality.

This second group is not always strikingly original though it writes more poetically and is to a certain extent more emotional. Its representatives have discarded romanticism and "heartrending" sentimentality in their lyrics, and have avoided empty rhetorical pathos. Their rich somewhat baroque metaphors tend in the direction of greater objectivity. Their work as a whole is more diffuse than the writings of the intellectual authors. Their writing has preserved an expressiveness, even a melodiousness and singable quality using themes which are similar to those of the essayistic group. In prose these include the dislocated existence of ordinary people. Others have achieved originality in poetic-fantastic visions, a thematic phenomenon rare in our literature up to now.

THE YOUNGEST LITERARY CREATORS

The youngest literary creators made their appearance around 1960. It is difficult, however, to draw the line between them and the "reserve" generation which immediately precedes them. Critics constantly mix them up using such confusing terms as "young," "younger," and "youngest." This generation of poets and prose writers should include such names as: Branislav Petrović, Božidar Šujić, Matija Bečković, Mirijana Stefanović and Mirjana Vukmirović, Jasna Melvinger, Danilo Kiš, Mirko Kovač, Filip David, Branimir Séepanović, Radomir Smiljanić, Zvonimir Majdak, Igor Zidić, Dubravko Horvatić, Mate Ganza, Alojz Majetić, Svetlana Makarović, Živko Čingo, Bogomil Djuzel, Radovan Pavlovski, Petre Andrejevski, Sead Fetahagić, and others.

It is difficult at this time to discuss and evaluate such a young and heterogenous group. I wish only to point out that they seem to resemble a "generation" more than my contemporaries, particularly in their need for mutual interdependence which is stronger and more immediate. Possibly circumstances have forced them into this. They must literally "break through" in order to have a chance to prove their capabilities.

Furthermore, there is a lively reaction against the previous generation in their poetry. One may consider this a direct revolt against the hermetic isolation, atrophied intellectualism and aestheticizing which have dominated our poetry in the last ten years. Another influence may also have been the worldwide success of the "fourth generation" of Soviet poets, in particular, Yevtushenko. Our youngest writers are producing an expressive, communicative lyric. They even seem to be "playing to the gallery," flirting with it and courting it. But at the same time their great obsession is Branko Miljković and his poetic adventure, and they are beginning to make use of European avant-garde techniques. And yet they lack culture and a knowledge of their craft and are too impatient to work at perfecting their own poetic idiom. They are thus easily led into dilletantism and facile versifying.

Our youngest writers' prose shows a broad interest in the fantastic and in black humor. In this respect it is a continuation of the work of Miodrag Bulatović, Momčilo Milankov and Bora Ćosić. But they are already displaying a greater objectivity. We find in their writings more classical elements, quieter narration, more rational composition and greater concreteness and richness of detail. They are even beginning a return to the fable.[37]

[37] See: Momčilo Milankov, "Naši novi stvaraoci," *Borba*, January 17, 1964.

4. OTHER LITERARY TRENDS

LITERARY MAGAZINES AND JOURNALS

THERE ARE CERTAIN isolated literary figures, as well as some smaller groups and circles of writers around reviews and journals, who are difficult to place in the macroscheme of contemporary Yugoslav literature. Not all of these have been included in our previous discussions of trends and currents, because they were often not integral parts of the most important literary groups and movements formed after the liberation. It is better to consider them as concurrent trends and to discuss them separately.

The most important literary journals and magazines which appeared between 1945 and 1965 in all our regional centers are listed in the Chronology of Yugoslav Literary Events. We will therefore pause to consider only those which have not been previously mentioned and which deserve attention.[1] One such example is *Književnost*. This was the first, and for a long time, the only Belgrade literary monthly. From 1950 to 1953, under the editorship of Eli Finci, the magazine participated in the opening up of our literature to new influences, though the brunt of this struggle was borne by *Mladost* and later by *Svedočanstva*. During the period of sharpened conflicts between the realists and the modernists in 1955 and 1956 *Književnost* tried to preserve a neutral and objective position. However, it did not succeed in this endeavor because it lacked a forceful group of collaborators. As a result it slowly slid to the periphery of events, and today, almost symbolically, even its publication is always late.

[1] These other literary trends have been discussed in greater detail in the appendix to the author's "Tokovi i struje u savremenoj jugoslovenskoj literaturi," *Delo*, 1965, no. 11.

Književne novine went through a number of phases, first as the organ of the Writers Union, then as the voice of the most conservative group of writers in 1952 Belgrade. After that it became a mixed forum and finally the platform for a new assemblage of moderate and conservative writers. Through the years this group became more and more divided and incoherent, oscillating between mediocre tolerance and rehashes of old polemics. The career of *Književne novine* is thus quite characteristic of other literary reviews and magazines which have appeared over an extended period of time. *Književne novine* has not had a basic literary line since it has been edited by such totally different men as Radomir Konstantinović, Miloš Bandić, Miodrag Pavlović, and Predrag Palavestra in the last ten years. Today it mainly attracts younger writers who are influenced by its traditional director, Tanasije Mladenović.

For the sake of completeness in recounting the literary situations of the early fifties, mention must be made here of the short-lived but very significant role of the magazine *Mladost* (1950–51). Little can be added to Zoran Gluščević's description of its merits, and his evaluation of the atmosphere of the period, which was published in *Delo* in 1965.[2] Another, as yet unmentioned, magazine, *NIN*, conjures up echoes of the past and its unique place in the liberation of our culture and society from dogmatism. With the exception of a few texts by Stevan Majstorović, *NIN* is best personified by Borislav Mihajlović Mihiz who was for two years its brilliant and lively critic. Mihiz effectively carried on the fight for modern literary values, and perhaps because of this partisanship his editorship ended too soon.[3]

It is also worth looking at the development of *Mlada kultura*. Sometime during 1953 this journal changed its views radically and switched from a realistic to a modernist line, not merely accepting but actively supporting modern values. This example illustrates the extent to which existing and sectarian prejudices prevented young Belgrade writers and critics from forming into groups. *Polja* too must be included in our list of innovators despite its reliance on outside

---

[2] Zoran Gluščević, *Delo*, 1965, no. 11, pp. 1518–23.

[3] Following the publication of the collection of critiques *Od istog čitaoca* (Belgrade, Nolit, 1956), Borislav Mihajlović has written only a few articles about literature in *Politika*, and given some interesting interviews.

collaboration. Though it revered surrealism and writers such as Miroslav Krleža, Oskar Davičo, and Dobrica Ćosić, there is no doubt that this review contributed greatly to the propagation of modernistic aspirations. In addition, it made an effort to introduce Macedonian and Slovene literature to the rest of us. Honorable mention should go in this endeavor to the stimulating atmosphere of *Tribina mladih* of Novi Sad with which *Polja* has ties.

Someday someone will have to undertake a closer study of the short but tempestuous history of the literary review *Danas* which is a fine reflection of our literary situation after 1960. *Danas* was published as a compromise, perhaps with too many concessions because of the very make-up of its board of directors composed of different generations and various aesthetic viewpoints. It therefore became neither the voice of one group or generation, nor an open forum for all. This lack of interior coherence, which made unified resistance difficult, quickly led to the demise of this journal. As early as 1963 *Danas* failed to receive its appropriation, and it finally ceased publication for as many bad reasons as there were good ones for continuing *Književne novine*. Despite its youthfulness, exhibitionism and cautious neutrality, *Danas* was an important landmark of a brighter and more vital literary moment than that of today.

Časopis has been published for years in Sarajevo. As a critical review it does not represent any particular literary stand. Instead it has attracted a number of the most promising writers of Bosnia. In addition, it also very tolerantly and intelligently carries texts from all over Yugoslavia. From time to time this has meant printing some of the bitterest opponents side by side, graphically illustrating that many of our differences and contradictions are exaggerated.

There are still other distinct literary groups which exist and have existed in Yugoslavia. Several examples, of these in the turbulent postwar period, are *Krugovi, Književnik,* and the groups formed around *Beseda* and *Perspektive* in Slovenia. *Nova misao* too belongs to this group. It has been only rarely mentioned, and then only incidentally and timidly. Since 1954, it seems that we have avoided evaluating it because it has been inevitably described as Djilas's mouthpiece. But I can see no reason why this should prevent us from viewing it objectively today.

Nova misao grew out of the attempt to reconcile opposite views which in 1952 were expressed in the violent conflict between *Književne novine* and *Svedočanstva*, a conflict which ended in the suppression of both these journals. As a result, we find adherents of both of them among the closest collaborators and among the editors of *Nova misao*. Their names are relatively well known. The work of the *Nova misao* group must therefore be considered in terms of the general overall aims of the newly founded review. These were to gather together all the progressive (not to say Marxist) views from various segments of Yugoslav scholarship, art and ideology. Of course it is easy to say after the Djilas "case" that *Nova misao* did not fulfill these expectations. But this was already evident after the first six issues. In fact, in July of 1953 I wrote in *Revija* that *Nova misao* had been "launched and abandoned."[4] It could not rid itself of factionalism in literature; at best, it hushed up some earlier excesses. On the other hand, it relied too early on the dogmatic authority of official party-state organs responsible for culture and ideology.

Finally, in 1956, it seemed as though a group of talented young Belgrade poets such as Branko Miljković, Božidar Timotijević, Velimir Lukić, Dragan Kolundžija with Dragan M. Jeremić as their theoretical leader were founding a new poetic movement — neosymbolism. Unfortunately, some of their interesting common ideas quickly died out because they lacked a voice and a manifesto and never produced anything tangible. This group also failed to incorporate neosymbolic traces in their later work.[5]

Other completely different groups also exist in Yugoslavia. In fact, it is difficult to place Mladen Leskovac, Boško Petrović, Aleksander Tisma, and Svetozar Brkić who joined them later. They jointly publish *Letopis Matice srpske* in Novi Sad but literarily each follows his own path. Since they are essentially immune to the turbulent influences of Belgrade literature, they are not extremists, but good modern writers and European intellectuals. And yet despite all this, and perhaps because of their aloofness and unaggressiveness, they remain too much in the shadow.

---

[4] "Neodredjeni bilansi," *Revija*, July 7, 1953.
[5] Dragan Jeremić, "Teze o neosimbolizmu," *Polja*, 1957, no. 2.

An entirely new trend in children's literature, especially in poetry has by now emerged and requires documentation. It is quite worthwhile and very original in many of its achievements. Among the trends influencing this writing are themes of modern urban life which are far more important than Lewis Carroll's surrealism. Irony, fantasy, and a deeper lyricism are condensed into an authentic, characteristic structure. Naturally we must single out Dušan Radović for special mention, but other good writers include Dragan Lukić, Milovan Danojlić, Brana Crnčević, Aleksandar Popović, Aleksandar Antić, Mirjana Stefanović, Ljubivoje Ršumović, and Zoran Popović.[6]

YUGOSLAV RADIO-DRAMA

Yugoslav radio-drama too is developing rapidly but imperceptibly, eclipsed by more traditional literary forms and our own theater and cinema. Little is known about this stepchild of Yugoslav culture except for Dušan Radović's radio play for children, *Kapetan Džon Piplfoks*, and some dramas of Radomir Konstantinović, Miodrag Djurdjević, Djordje Lebović, and Zora Direnbah. Finally some local and foreign radio-drama festivals in Western Germany and Poland and Aleksandar Obrenović's and Nebojša Nikolić's success in the Prix Italia brought them to our attention. It is obvious today their amusing and inspiring plays deserve closer analysis.[7]

Actually, radio-drama began only after World War II in Yugoslavia. Though the first of these plays was performed in 1949, we cannot date the presence of drama in Yugoslav radio programming until 1951 or 1952. Up to now, this kind of drama is not written in response to popular demand or program politics, but for a limited audience and for festival performances. The circle of radio authors is not very wide as yet and only thirty writers have contributed more than one work each. Yet in spite of this, there are many good radio dramas and a few writers stand out.

In Yugoslavia as in most other countries, radio drama is almost

---

[6] See *Dečja poezija srpska* (introduction by Bora Ćosić), Novi Sad, Matica Srpska, and Belgrade, SKZ, 1965.

[7] See *Der Flug des Ikaros* (anthology of Yugoslav radio-drama published in German), Horst Erdman Verlag, 1964.

exclusively written by the young and the middle generations. Among them we find some of the most distinguished names of Yugoslav prose and drama. I am, of course, thinking of original radio plays and not of adaptations of other literary works. Yugoslav authors are thus trying their hand at a new medium which has its own rules of the game. In radio-drama some of them, such as Radomir Konstantinović, Aleksandar Obrenović, Miodrag Pavlović Vojislav Kuzmanović, have found the proper medium for expressing things which they were unable to say in any other form.

It would be an exaggeration to say that we have mastered the language of radio. Even the best creations of our radio writers are more significant for their content than their technical qualities. This is proven by the fact that worthwhile literary texts are found among our radio-dramas. Some of these belong to the best postwar literature, and in any case share some of its same basic qualities.

A panorama of Yugoslav radio-drama was published in Western Germany under the title *Icarus's Flight*, after the radio-play of the same name by Radomir Konstantinović. Unfortunately, Milo Dor, who is known as the most agile translator of works of this kind into German, has only made a collection of Serbian and Croatian radio-drama. The works of the Slovenians, from Vasja Ocvirk to Matijaž Kmecl, are missing as are those of the Macedonian writers Tome Arsovski and Tasko Georgijevski. This mars the completeness of the picture as does the omission of the works of Miodrag Petrović, Djordje Lebović, Vojislav Kuzmanović, and Zvoninir Bajšić. But those works which are included nevertheless acquaint us with the nature of this writing.

The subject matter of Yugoslav radio-drama ranges from World War II to ancient myths, and from the preoccupations of Miodrag Djurdjević and Mirko Božić to those of Jovan Hristić and Radomir Konstantinović. Contemporary, postwar, socially committed and relevant themes are preferred in Yugoslavia, as elsewhere in the world. But Yugoslav authors strive to represent the contemporary scene on a more general level as well. Psychological drama punctuated with humorous or poetic accents, dominates and is given a natural and modern treatment. Within this framework the following questions are discussed: the relationship of the individual to society, the moment of decision (Miodrag Djurdjević); the question of responsibility and the limits of personal freedom (Mirko Božić, Marijan Matković); the causes and meaning of the collective destruction of man (Zora Direnbah); action and contemplation (Jovan Hristić); the ties between men and women (Ivan Ivanac); the conflict between soaring human desires and everyday reality (Aleksandar Obrenović, Radomir Konstantinović).

There is great openness in stating and developing these important human dilemmas, and it is done without oversimplified patterns and dogmas. On the contrary, in the very approach of each author we will find the kind of relativity which is intimately connected with modern views about the complexity of life. Yet, the essential core of these texts is not superficial relativism. In the profusion of dependences of chance, and in the tangle of life, the authors are seeking a deeper meaning and reliable human values. Although conclusions are not always formulated, the search for them continues in terms of a broadly understood, free and commonsense humanism.

I think that our radio-drama is to a large extent essayistic, a trend which I have identified as the main innovation in contemporary world prose, and which corresponds to the very phenomenon of radio itself. There are conversations and discussions, attitudes are defined without the need for the fable or traditional hero, and the whole is held together by the intellectual temper of the text. Sometimes such a text lacks an immediate dynamic, which is often the case when our writers use symbols. At times this poetic symbolism lacks communicative power or threatens understanding with "modernistic clichés," and yet thought-provoking ideas are conveyed.

Radio-drama in Yugoslavia is not tied to the avant-garde theater of Ionesco or Beckett. Humorous accents in the tradition of Giraudoux's mockery of ancient myths dominate particularly in Jovan Hristić, Zora Direnbah, Aleksandar Obrenović, and Ivan Ivanac. Originally this trend was first manifested in Belgrade children's radio-drama, presented by Dušan Radović in *Kapetan Džon Piplfoks*. Other similar works like Nebojša Nikolić's *M'sje Žozef* remain to be collected into a variegated interesting anthology filled with poetic humor and pure fantasy, free of false pedagogy, and intended above all for "older" children, or for all of us.[8]

A TYPOLOGY OF CURRENT YUGOSLAV LITERATURE

In Chapter Three I commented on the global dimensions of the main literary currents and trends in postwar Yugoslavia. A survey of other trends brings us to the conclusion that such a classification is aesthetically provisional and has been primarily dictated by events in our literary life. Here is the most convincing proof that literary life itself is a mixture of literary and nonliterary factors.

If we wish to discuss the basis of literary, artistic, and aesthetic standards, we have to return to the kind of typology I mentioned at the beginning of the preceding chapter. Using stricter aesthetic criteria we discerned that traditionalism, the poetico-fantastic, and intellectual currents are all tendencies in Yugoslav as in other European literatures. But regardless of their presence, these tendencies did not directly influence postwar Yugoslav literature, and therefore these distinctions are not very useful. Even if the description of literary life were not the main focus of this book, only a typology based on postwar literary life yields verifiable insights and explanations. A typology with an appendix of literary occurrences, in the form presented in this book, becomes an essential precondition for aesthetic classification, since it places literary works in historical context. Literary values, it turns out, cannot be abstractly appraised but must be based on concrete events and occurrences.

What is most significant, our typology has not been "made up," invented or constructed. Another typology may order the sequence of currents and trends slightly differently. My sequencing is historical though not strictly chronological. I selected primarily those currents and tendencies which were outstanding historically, sociologically, and politically and which in the last analysis, were strictly literary, artistic, and aesthetic. In other words, I was interested in the more obvious groups, which lasted longer, which gathered more

---

[8] This section on Yugoslav radio-drama is quoted in the introduction to the earlier mentioned anthology, pp. 8–10.

adherents, and which participated in or precipitated external or internal events which had literary repercussions, and which influenced the development of Yugoslav literature. I have tried to describe these groups using the names given to them in our literary community.

When I presented the first version of this typology for public discussion, it was criticized as an inadequate sketch of the entire history of postwar literature. See particularly the discussion in the November 1965 issue of *Delo*. This article misinterpreted my "Tokovi i struje u našoj današnjoj literaturi," which appeared four months earlier. That text describes only the main, most obvious literary trends, and currents in our literary life. In other words, my perspective does not claim to be integral; it is narrow and partial. It deals with macromovements and those influences which exist or continue to exist in our postwar literature. Such a justifiable critique is a result of the absence of a history of Yugoslav literature, a fact which we mentioned earlier and which means that every text is received and thus judged as if it were meant to be a complete history. Furthermore, this typology, with appendix, was incorrectly assumed to imply a hierarchy of merit.

In spite of all that has been said, there is a hierarchy of values dominating literary evaluation in Yugoslavia. Because it has never been spelled out it is all the more dangerous. Nevertheless the ordering of works and individuals according to this fictitious hierarchy is well known. Let us therefore look at this more closely.[9] If we compare this fictitious hierarchy with our typology we find supremacy has been given to certain trends and currents, to particular means of expression, to the momentary, ideological significance of a certain literary phenomenon, while the inherent aesthetic value of the work has been left out. The magnitude of that error is all the more serious because all artistic means of expression are equally valuable, and the significance of a work of art and its creator is not determined by its instantaneous popularity.

Misjudgments and errors of this kind could have been avoided, if

[9] Cf. the author's essay "Hijerarhijska lestvica vrednosti i savremena jugoslovenska literatura," *Delo*, 1965, no. 6.

our classification were less rudimentary, and aesthetically more differentiated and specific. In the preceding chapter we saw how writers of very diverse creativity and style were allied in the same "movement," "group," or "current." Vivid examples of this are Belgrade modernism and Belgrade realism, both of which are extremely heterogeneous. An artist's belonging to the group cannot possibly provide a basis for aesthetic judgment; in this case, such a criterion may even be misleading.

The outside observer is confused by the relatively large number of misjudgments about such a small list of literary works and figures. Yet, it is quite certain that there are no longer "damned poets." The question is whether, with the exception of Dis and Djordje Marković Koder, they ever did exist in such a modest literary production as ours. Even then Dis was perhaps not completely damned and in the case of Koder we have first to determine whether he was a poet or a paranoiac. Our literature is far from being diversified, if one considers number of works and genres. However the hierarchy of values by which we judge literature is fluid and uncertain.

In the first place there is something wrong with the ordering of the hierarchy of values. While it coincides by and large with the chronology revealed earlier by our typology, it underemphasizes the value of Oskar Davičo, Mihailo Lalić, and Branko Ćopić, and to a certain extent Miodrag Bulatović and Branko Miljković, while overemphasizing the majority of writers of social literature as well as the first postwar literary generation. In practical terms this means that the older writers are considered more significant than the younger ones. To a certain extent this principle is understandable and can be observed in all countries and throughout all periods. What is surprising is the very literalness with which this principle is applied in postwar Yugoslav literature. In other words, the conventional order of things is overemphasized.

Furthermore, in those cases where two writers have similar rank on this traditional scale, the more conventional writer is valued higher. The critics' opinions of them are less extreme and divergent, and the public also accepts them more readily. For this reason an older poet such as Desanka Maksimović ranks above Vasko Popa, particularly after her new collection *Tražim pomilovanje*. The group of prose writers of the middle generation is similarly considered on an equal footing with the leaders of our early post–World War I modernism. One can barely find examples, and those mainly at the top of the hierarchy, where writers of the same generation are evaluated differently. We are here referring to the oldest writers as well as the "prugaši." Generally writers are evaluated on the basis of popularity or even more superficial criteria. The most tangled situation therefore exists at the bottom where we find the young and youngest writers. Unfortunately this whole group is evaluated as a single entity.

Beyond the top of the scale occupied by the strongest and most easily recognized figures of contemporary Yugoslav literature, individual ranking ceases. Further down we find collective and group evaluations, a fact which is much more evident here than in my typology. At the very bottom evaluation becomes a mechanical ordering of the most diverse young writers of several generations. When a large group of different creative spirits finds itself in this position, we must conclude that certain nonaesthetic criteria have been taken into account.

Another glaring defect must be pointed out. Those writers who were or are still outside the main literary currents and who cannot be evaluated by our typology are not even found in the hierarchy or if they are, they by definition occupy a rank lower than they deserve. While this applies particularly to critics, there are cases among prose writers as well. Take for instance Dragoslav Popović, who has undeservedly remained in the shadow of Dobrica Ćosić, Antonije Isaković and others, and is obscured by Vojisalv Čolanović and Branimir Sćepanović as well. Among the younger prose writers, the most unjustifiably underrated are Živojin Pavlović, Radomir Smiljanić, Aleksander Tišma and some others who work far from the literary limelight, who are engaged in other activities, or who have not had their books printed by publishers who advertise well.

While currents, directions and groupings have provided an informal basis for the classification of literary merit, a much more serious drawback of this kind of an evaluation is that it underrates, works with "intellectual" and "fantastic" orientation. Both of these trends became more apparent in the postwar period of Yugoslav literature.

Finally, the writers of traditional literature are ranked disproportionately high by the members of social literature because of certain historic "services" which cannot be discussed entirely objectively. This observation does not apply to such "folksy" writers as Branko Ćopić, whose works are widely accepted because of their social color.

There are various additional obstacles to a more responsible and objective evaluation of the literature of the Yugoslav peoples. On the one hand, we cannot strictly rate writers from the smaller republics on the basis of some kind of a quantitative popularity measure since the number of readers and critics are considerably greater in the larger and more culturally developed regions. On the other hand it would be just as dangerous to overemphasize the position of these writers in their national culture because they are fewer in number and there is less competition. Few of them in fact manage to cross provincial boundaries and only with great difficulty since their writing lacks a broader context. Andrić and Krleža are the only ones who have an undisputed position throughout the entire country, which varies according to republics. In Slovenia, for instance, Krleža's influence on the cultural elite was primarily felt before the war. Andrić is read almost like a foreign author such as Moravia or Tolstoy. Davičo has left practically no trace. Foreign authors like Faulkner, Giraudoux, Kafka, Sartre, and Heidegger have been the primary postwar influence on Slovenian contemporary writers.

A few other facts must be borne in mind in reviewing our hierarchies. In spite of the fact that two decades have passed since the war, many writers are still excluded while others enjoy a puffed-up reputation all because of purely political reasons. Miloš Crnjanski and Rastko Petrović, as well as Ristić's "Dead Poets," have been particularly affected by this kind of neglect.* The tendency to rediscover the value of some interesting and significant literary figures who are not so current is also striking. This is exemplified by the case of Stanislav Simić in Zagreb.

Among critics it has been easier to find a place for the older generation, while the younger ones have been lost in the shuffle. The

* Miloš Crnjanski has returned to Belgrade from London and is now published. — *Ed.*

fact that some of them have received official recognition, a kind of charter for their life's work, has however been instrumental in raising the dignity of criticism as a whole. Critics are a peculiar species, whom artists as well as the public venerate but dislike. Besides, Yugoslav criticism remains too much under the influence of Skerlić and Matoša who laid the ground work and cleared the national literary terrain. Contemporary critics suffer because they are always being compared with these two classic figures. Such a comparison is prejudicial and puts a brake on the evolution of criticism, and thus indirectly on the development of literature itself.

I have already mentioned that the evaluation of the younger writers is totally chaotic. This may be excusable for beginners. But it is curious that this ignorance also applies to those writers who have published several books worth noticing, who have been active in the literary community during the entire past decade, and who are really no longer "young." In fact, the entire "reserve" generation is caught in this predicament.

Until 1954 or 1955, the Yugoslav literary situation was relatively clear, not to say sterile, because of the demands of socialist realism. Since at that time proportionately fewer of the young writers entered the field, they were noticed even when they were attacked. Their presence was a fact, undenied and undeniable. All of Belgrade, for instance, was familiar with Miodrag Petrović's 87 *Pesama* and some of the poems in Popa's *Kore* while everyone certainly knew about his eight-legged horse.* During a relatively short period in the late fifties, many young authors entered the literary scene. From then until now their work has not been justly appraised, or accepted, either by the public or by the critics.

There seems to be no way of bridging this gap. Miodrag Bulatović and Branko Miljković are the only two writers from this "reserve generation" who are better known. Bulatović was very badly received by the critics, in particular by the more respected group whose leader was Borislav Mihajlović. It was only after some of his works were translated into German that he began to receive some recognition at home. Unfortunately, even this respectability had its

* Subject of a modernistic poem. — *Ed.*

thorny sides. It manifested itself in jokes published by satirical magazines and thus had little concrete value. The greatest contribution to Branko Miljković's success was the October 1960 Belgrade Prize which he won for his book of poems *Vatra i ništa*. It is ironical and sad, but true to say that his relatively high position in the value hierarchy, especially compared to Borislav Radović and Velimir Lukić, is due in large measure to his suicide, which occurred in Februrary of 1961 shortly after he had received the prize. The newer writers, representatives of the youngest literary generation, are attempting to rise in the hierarchy by some other means. They are supplementing their creative work with more public activities, such as writing for satirical magazines and for television.

So much for an analysis of the value hierarchy in Yugoslav literature. Our pyramid is relatively open, but it is chaotic. We have demonstrated that value criteria adhere strictly to the historical typology. They are not inherent in the work of art nor are they up-to-date. They follow the line of least resistance and so include the easiest and least adequate considerations, as though events retarded their development.

5. LITERARY POLITICS

THE POSITION OF CULTURE IN YUGOSLAVIA

YUGOSLAV POSTWAR literary movements cannot be explained without looking at the social context. Here we have to consider two factors of literary life, writers' groups and literary politics.[1] Literary politics in Yugoslavia is determined mainly by the Communist party. This fact distinguishes socialist literary life from that in capitalist countries.

Usually literary politics constitutes one particular aspect of cultural politics in general. We will therefore first examine the general perspective of culture as a whole. To avoid an extended discussion about the meaning of culture, we shall use the word in its everyday sense. This means we shall not examine science and technology, but limit ourselves to what is called the humanistic sphere. More specfically, we shall discuss the products of mass culture and then the works of high and "pure" art.

Until very recently the role of culture in socialism has not been clearly formulated. A discussion in *Socijalizam* during 1966 to which Vanja Sutlić[2] contributed probably provided the most fruitful way of viewing the relationship. To confirm the conclusions arrived at, we must look at the Communist party's attitude towards culture during the past thirty years. Certain enigmas are clarified by such a review, especially if we remember two key occurrences which we

[1] Editorial discussion in *Socijalizam* on the topic "Savez komunista i kultura"; participants: Krste Crvenkovski, Vukašin Mićunović, Veljko Vlahović, Stane Kavčić, Boris Ziherl, Beno Župančić, Vanja Sutlić, Vatroslav Mimica, Boris Hudoletnjak, Vjekoslav Mikecin, Sveta Lukić, Oskar Davičo, Latinka Perović, Živan Berisavljević, Dušan Popović, Kiro Hadži Vasilev, *Socijalizam*, 1965, no. 9.

[2] Vanja Sutlić, *op. cit.*, pp. 159–162.

have mentioned several times in earlier parts of this book. The first is the well-known 1930's encounter between *Književne sveske* and Krleža's *Pečat*. The second is the liberation of Yugoslav society from dogmatism between 1950 and 1955 which took the form of a polemic against socialist realism. The attempt at that time was to formulate a different kind of social understanding of art, which would be closer to socialism and cultural creativity. Finally today, it seems as though we are on the threshold of a third period in which cultural problems are increasingly interpreted in economic terms.

During this whole lively and complex period the party in the person of "agitprops" [ideological commissions] and ideologues, paid a great deal of attention to phenomena of "higher" art and their ideological interpretation. Such interest was quite understandable during the prewar period because the party contained the intellectual elite. Work on literary magazines and periodicals as well as in other artistic spheres were one of the few legitimate channels of activity for the barred party. Such surveillance was also valid during the unconsolidated period immediately after World War II and for some time after the Cominform expulsion when a new socialist society had to be defended.

However the party's preoccupation with art and the highest forms of cultural expression has not diminished even today. Such a concern is now unbalanced primarily because our practical ideologues, politicians and public workers pay so little attention to our culture as a whole. The media of mass culture and their impact are rarely thought about. Television, a powerful medium of mass communication, and potentially the most ideal contemporary transmitter of mass culture and ideology, has never been thoroughly analyzed in Yugoslavia. Not to mention cultural problems in the provinces. There, culture has been left to itself, to the mercy of chance or some Samaritan initiatives such as the publication of *Bagdala* in Kruševac, or the "Slobodiste" in the same town, or the Park of Sculptures in Vrnjačka Banja. From all of this one must conclude that in Yugoslavia the cultural marketplace, cultural needs, and the social function of culture are not well understood. More systematic examinations of these questions, which may produce or suggest certain answers, are made in vain.[3] Improvisation is the norm and basis for commentaries and conclusions devised by cultural workers, journalists, politicians and officials. Each selects a particular isolated fact which interests him and brandishes it like a club.

Our discussion will become clearer if we are aware that there are no investigations into the existing ideological multiplicity in our society. Momentary political needs illuminate one or the other element, but I am not aware of anyone providing a more complete picture of this Yugoslav ideological multiplicity. On one side, there is a powerful trend toward technocracy, or Americanization of our working intelligentsia. On another, there continues to be a persistent desire for "strong-arm" ideology of the Stalinist bureaucratic-dogmatic school. While on a third, our ideological formulations are being squashed by our nationalistic particularisms. These are not the product of a traditional "mentality" but are rather the result of local economic interests. Each of these nationalisms is merely one manifestation of particularism.

YUGOSLAV ATTITUDES TOWARD CULTURE

There is no need to underline the fact that a complex sociopolitical situation has certain consequences in the cultural field as well. Let us examine one phenomenon in the eastern region of Yugoslavia. Dobrica Ćosić and others christen it the revival of the traditional *čevabdžija* or "petit bourgeois, tavern-keeping" Serbian mentality.[4] What they are referring to is a form of classical Balkan provincialism which has re-emerged during the past ten years. It appeared in the fifties during the transition to political self-government following the more centralized period of administrative socialism. It heralds an atmosphere of overall social liberation, and a transition to a more

[3] This is further supported by the findings of *Jugoslovensko javno mnenje*, the journal of the Institute for Social Studies in Belgrade, which publishes the statistics of its annual public opinion polls on current Yugoslav social issues.

[4] Dobrica Ćosić, "O civilizaciji, naciji, i drugom" (introductory remarks to "Razgovoru o kulturi i urbanizmu zapadnomoravskih gradova," October 1965, Vrnjačka Banja), in the collected works of Dobrica Ćosić, vol. VIII, Belgrade, Prosveta 1966, pp. 203–18. [*Čevabdjia* in the original text is the owner and usually cook in popular local cafes specializing in grilled meat balls — *Trans.*]

diversified "peacetime" way of life. Urbanization, too, covering everything from the problems of urbanism to human behavior, seems to have been a favorable breeding ground for this type of mentality. The phenomenon to which I am referring is not an expression of a classical peasant "Weltanschaung" nor is it fully explained by petit bourgeois ideology. For these views of the world have their own established code and values. But here, in the transition from one developmental phase of our society to another, in the tension among village, town and city, only the most negative aspects of the classical peasant and provincial mentality have come to the fore. Unfortunately, this "philosophy" of life does not have stable positive norms. In fact, it negates all fixed norms. According to it life is reduced to mechanical living and to something temporary. Its deeper meaning lies in "standardization" which is accompanied by man's entanglement in the web of petty activities; it is a unit of semiresponsibility and irresponsibility. In short what we have is a low-order combination of hedonism and pragmatism.

The main propagators of this philosophy are the bureaucrats and the tradesmen, in general the entrepreneurs and a segment of better-paid experts. From our point of view, it is an outgrowth of Stalinism, of the Stalinistic interpretation of authority and the over development of the political hierarchy. Another influential factor in the formation of this "philosophy" is a universal low-order Americanism, which invaded Yugoslavia during the past decade. This combination of ostensible opposites is obscured by Balkan "petit bourgeoisism," which represents the worst in personal petty views. It is obvious that those who live by the values of a hedonistic-pragmatic philosophy seek the most inferior aspects of culture, from folk music to "kitsch" and "schund" ["bad" literature]. But what is even worse is that these groups belong to the most vocal elements of our social life and can influence the development of a general anticultural point of view.

In spite of the anticultural attitude of some segments of the population, Yugoslavia does not lack programs and ideas about culture. Here the Program of the League of Communists is of prime importance. The general ideas expressed in this document have

been analyzed by Vanja Sutlić.[5] Urbanization and cultural development must include the civilizing of our environment and an appreciation of classical cultural values. This process should also provide
for the creation, propagation and acceptance of new, individualistic
values which portray the contemporary social and human condition.
In practice however a vacuum exists between these very general
ideas and everyday Yugoslav life. Although we expect to encounter
an established philosophy of everyday life with concrete moral
norms and a vivid cultural conception, these do not exist. As a result,
the socialist superstructure in Yugoslavia has not been fully built.
At a symposium devoted to the problems of culture and urbanization
I wrote the following:

> I do not consider it an exaggeration to say that after 1945, no new
> philosophic, cultural and urban conceptions have been developed which
> are both sufficiently general and concrete to become part of everyday
> life. Even if there are formulations to the public, these have not been
> specific. We seem to be lacking a system for transmitting ideas and initia-
> tives which fosters genuine closer ties between the artist and the citizens,
> so that culture can humanize life and work.
>
> All of this is the failure of society as a whole, including avant-garde
> politicians, ideologues, writers, artists, scholars, and philosophers. Neither
> concrete positive concepts nor legal means for their realization are availa-
> ble. Our attempt to hide this fact has resulted in the current situation.
> If we wish to refer to its "philosophy" as provincialism, then we have to
> be aware and admit that provincialism is above all rampant in Belgrade
> and that it exists in all of us.[6]

THE ECONOMIC CONCEPT OF CULTURE

New Yugoslavia is a society of strained disproportions, which are
increasingly felt in culture. They cannot be solved by optimistic
phrases about self-government in culture, because these disproportions are not being analyzed or even discussed. Though the Communist party is in power, it is acting as though it were not responsible in the cultural sphere. Our official ideology pays unhealthy

[5] Program SKJ, Belgrade, Kultura, 1958.
[6] Sveta Lukić, "Provincija i provincijalizam," *Polja*, 1966.

and exaggerated attention only to the very highest forms of culture, art or philosophy and leaves popular culture to its own devices.

In short, in contrast to the American concept which treats culture as part of industry, we still adhere to the Stalinist idea that culture is part of ideology. Moreover our culture sometimes becomes a testing ground for various ideas which cannot be tried out in other fields such as economics, or in foreign affairs.* As a consequence our society vaccilates more and more between two concepts of culture — the American and the Soviet.

During the last two years, official headquarters has increasingly made public and semipublic ideological evaluations of certain theoretical works in culture and philosophy. Usually these evaluations are from what Lukacs correctly considers the Stalinist point of view.[7] Verdicts against the philosophical journal *Praxis* during 1965 and 1966, for instance, clearly show how easily the leading ideologues of the League of Communists are able to discredit members of the party intelligentsia as a whole. And this is being done with great lack of subtlety and concern for the real content of the works criticized. On the theoretical level these attacks are remnants of the old dogmatic "ideology," but in practical life they are something quite different, and no one pays any attention.[8]

Since 1965, or the beginning of the economic reform, economic mechanisms have been offered as the panacea for all economic as well as societal problems. Improvised formulas with an economic cast are applied to the cultural sphere as well. *Ekonomska Politika*, for example, trotted out vulgar economism when it commented on our current cultural problems. No wonder that this provoked an extreme moral-romantic reaction among creative artists who expressed their views in *Književne novine* and in discussions on tele-

---

* The author is referring here to the fact that literature may be relatively free but that this is not the case in other areas of society, such as economics and diplomacy — *Ed.*

[7] Georg Lukacs, "Pismo o staljinizmu," *Naše teme*, 1962, no. 12.

[8] Gajo Petrović, "Kritika u socijalizmu," *Praxis*, 1965, no. 3 and "O nepoštednoj kritici svega postojećeg (uz jednu *Vjesnikovu* ocjenu")," *Praxis*, 1965, nos. 4–5; "Dvije i po godine Praxisa," *Praxis*, 1967, nos. 1–2; Rudi Supek, "Partija i inteligencija," *Praxis*, 1965, no. 3; "Još jednom o alternativi — staljinistički pozitivizam ili stvaralački marksizam," *Praxis*, 1965, no. 6.

vision.[9] Doubtless there is a need for stronger ties between art and "consumers," and for a switch from dependence on state budgets to self-financing. A purely economic approach to culture does not, however, consider the essence of culture, which it eagerly emphasizes in theory, and it is even less sensitive to the availability of finances.[10] This can best be illustrated by replies from a Yugoslav opinion poll on the financing of culture (see Tables 1, 2, 3).

TABLE 1

QUESTION: *How should culture be financed (libraries, publishers, cultural centers, theaters, cinemas, museums, performances, etc.)?*
REPLIES: (1) The community as a whole should finance culture.
          (2) Both the community and the consumers should finance culture.
          (3) Culture can be supported entirely by its own consumers.
          (4) Undecided.

Percentage of Replies	SFRJ	Slovenia	Croatia	Voyvo-dina	Serbia	Bosnia-Herce-govina	Monte-negro	Mace-donia	Kosovo-Metohije
(1)	23	21	27	33	22	22	22	10	22
(2)	33	38	32	37	30	26	34	33	37
(3)	4	4	4	7	3	2	12	6	1
(4)	40	37	37	23	45	50	32	51	40

TABLE 2 [11]

What is the reason for your reply to question number 1?

Percentage

"The community as a whole should support culture."
1. Because culture is important to the community and to the individual   25
2. Culture cannot support itself (big expenditures, uninterested consumers)   47

[9] Cf. Petar Džadžić, "Kulturne prilike" (I–IV), *NIN*, February 5, 12, 19 and 26, 1967.
[10] See Mito Hadži Vasilev, "Teorijski aspekti društvenog položaja kulture u socijalizmu," *Socijalizam*, 1968, no. 3.
[11] Jugoslovensko javno mnenje 1966, seria A, "Rezultati anketnih istrazi-vanja," Institut Društvenih Nauka, Belgrade, 1967, pp. 130–42 (results and comments on a poll on financing Yugoslav culture).

TABLE 2—*Continued*

3. Other	16
4. No reply	12

"Both the community and the consumers should finance culture."

5. Culture benefits society and the individual	16
6. Culture has insufficient income from its consumers and therefore needs help from the community	47
7. Other	16
8. No answer	21

"Culture can be supported entirely by its own consumers."

9. So that in all phases of our society rewards are made according to efficiency and cost	23
10. Those who use culture should pay for it	34
11. Other	22
12. No answer	21

For the economic mechanism to function efficiently in making literature and culture available to the public, it is necessary to provide stable institutions which will actively bring the consumer in contact with culture. In addition, Yugoslavs will have to be offered a more attractive philosophy of everyday life. I once suggested: "Let us worry about life rather than about the Communist future." Such a philosophy will help people understand that culture means to develop one's own personality. Such a philosophy will help Yugoslavs seek out more serious cultural values and acquire a need for them.

Culture suffers because it lacks a public and the public suffers without culture. The purely economic approach must not overlook where we stand in art and culture. We must also resolve the frustrating contradictions between American-postulated practice and Stalinist theory, between the extreme emphasis on economic criteria and ideological suppression.

TABLE 3

How do you think culture should be financed (libraries, publishers, cultural centers, theaters, cinemas, museums, various performances, etc.)?[b]

SOCIAL PROFESSIONAL CLASSIFICATION PERCENTAGES

	Highly skilled and skilled workers	Semi-skilled and un-skilled workers	Highly quali-fied employ-ees	Moder-ately quali-fied employ-ees	Less quali-fied employ-ees	Agricul-tural workers (self-employed)	Other self-employed: artisans, restau-rateurs	Pen-sioners, invalids, etc.	Students (school and uni-versity)	House-wives (agri-cultural)	House-wives (non-agri-cultural)
The community as a whole should support culture	27	21	25	30	28	20	14	27	21	14	19
The community and the public (consumers) should finance culture	51	31	72	49	46	22	45	30	72	12	22
Culture can be supported by its own consumers	6	4	1	9	3	10	0	5	1	5	3
Undecided	16	44	2	12	23	48	41	38	6	69	56

THE PARTY'S LITERARY POLITICS IMMEDIATELY
AFTER THE LIBERATION

Paradoxically, Yugoslavia has no program for culture as a whole, and for this reason there cannot be a cultural policy. Yet our ideologues and politicians have a definite influence on norms and programs of creativity in literature and art. At the risk of repetition we will therefore have to review the entire postwar period from the point of view of the relationship between party and literature.[12]

Immediately after the war certain very general principles of art, its relationship towards reality, its place in society and its immediate tasks were spelled out. Some of these were formulated in the period of prewar social literature and in the conflict between *Književne sveske* representing the official position of the Communist party and *Pečat*. These socialist-realism principles were further refined during the struggle for national liberation. The infamous Zhdanov reports * transformed them into Stalinism in art and culture and thus legitimized party control of literature. One must not forget that this very negative extreme was the fruit of ten years of "literary politics" in the Soviet Union and that efforts were made to export socialist realism with all its Soviet extremes to the Eastern block countries.

In Yugoslavia, however, there were still many older bourgeois writers, as well as traces of avant-garde symbolism and German expressionism which counteracted Soviet extremism in literature. Finally, the prewar spirit of social revolt was preserved in social literature. Thus Yugoslavia still had literary variety in 1947 while all such phenomena were liquidated in the Soviet Union as early as 1930–32, and quite definitively by 1934 when socialist realism was proclaimed during the First Congress of the Writers' Union. The party therefore, even though it was involved in the creation of a new literature in a new society, did not insist on the principles of socialist realism too rigidly. In our country a milder formula emerged called *national realism*. This variation came about because

[12] The following text was published under the title "Partija i književnost" in the journal *Encyclopedia moderna*, 1967, no. 3–4.

* Andrei Zhdanov, 1896–1948, was Stalin's Party chief for Leningrad who after World War II ruthlessly destroyed new literary and musical trends by demanding continued conformity to the dictates of socialist realism — Ed.

our art needed to express our own specific social situation and because there were many uncompromised artists, partisans, and "loyal"
citizens, who were once again allowed to publish.

The Communist party adopted this milder formula and publicized
it through Radovan Zogović's speech at the First Writers' Congress
in 1946. His report is characteristic of literary policy during the first
postwar period. In addition to laying down general formulas and
defining tasks, it summarized the literary activities of our writers
since 1941, rated their political behavior during the war, and issued
visas for those who were permitted to write in the new Yugoslavia.

In the period right after the war literature was under the federal
ideological commission, the Agitprop. Its leading functionaries cen-
sored literature at all levels from recruitment of editors to editorial
boards to the selection and revision of texts. They also publicly criticized theatrical performances, checking on their ideology and often
banning or changing them, thus influencing style and repertoire. In
films, Agitprop personnel meddled in everything including the choice
of actors and the final approval of the sound track.[13] There is no
doubt that such direct censorship was the result of Soviet influence.
The major censors were distinguished prewar Communists, early
fighters, and intellectuals. Often they were publicists who dabbled
in art but there were also a few like Radovan Zogović who remained
artists.

We are not entirely incorrect in calling this the "verbal" period
of literary censorship. One word pronounced by the "top" determined the destiny of a work or of an individual. The most significant
cultural questions were settled verbally and behind closed doors.
There is not even a bibliography of Yugoslav literature for the years
1945–50. It is therefore difficult to study the literary situation of this
period. One more thing needs to be mentioned. Contacts between
writers and ideologues were sometimes diverse and informal so that
the party did not always have to meddle in literature officially. At
times this influence was brought to bear by those writers, who were
considered to have official sanction and who frequently took advan-

[13] The famous discussion which followed the first three premieres of the Yugoslav Dramatic Theater (*Književne novine*, July 13, 1948) is a typical example
of this.

tage of this status. Representatives of prewar social literature come to mind here. But at the same time a type of person emerged who voluntarily wished to serve as a link between the party and literature. These people were particularly dangerous when they raised certain questions and then answered them in the way in which they felt the party would have responded. This negative habit has persisted to our day and has become more deeply entrenched.

THE PARTY'S ROLE IN THE LIBERALIZATION OF LITERATURE AFTER 1950

We know that the second phase of development of our postwar literature begins in the fifties. At that time political polemics against Stalinism and our own dogmatism were transferred to the literary arena. It was not until 1952 and 1954, however, that the isolated voices of the literary rebels began to be united. Parallel with and as a result of this campaign, different ways of writing were permitted. In Belgrade this development was heralded by the appearance of *Mladost* and later the fight between *Svedočanstva* and *Književne novine*. Proof of the growing pains which accompanied the process of liberalization was the brief appearance of these literary periodicals and similar ones in Croatia (*Krugovi*) and Slovenia (*Beseda*). Recently discovered shorthand notes of the 1954 founders meeting of *Svedočanstva* provide illuminating insights into the atmosphere of those years. The final speaker after the initiating committee was Bora Drenovać, representing the Agitprops, who gave his blessing to the journal because he "personally had confidence in those" who had taken the initiative.[14]

The paradox of the whole situation was not only that the ideological commissions first approved the founding of these freer periodicals but that they later banned them. Wasn't their development, after all, in accordance with original intentions? How can this paradox be explained? The fact is that both the politicians and ideologues at the time needed proof of freedom of ideas in literature and culture

[14] See the stenographic notes published under the title "Početak *Svedočanstava*," Delo, 1967, no. 2.

in order to undermine Soviet dogmatism. However too much independence of mind in domestic literature went beyond official plans and desires. The League of Communists of Yugoslavia was more interested in scoring a foreign policy goal against the Soviet Union than in securing genuine internal freedom for Yugoslav culture.

Such an assessment is supported by none other than Milovan Djilas, the party ideologue most concerned with artistic and aesthetic questions. In his book *Legenda o Njegošu* (1952) he says: "Leave politics to us politicians, while we leave aesthetics to you writers. It is obvious which of these is more important." Going even a step further and reducing matters to the absurd, Djilas also praised Andrić as the writer who had most profoundly described contemporary reality.[15]

Consequently the following conformist literary formula becomes prevalent: "The further into the past and away from the present the better." This is a many-sided formula, which however provides enough room for maneuver, and enables literature to do some experimenting. It also protects it against risks arising from touching sensitive points. No one objected to this slogan. In looking over the periodicals and polemics of those years, one has the distinct impression that our writers as a matter of fact were anxious to fall into this formula. It would have been more normal for literature while actively fighting the dictates of socialist realism so chose temporarily a more militant extreme. Instead this passive formula spread and became a permanent attitude.

In making this evaluation we must not, however, forget that there was in fact an event, the "Djilas case," which seemed to spring from more militant leanings and which culminated in the Plenum of the Central Committee held January 20, 1954. At this Plenum and later in public, Oskar Davičo's poem *Čovekov čovek* was identified with "Djilasism" in art. For a few months there was under cover "revanchism" spearheaded by the dogmatic forces which culminated in party witch hunts, especially among writers and at the University. Then toward the end of 1954 Kardelj made his statement about

[15] Milovan Djilas, *Razmišljana o raznim pitanjima*, Belgrade, Kultura, 1951, pp. 46–47.

freedom of creativity and party noninterference in questions of artistic style. This formula turns out to be identical to the resolution of the Soviet Communist party of June 18, 1925.[16] We have here a Party response which was not borrowed but an indication that the Yugoslav situation in 1954 was similar to that in Soviet Russia in 1925. Later, at the beginning of 1955, two new reviews, *Savremenik* and *Delo*, were founded in Belgrade, thus setting the stage for the modernism-realism fight.

It is unnecessary to point out that the League of Communists was the prime mover in founding these journals. The publication indicated, for the first time, an interest in the internal cultural situation. It also legalized a process which could no longer be stopped but which could be slowed down or redirected. Foreign policy considerations continued to be influential, demanding proof that the Djilas case with its polemic against dogmatism was not a return to Stalinism. The expression of conflicting ideas continued unabated and was increasingly fruitful. The existence of varied points of view was used by the party not only in culture but also to prove that our society in general was becoming more liberal. Naturally this argument was false because the example came from a restricted area, cultural debate, and did not apply to social questions at all.

Until a few years ago Yugoslavia was a country primarily concerned with foreign affairs. Domestic policy, including economic and cultural questions, were an incidental by-product of external commitments. This subordination continued even after internal problems could no longer be solved by external dictates alone. The second phase of our postwar literary development proves that the problems of culture as a whole, and literature in particular, were closely tied to this syndrome. The particular character of our literary development is additionally a result of the brief duration of Stalinism in Yugoslavia. De-Stalinization began early and progressed gradually and slowly. This progress which is determined by Yugoslav-Soviet foreign relations can be summed up in the following way: Soviet dogmatism directly orders artists to create in a certain way,

[16] Resolution of the Central Committee of the Serbian Communist Party (b), June 18, 1925. "O politici Partije u oblasti umetničke književnosti, *Delo*, 1957, no. 11.

while in Yugoslavia, society, through its politicians, ideologues and official artists, reaches an agreement with creators on what not to do. Either form of intervention however, makes artists passive.[17] The November 1954 plenum provides the first accounts of our fight against socialist realism as the cultural arm of Stalinism. This plenum is thus historically significant, not only for Yugoslavia, but for socialism everywhere. At the same time it timidly and indirectly proposed the criteria of our aestheticism. It is characteristic that in 1954 a writers' plenum openly discusses socialist realism in the Soviet Union, while we ourselves were compromised by the Djilas case. The situation is not basically different today. It is time we realized that we are very frank in international questions, but not in domestic matters. The right of radical criticism seems to belong only to selected individuals and certain social groups.

PARTY NON-INTERVENTION, FROM 1955 TO PRESENT

After 1955, the party no longer interfered in literary questions, as long as they were purely literary. From time to time since then the party has exerted informal pressure through its "own" people, and possibly there has been some influence on the work of periodicals or publishing houses. But in every case of informal pressure, official artists had to fight for the party's line using argumentation rather than threat. Party authority alone was no longer sufficient to bring results, nor did the party itself insist on this.

The period from 1955 to 1960 was the best and the most stimulating period in Yugoslav literature. The League of Communists intervened directly only in cases in which literary works might have an effect on foreign policy, particularly on relations with the Soviet Union, or in those internal situations where censorship might have degenerated into the settling of personal grudges. In short, it intervened only in borderline cases. Here are some examples of such borderline cases and the party's response. Take for instance the party's negative response to those serious critiques of socialist real-

[17] *Umetnost i kriterijumi,* p. 192.

ism which were written in 1957 on the occasion of the fortieth anniversary of the October Revolution, and in 1962 when the Yugoslav introduction to *Doctor Zhivago* was published.[18] Then there was the interference with the election of delegates to the 1958 Belgrade Writers Congress. In spite of the fact that this congress was to battle dogmatism, the "voting machine" of the Serbian Writers Association did not elect certain prominent writers, merely because they belonged to the modernistic camp. On the other hand, Ćopić too was punished when he published his criticism of our literary situation in Moscow's *Literaturnaya gazeta.*[19]

In general, however, the interference by the League takes on a new more moderate coloration in this period. The party takes stands and makes evaluations, but this does not necessarily imply arrest, banning of journals, or party penalties. If in this period members make errors they are not summoned to an ideologue or to the politicians. In this way, a relatively coarse sieve made literary freedom and freedom of thought more and more possible. The League's liberalization is evidenced by a number of literary works and even critical texts. Borislav Mihajlović, the critic, noted in a *NIN* interview that Yugoslavia had some of the most abstract belles lettres in the world.[20] As I pointed out earlier in the analysis of our postwar literary movements, I personally believe that our literature is noncommital toward our epoch. Yugoslav literary and cultural life grew more self-reliant toward the end of the fifties. The press was the first to gain independence and autonomy, followed by publishers and publishing houses. Writers' organizations lost much of their previous power. A stratified audience guarantees that our literature is of a high quality, but it does not in fact have any impact on the larger mass of people.

Ideology and the cultural apparatus slowly separate in this same period. The apparatus run by writers solved practical questions

[18] In addition to Šinko's and Vidmar's text, see also: Nana Bogdanović, "Boljševici reči"; Dušan Makavejev, Film-neustrašivost; Vladan Radovanović, "Šostakovič i stvaralaštvo (above articles in *Delo*, 1957, no. 11) Boris Pasternak's *Doktor Živago*, Belgrade, Prosveta, 1962 (the author's introduction in the Cyrillic edition of *Pasternak i roman*).

[19] *Literaturnaya gazeta*, July 15, 1960.

[20] Borislav Mihajlović: Interview in *NIN*, December 17, 1957.

and held the purse strings. "Ideology" consequently had only to be consulted when essential issues needed clarification and solution. Ideology which now operates in a vacuum, lacks constant contact with and relation to reality. As a result of this cultural policy-making has gotten lost in different bodies, between producers and consumers.[21] Before, Agitprop and ideology were directed by the elite cadres, who had gathered around the party in the turbulent thirties and the war years. Now this has changed because Yugoslav society has become differentiated. With a few exceptions the old ideological cadres no longer exist. The elite which forged the party and postwar intellectual youth have gone off to do other things. They have become engineers, doctors, scholars and artists. Only the minority with questionable talent have chosen professional party and political work. Unfortunately those who select party cadres do not understand this simple fact. Out of habit they continue to recruit replacements for ideological and cultural work from that same minority with inadequate talent and preparation.

In summary then, ideological interference on the part of the party is not continuous or direct today. Economic correctives, not to say pressures, seem to have taken the place of some earlier types of interventions. In everyday life there are still petty censors, members of various councils of cultural institutions who are professionally concerned with ideology. It is therefore sometimes difficult to determine whether their meddling is a result of a personal decision or if it emanates from "above," as the result of conversations and decisions in some ideological commission. More important is seems to me is the desire to remove literature from the party agenda. This desire results from a combination of economic and conformist tendencies.

IDEOLOGICAL ASSESSMENTS TODAY

Recently, after an interruption of several years, it is once again fashionable to make ideological evaluations of literary works. For the time being these appraisals are oral rather than written, and if they are printed it is generally in pamphlets and interviews rather than

[21] Cf. Latinka Perović, "Društveni položaj kulture u Jugoslaviji, *Delo*, 1964, no. 12.

in serious texts. But we cannot ignore them because oral and improvised criticisms have always been very important in Yugoslavia. They merit our attention above all because they are extremely negative.[22]

Current ideological evaluations make three points. First, they criticize modern Yugoslav literature as bourgeois and reactionary, because they reflect Western influences or preach nationalism and chauvinism. This kind of argumentation is found not only among ideologues but also among old revolutionary writers and former front-line fighters, who were active in social literature, and have always tended toward traditional literary-aesthetic views. In fact this coincidence should not surprise us. We cannot expect much more of men who were shaped before the war, during the revolution or immediately afterwards, in the midst of harsh political, literary-political and other battles. These battles were always divisive: "for" and "against," "yes" or "no." Naturally many of these men developed a defensive psychology and they are the ones today who have been called on to judge what is progressive or what endangers socialism.

There is also another point of attack. Those writers who fifteen years ago fought bitterly against our own and Soviet dogmatism have a way of discovering "Zhdanovism" in Yugoslavia today. This is understandable as we have pointed out because the extreme opposite of Zhdanovism has some of the same characteristics. Writers like Oskar Davičo and Marko Ristić have always wanted to destroy Zhdanovites with Zhdanovist means, such as administrative censorship and ideological disqualification. Today they are applying these methods to new quite different opponents. Besides, our anti-Zhdanovites have acquired the habit of covering up certain "sticky" questions, fearing that discussing them openly will lead to "awkward" repercussions. They seem to have been worn out by the battles waged ten to fifteen years ago.

The third current of criticism, unscrupulous in its aggressiveness, lets ideological epithets fall where they may. Unfortunately some younger men, humorists and poets, have found themselves among

[22] Cf. Sveta Lukić "Idejne ocene ili ideološke diskvalifikacije," *Borba*, June 15, 1966.

the attacked. The critics are a circle of writers, who have only recently struggled to the top and are now greedy for praise, recognition and reward. They seem to be afraid, with some justification,
that their pinnacle will turn to dust and ashes tomorrow. Even if
they are not directly careerists, they engage in private antagonisms
which are faddish and petty. They express these primarily in public
outbursts in clubs and cafes rather than in their writing.

It is not difficult to discover that these quasi-ideological judgments
contain no serious rational arguments. What is noticeable is that
the first line of attack seldom uses Zhdanovism. The two older attack
strategies also give opposite ideological evaluations of the same literary works. But through the years they have unintentionally become more similar. Today, in almost every respect, these two currents coincide. A vicious circle has resulted from which there is
no escape even by means of the third tactic.

What then is the real basis for such ideological practice? In the
process of fighting dogmatism, both Yugoslav and Soviet, and parallel with the development of our new literature, we abandoned
"classic dogmatism" which often turned into condemnations of literature. Along with this the evaluation of ideological content died as
well.

Any analysis of ideological developments vis-a-vis literature must
take into account the overall situation in our society. Yugoslavia's
developmental path since 1945 is a unique social experience and
raises many complex questions. In judging new literary manifestations therefore caution and flexibility are essential. It is probably
correct to say that certain contemporary literary works express insights of a livelier more fluid strata of Yugoslav society. Others reflect the self-satisfied feelings of some people, for whom all difficulties have been solved, mainly because they have given up on them,
and for whom no important existential questions remain. The third
group finds its models and its public among the old revolutionaries,
our dissatisfied "solunaši" * who are crushed by the dialectic of
development.

It may be best, in fact, to devise some evaluative formulas, or

* World War I veterans of the Solun (Salonika) front seeking special privileges — Ed.

terms, which would represent the outlook of these layers in Yugoslav society. Classical ideological categories are sufficient to fulfill this task. Let us take for example the concepts revolutionary/reactionary. If they are applied to literary works honestly, some conclusions can be drawn. It is obvious that our new literature contains no strikingly revolutionary books, but it is even clearer that there are few reactionary books.[23] If we want to use these qualifiers, then we must include all literary output and not merely hang epithets on younger and less well established writers. These criteria must be applied more systematically as well as more precisely than has been the rule in political speeches and reports.

Current ideological evaluations which are capricious and improvised are useless without real analysis and without theoretical foundations. The two opposing currents of censorship, Zhdanovite and anti-Zhdanovite, seem to be engaged in a friendly match somewhere on the periphery of reality, although they give the appearance of being pitted against one another. Their discussions sound like the grumbling of old men, though they are not without danger. It is amusing to notice how the protection of narrow personal interests is uppermost in these men's minds. All are striving collectively to maintain the literary status quo so it may remain moderately free and moderately problematic. Such behavior is reminiscent of salon ideology, if I may be permitted to use an old-fashioned expression.

Our discussion elucidates the idea that tolerance is the cornerstone on which cultural and ideological politics must be built during this period. Above all, we must define its lowest common denominator so that ideological evaluations and interventions do not injure the very root of artistic creation, or denigrate the value of the individual, as was the case during Stalin's time. Finally, in ideological work it is essential to seek rational arguments and then to use them. Ideological evaluation, regardless of what it is or where it originates, must be conscientiously planned and based on rational criteria in order to be effective and beneficial.

[23] Cf. *Estetička čitanka*, pp. 120–21.

6. LITERARY CRITICISM

THROUGHOUT HISTORY we can distinguish three types of criticism depending on the rigor of their approach. Although they are not entirely separable, we shall isolate them for clarity's sake. The first is ontological and philosophical and is exemplified by Heidegger, Sartre and Blanchaux. This approach uses specific examples to demonstrate the meaning of art compared to other human activities. This kind of criticism may miss what is specific in a work of art, because it uses the journey through art to prove its own general concepts.

The philosophical-ontological type of criticism is resented for its romanticism, and is accused of relying too much on prophecy and intuition. Naturally it employs no specific method, or scientific standards of verification. For this reason, its approach is basically common sense and dialectical, which means that it is speculative. It does not, additionally, establish definite premises and final conclusions.

This type of criticism makes some very fruitful predictions. In a more rigorous form its ideas can at least be used as working hypotheses to determine the relationship between artistic phenomena and the poetic unity of a work of art. Philosophical criticism is thus at its best when it is used to interpret thoughtful, reflective poetry; painting, and contemporary "black humor" literature. In other words, it is most effective dealing with some kinds of artistic creations.

The second type of criticism is exact, or scientific. Only two of its orientations, the sociological and the formalistic, have so far produced worthwhile results. In the field of sociological criticism the most serious work has been done by Marxists. But certain Western critics, such as Hauser and Kazin, must also be included among these because of the objectivity of their research and its closeness to Marxism. The contribution of sociologists such as Adorno, Lipzeller, Dufrenne, Divino, and Escarpit has not been evaluated or widely used.

One can say with some justification that this type of criticism vacillates between tradition and sociological aestheticism and a modern sociology of art. The method is general, common sense, with certain dialectical influences which it has absorbed from historical materialism. This means that it contains many of the elements of philosophical-ontological criticism. I have written the following about the relationship between this type of criticism and historical materialism:

> Historical materialism attempted by using some quotations from Marx, Lenin, and Engels to show that its laws apply to art and then used art to illustrate those laws. As a result, art was automatically reduced to a "social equivalent" and then had to depict the typical socioeconomic realities of an epoch. Even such outstanding Marxists as Mehring, Lafargue, Plekhanov, Lukacs exhibit such tendencies.
>
> The younger generation of critics, who appeared just before or after the war, like Gramsci, Lefebvre, Goldman and Anders, studied literature as seriously as these early Marxist thinkers and knew it thoroughly.[1]

Sociological criticism's strong point is history and the historical approach. Since it does not limit itself to an analysis of one social environment, it presents a work in relation to the period in which it originated and in relation to subsequent periods. Sociological criticism is a powerful approach in unraveling controversial questions, especially when these questions arise from deficiencies in the works themselves. It explains these in terms of the artist's relationship to his epoch, or as Goldman puts it, "the writer's individuality and the external conditions of his life." Sociological criticism is most successful in interpreting average artworks, especially those which have little value, such as kitsch and schund, and which constitute the so-called current output. However, in "high" art it is most successful only in critical realism.[2]

[1] *Umetnost i kriterijumi*, pp. 11–12.

[2] Cf. Lucien Goldman, *Dijalektička istraživanja* (translation), Sarajevo, Veselin Masleša, 1959.

The second type of exact criticism is formalistic, or instrumental, and has received much greater attention in the West during the last decades. Today this kind of criticism is under fire in the Anglo-American countries where it reached its greatest development. Its treatises however lack "general perspective." In all sciences, certain general theories have to be established.[3] Today the criticism of criticism seems to demand a total or philosophico-anthropological approach to a work of art. In practice, such an approach is either Christian or Marxist, as Svetozar Petrović convincingly points out.[4]

The scientism of instrumental criticism is also attacked on the grounds that it leaves no room for the individual critic's talent and intuition. Spitzer and Staiger consider the first step of criticism a certain "hunch" which does or does not exist.[5] This is an assumption which is difficult to prove. With all its faults, this type of criticism is strongest when it deals with pure forms of art, particularly poetry. It is also more efficacious with realistic lifelike literature and the fantastic than with essayistic or cerebral literature.

Both types of exact criticism use the scientific, scholarly approach and thus represent the last word in science as applied to art. Since it however also utilizes philosophical, commonsense, and dialectical methods as well as intuition, it cannot make generalizations or prove these rationally and with confidence.

We are thus left with concrete, empirical criticism which may be called "artistic" criticism. It is not an impressionistic or evocative orientation, nor everyday journalistic criticism, but extremely diverse and permeated with exact and philosophical criticism. Its representatives include T. S. Eliot, Virginia Woolf, Marina Cvetayeva, Roland Bart, and François Mauriac.

Various varieties of this criticism can be distinguished according to their aesthetic concepts. Each one has its basic principles. The artistic critic has not formulated them, they are the "fabric" of his work. Theoretically they are not solid. Essentially we are talking about a certain "naïve" approach to art and a "feeling" for art, which

[3] "Ka kritici kritike," *Razlog*, 1964, no. 4, p. 348.
[4] Svetozar Petrović, "Kritika i djelo," *Zora*, Zagreb, 1963.
[5] Emil Staiger, *Die Kunst der Interpretation*, Zurich, 1955; see also Ždenek Škreba's comments on this book in *Umjetnost riječi*, 1957, no. 1.

are not infallible. A genuine, solid critic has the ability to stand off and refute himself; he is able, thanks to his immersion and flexibility, to appreciate and accept different artistic directions, to reconcile himself to them, and to be just in his principled prejudice. Concrete criticism serves art rather than vice versa.

This type of criticism collects contemporary material and thus complements the history of art. This fact emerges from a review of the history of art criticism. In his significant book *The History of Art Criticism*, Lionello Venturi follows Croce and unites the history of art with art criticism: "The history of art and art criticism, strive towards the comprehension of a work of art, which cannot be attained without an understanding of the conditions surrounding its creation. And there is no comprehension without judgment. Judgment is the final goal of criticism and art history.[6]

POSSIBILITIES FOR SYNTHESIS OF DIFFERENT KINDS OF LITERARY CRITICISM

Obviously there is no one ideal integral criticism which combines the most worthwhile qualities of all types of criticism. We can imagine such a criticism, but how can it be realized? And should our efforts even be devoted to this end? There is no clear answer, despite the argument that a synthesis is possible because each type of criticism, to a greater or lesser extent, contains elements of all others.

In the meantime, though it may not be ideal, each type of criticism is practiced. They exist, with all their good and bad sides and get at some of the essence of art. Valéry's speculative idea which Sartre mentions in his discussion on imagination is once again confirmed: "Everything exists in everything else, if only we continue to the end."[7] But according to others whose standards of scholarship are flexible, criticism is far from being scientific and never will become a science.

Let us look at a narrower field, therefore, comparing sociological

[6] Lionello Venturi, *Istorija umetničke kritike* (translation), Belgrade, Kultura, 1963, p. 17.
[7] Jean-Paul Sartre, *Imagination*, Felix Alcan, Paris, 1936.

criticism with instrumental criticism (language, style, structure). It may be that these two criticisms are the only two rational approaches to art today. Attempts have been made to bring them closer together or at least to use them concomitantly. In 1927, Boris Arvatov pointed out the need for uniting the formalistic and sociological methods, and those who agreed with him, even called themselves by a new name, "forsocs" [*formalistic-soc*iological critic*s*]. It appears that historical and structural elements can be related. The levels of a work of art as outlined by structural critics such as Wellek, suggest this to us: "A closer analysis of a work of art will show that it is best to think of it as not merely one system of norms, but rather a system which is made up of several strata, each implying its own subordinate group.[8]

Wellek constructs these layers according to the outline of the Polish philosopher Roman Ingarden:

1. sound-stratum
2. units of meaning
3. the objects represented
4. stratum of metaphysical qualities.[9]

Such a synthesis would provide a much more complete theory of literature with more scientific elements than other current theories. In such a theory of literature containing means of verification, philosophical criticism would help to generalize and concrete criticism would provide specific examples of works of art and artists and thus generate inexhaustible new material.

Wellek meanwhile underlines the possibility of a more far-reaching synthesis, which would unite philosophical criticism and even meta-aesthetics, with exact, structural criticism. His conclusion about a work of art is:

It is a system of norms of ideal concepts which are intersubjective. They must be assumed to exist in collective ideology, changing with it, accessible only through individual mental experiences. . . .

[8] Rene Wellek and Austin Warren, *Theory of Literature*, 3rd ed. New York, Harcourt, Brace & World (Harvest Book), 1963, p. 151 (Serbo-Croatian translation, Belgrade, Nolit, 1965).
[9] Roman Ingarden, *O dziele literackim* (Das Literarische Kuntswerk), Warsaw, PWN, 1954, pp. 52–57.

There is no structure outside norms and values. We can not comprehend and analyze any work of art without reference to values. . . .

Structure, sign, and form are three aspects of the same problem and
cannot be artificially isolated.[10]

Wellek's conclusions provide additional material for a discussion
of evaluative criteria. In my *Umetnost i kriterijumi*, which surveys
the most dissimilar contemporary critics, I conclude that basic criteria are discoverable only through a study of both criticism and the
work of art itself:

Regardless of their aesthetic orientation and their other differences,
all critics discover something which is common in a work of art. Look at
the Belgrade critics and essayists, such as Stanislav Vinaver, who bril-
liantly reconstructs Rabelais, Villon and the German romantics. He does
it freely, seemingly nonchalantly, and yet completely. The same effect is
achieved by Isidora Sekulić, a writer whose great erudition is combined
with an exceptional feeling for poetry as the essence of art. Zoran Gluščević writes with amateur adulation about Goethe and German romanticism. Zoran Mišić speaks clearly and systematically without simplification
about his two poets Miodrag Pavlović and Vasko Popa and about Serbian
poetry in general. Borislav Mihajlović has demonstrated brilliant insight,
in which capricious partiality and objectivity are paradoxically combined,
in dealing with the essays of Marko Ristić, the novels of Dobrica Ćosić,
Andrić's *Prokleta avlija*, as well as with the poetry of Miodrag Pavlović
and Vasko Popa. Miodrag Pavlović, following modern structural criticism
and at the same time being comfortable in his own domain of poetry, has
seriously studied Vasko Popa, Vladislav Petković Dis, Milan Rakić and
Milutin Bojić while disproving many established opinions about them. An
impressionistic criticism can be found in the texts of Petar Dzadzić studying the relationship between Andrić's earlier and later works, Miroslav
Krleža's "man in revolt," as well as Miodrag Bulatović and Branko Miljković. Among the young ones, whom I like and whom I have been in a position
to follow more regularly, I have observed similarities in the critiques of
Miloslav Mirković, a great lover of poetry, in the work of Muharem Pervić, a serious contemplative, in the rebel and pamphleteer Miroslav Egerić,
and in the lucid Zoran Petrović.[11]

---

[10] Wellek and Warren, *op. cit.*, pp. 151–52.
[11] *Umetnost i kriterijumi*, p. 122.

YUGOSLAV IMPRESSIONISTIC
AND AESTHETIC CRITICISM

In spite of these exceptions, postwar criticism as a whole in Yugoslavia is still monotonous and uniform though there are some regional differences. Critics in Belgrade, Sarajevo and Skopje primarily practice concrete criticism. In Zagreb there is a tendency to work in the scientific, instrumental tradition, while in Slovenia the philosophic current is more evident, as exemplified by critical writings in *Perspektive*. Our historical review of literary life gives reasons for these divergences.

By and large criticism in Yugoslavia is aesthetic, even aestheticising. The majority of critics go to extremes in stressing the independence of the literary work. This criticism takes itself too seriously as an academic discipline, and is embellished with the faddish terminology of aestheticism. In spite of all this its basic approach to a literary work, however, has remained impressionistic. Attempts at formal analysis remain superficial, excursions into sociology are rare and journalistic, while the philosophizing of Yugoslav critics is amateurish. Quite logically such criticism has pushed our literature into the arms of aestheticism more perhaps than it would have gone on its own account.[12]

An examination of Belgrade criticism of poetry after the war proves some interesting facts. Take for instance the anthology *Savremena poezija*.[13] Here the criticism is best when it deals with individual poets and their works. Being ahistorical it avoids strict literary evaluation and concentrates on the interpretation of the poet's own world, his visions and his message. For the last ten years this has been the central tendency in Belgrade.

The younger critics, who are the only active ones at present, rarely keep track of contemporary poetry as a whole. They limit their interest and choose according to more personal preferences. Each one deals with a few of his own favorites. In Belgrade, recently for instance, a dozen serious modern critical works of this personal type have been written. There have been portraits, essays, and studies

[12] Cf. Sveta Lukić, "Opredeljivanje," *Vidici*, 1964, nos. 81–82.
[13] *Savremena poezija*, pp. 11–12.

about Dušan Matić, Milan Dedinac, Oskar Davičo, Skender Kulenović, Vasko Popa, Miodrag Pavlović, Branko Miljković and Borislav
Radović. Naturally there are other poets who are equally good,
who have not been written about or received the kind of interpre-
tations they deserved. I am thinking in particular of Desanka Maksimović, Aleksander Vučo, Radovan Zogović, Stevan Raičković and
some others. However, on the whole our contemporary poets have
had better luck than their predecessors from the interwar period
who are still awaiting interpretation.

One immediate result of this subjective type of critique is that it
emphasizes, perhaps even overrates poets. While pointing out its
best aspects, we must take exception to the fact that this criticism
lacks a theoretic and historical point of view. In principle, it is
difficult to write about living writers and about phenomena which
are still in the process of development. One cannot expect defini-
tive literary-historical appraisals from contemporaries. Our postwar
criticism, however, has practically abandoned any attempt at historical treatment of contemporary poetry. The reason for this is
that the critics were involved in various literary struggles and themselves took one or another "warring" side, so that no one remained
"outside the barricades." Subjectivity is thus professionally unavoidable, and it is certainly not as bad as sterility.

Lack of a more general point of view makes serious efforts towards
synthesis impossible. Theoretically, our criticism is unaware of the
close ties between criticism, theory and history which are justifiably
stressed today.[14] In practice we have additionally forgotten that it
is time to examine quite honestly the direction we have taken.

The situation in the criticism of poetry indicates that our active
criticism has arrived at a crossroad. And yet, after defending literature as literature, and the analysis of the phenomenology of literary
works, critics still hesitate to take sides. While contemporary Yugoslav literature is fraught with many problems, it is mature enough
to be subjected to broader analysis and stricter evaluation. Unfortunately, no one has undertaken such an analysis and the only dis-

[14] Lionello Venturi, *op. cit.*, pp. 289–92.

tinction between our critics is their language and style rather than their approach.

To reiterate, Yugoslavia lacks philosophical criticism which deals with "ideas," "messages," and morality in the narrower sense of the word. We also need sociologically based criticism, as well as criticism which examines the structure of literary works. Even the old-fashioned, formalistic "line by line" analysis is valuable in certain contexts. These different ways of looking at a work of art provide a more rational approach to the phenomenon of literature, to that which is truly artistic in literature. Any kind of more precisely defined approach is welcome in our current situation because it will help counterbalance relatively widespread and dangerously pretentious superficialities. Besides, there is no method which is not fruitful if carefully done. What is more, all methods lead to similar results.

For almost two decades now we have been in need of another Skerlić. What made him outstanding as a critic were not only his views, but more importantly his evaluative ability which purged literature of numerous false giants who are even today mixed in with real writers. They are the ones who are scheming and conspiring. Wrapped in the trappings of local, national, political or cosmopolitan slogans, they are also more dangerous than they were in Skerlić's time. Such a situation needs no further elaboration if one is aware of the fact that in Yugoslavia even the most obscure writer can inflate his value by collecting large numbers of positive reviews, including a few published in distinguished newspapers and journals.

WRITTEN AND ORAL CRITICISM

Ten years ago, in a reductio ad absurdum, I observed that our criticism could be classified into only two categories: written and oral.[15] Oral criticism includes conversations in clubs and among circles, and camps, in general anything that used to be called the "literary marketplace." This informal web has for years dictated conditions in

[15] See Sveta Lukić, "Vrste književne kritike kod nas," *Borba*, September 27, 1958.

our criticism and literature. It usually reinforces opinions expressed in public written criticism, but in a more witty and expressive way. Why the spoken word is still so powerful in Yugoslavia is a question difficult to unravel. Perhaps it comes from a veneration for the written word, from dogmatism, or out of cautiousness bred by past experiences. Though it is difficult to explain, such semiprivate criticism may be worthwhile in our milieu where everyone knows everyone else and gossip flows freely.

Curiously enough this oral criticism decreased noticeably after 1956 when Yugoslav literature was suddenly permeated by an atmosphere of hard work and writers started producing and publishing on a large scale. Unfortunately oral criticism was not replaced by published criticism in newspapers and periodicals. Flooding the market today are books with meager annotations, compromised awards and dubious advertisements. They are rarely greeted with a competent critique.

Silence now reigns between literary friends as well. Writers live side by side, locked within themselves, as if they were at the opposite ends of the continent, sincerely chit-chatting even about unimportant topics. One would expect that writers, whether they are accepted or just beginning to publish, would demand oral criticism. But our authors blush more easily after each book and have increasing doubts about the honest intentions of the critics. It is probably easier to doubt them than to doubt oneself. In this way the author automatically comes to lean on the support of anonymous and bloodless "admirers."

Both writers and critics have unexpectedly withdrawn into their own four walls, relying megalomaniacally upon their own strength. Perhaps this has come about because there is no one with whom to exchange ideas and experiences, or perhaps because there is no wish to do so. The talent for criticism and self-criticism, and a sense of proportion, of one's own limits and the limits of others, has been lost. A number of older writers, among them Andrić, who is by now considered a national monument rather than a living man, prove to be exceptions to this state of affairs. Few Yugoslav writers have attained such calm assurance in their work and in their behavior.

Beginning in 1963–64, both in criticism and in literature there has

been a new wave of bannings, prejudices and condemnations. These
contained a number of recurrent aesthetic and ideological ideas as
well as some new problems.[16] Take for example the attitudes expressed in certain closed discussions about such new Yugoslav films
as *Grad* (the work of three authors: Kokan Rakonjc, Marko Bapc
and Živojin Pavlović), *Povratak* by Živojin Pavlović, and *Čovek iz
hrastove šume* by Mića Popović. This kind of criticism soon spread
to literature. It made sociologically unfounded and empty accusations about foreign influences affecting some of our higher art and
culture, allegations about the spread of foreign views (whose, when,
or whom, and what form?) and spoke of ideological disorientation.
This was followed by inaccurate figures, and phrases about "the
wasteful use of societal funds" to support works of questionable
artistic merit.

After that came a brave, theoretically pretentious explanation of
basic criteria for the evaluation of works of art. According to this
theory, art deals with general human themes, but it must also present the spirit of the country and the society in which it originates;
art must instill faith in human values, otherwise it is not justified
aesthetically; art is for all men; art is sincere (sincerity meaning confession), art is antimythological, etc., etc.

Theoretically these opinions remind one of a kind of classical
aestheticism or a vulgarized Lukacs, during his period of concessions to socialist realism.[17] However practically, because they were
used to banning certain works of art, they bear the mark of low-
down dogmatism.

I have no idea yet what these concepts mean nor how to relate
them to the bases of culture in our society. One thing is nevertheless certain: though they show signs of pragmatism, they are not
merely pragmatic. Dobrica Ćosić's lone fight against interference
illustrates this point, because throughout this period literary and art
critics either remained on the sidelines or even led the witch hunt.[18]

[16] Dejan Djurković, "Proces," *Delo*, 1963, no. 12 (on the censoring of the
film *Grad*); compare also the author's article in *Gledišta*, 1964, nos. 7–8.
[17] Georg Lukacs, "Post scriptum" (translation), *Politika*, November 29, 1958,
and *Pregled*, 1958, no. 10.
[18] Dobrica Ćosić, "Predlozi za razgovor," *Gledišta*, 1964, no. 5.

THE TASKS OF LITERARY CRITICISM

A positive way in which literary criticism could modernize its old-fashioned "methods" is through a careful and systematic analysis of contemporary developments in Yugoslav literature. Two decades have passed and there is no excuse for the continued absence of such an analysis. In 1965, a number of articles and essays tried to be specific in evaluating literary movements and their results. No one, however, was accustomed to such a precise approach. These pioneering studies therefore provoked violent opposition.

The already mentioned *Delo* panel of fifteen critics is an excellent example of the common resistance to objective studies. Though the panel was not quarrelsome and had more substance than previous discussions, it had the same deformations which we have already decried. Instead of using texts as starting points only, they became the focus of a discussion which turned at times into a trial of the authors of those texts. In addition, some members of the panel, speaking superficially and pretentiously, did not even look at the list of works of postwar Yugoslav literature. They justified this oversight as amateurish perfectionism, claiming it was better not to have a history of literature if this were not perfect. Such perfectionism is merely spiritual laziness which refuses to study and generalize about relationships between criticism, history and theory of literature and makes arbitrary claims about the state of current literary history. It appears, though not consciously, as if we had agreed to ignore the essential questions of the postwar period. Those who break this unwritten law will unavoidably have to bear the burden.

The complacent behavior of some of our criticism goes even further. During the last two years it has been possible to say anything and everything without having rational arguments, moral principles, or a sense of professional responsibility. For instance, some of those who participated in the panel exaggerated the significance of their own publications, as well as the circle and little groups to which they had at one time belonged.

One wonders, in connection with this: who really won the postwar battle? It is too simple to say that it was modernism. And yet, if we look at the question historically, it is indeed true that modern tendencies predominate. The *Delo* panel confirms this indirectly, since critics of different orientations vied with one another to show how much each one had contributed to the victory of modern ideas. But in a much more basic sense what we have here is a Pyrrhic victory.[19]

[19] Concluding comments in *Delo*, 1965, no. 11.

7. LITERARY ORGANIZATION

SOVIET WRITERS' GROUPS IN THE 1920'S

THE FIRST PHASE of our disappointment with socialist realism, which occurred between 1952 and 1956, was in many ways similar to the Soviet literary situation during the twenties.[1] At that time, when Alexander Voronski[2] started *Krasnaya nov*, literary life in Moscow and Leningrad began to expand. Many and diverse literary groups were active. Among them were the LEF futurists and "Serapionov's Brothers," the "Pereval" realists and the "smithy poets" as well as RAPP[*] and the *Na postu* group. All espoused different ideas, and literary life was therefore anarchic and heterogeneous. One group was interested in schools for illiterate representatives of future proletarian literature; others were largely avant-garde; while a third was narrowly and exclusively literary.

These groups participated in various polemics, and fought among themselves. Topics discussed included the meaning and purpose of art in general; whether a new proletarian art and culture can adequately express the new proletarian society; who should create this new art — "fellow travellers" or "proletarian" writers; and how its development can be structured and what the role of the party is in this process.[3]

[1] An elaboration of this situation is provided in "Književnost u socijalizmu," *Encyclopaedia moderna*, 1967, No. 5–6.

[2] *Krasnaya nov*, journal of art, literature, science and current affairs, editor-in-chief A. Voronski, Moscow, Gosizdat, 1921, no. 1.

[*] Russian Association of Proletarian Writers, which presumed to speak for the party in literary affairs — *Ed.*

[3] See *Raskrsnica književnosti*, a compilation of texts which grew out of a discussion of these questions, *Delo*, 1957, no. 11.

Positions crystalized on the question of who should create the new literature. The *Na postu* group demanded that the party take a stand, since they considered its resolution on tolerance and freedom of expression a sign of weakness and capitulation to bourgeois elements. They could hardly wait to have their say during the period of farm collectivization at the beginning of the first Five Year Plan. Voronski was at that time declared a Trotskyite while Pilnyak and Zamyatin were both attacked. The debate turned so acrimonious that the old division of writers into "fellow travelers" and "proletarians" was swept away and "allies" and "enemies" emerge instead. Writers were forced into public self-criticism and their reeducation began, with the campaign continuing in issue after issue of the newly founded *Literaturnaya gazeta*.[4]

The period 1929–32 culminated in a reign of RAPP terror, which resulted in a central committee decision to disband all literary groups.[5] It seemed as though the party wanted to stop RAPP's advances. Yet, in fact it turned out that this suppression was a result of a different kind of fear.

A recent anthology, edited by Alexander Dementeyev,[6] entitled *An Outline of the History of Soviet Journalism (1917–1932)* sheds new light on this period. It contains articles prepared by the Institute for World Literature of the Soviet Academy of Sciences. Disregarding its evaluations, it reflects the wealth of literary trends and currents of Soviet literature in the twenties. Writers were organizing spontaneously and literary life existed without a monopolistic Writers Union. Though these lively currents produced serious conflicts, political provocations and insinuations, restrictions and prohibitions, the important fact to remember is that a dynamism existed. Thanks to it, literary pluralism was able to develop without imperiling the basic rights of existence for others, since the freedom to create and to criticize daily life was guaranteed.

[4] *Literaturnaya gazeta*, official publication of the Soviet Writers' Union (first issue published April 22, 1929).

[5] The groups were dissolved following the resolution VKP(b) April 23, 1932, "O reorganizaciji književno-umetničkih organizacija"; see also the article on the critics' role in RAPP, *Proletarskaya literatura*, 1932, no. 1–2.

[6] *Ocerki istorii russkoi sovetskoi zhurnalistiki*, Moscow, Nauka, 1966.

Some of the best works of art appeared in that decade. Such an exceptional rush of creativity can only be explained by a pluralistic atmosphere and writers' groups associating because of literary "affinities." The atmosphere surrounding the First Congress of the Union of Soviet Writers, held in 1934, is particularly interesting in assessing the mood of the period.[7] The first congress was expected to encourage greater tolerance and a freer atmosphere in literature, coming as it did after the RAPP excesses and after the apathy and delays of the preparatory period. The outspokenness of numerous writers at this congress were evidence of such an expectation. Even the bitterest Russian emigres were predicting that conditions for creative writing in the USSR would be improved after the congress. European leftist intellectuals, among them Gide, Arragon, Malraux and Nerval, who on the eve of Hitler's expansionism had come closer to the USSR, even more eagerly anticipated this expansion of freedom.

SOVIET LITERARY ORGANIZATION DURING THE SOCIALIST REALISM PERIOD

These hopes were dashed, however. Instead, socialist realism cannonized itself as the exclusive form of literary life, and as the only recognized system of criteria, norms and programs for artistic creation. The Minsk plenum of the Soviet Writers' Union held at the beginning of 1936 played the decisive role here. It settled accounts with Bukharin, Pasternak, and modern Soviet poetry, while at the same time disapproving the RAPP excesses.

Two parallel ideas were promulgated at the congress. First, the proclamation of Soviet realism and second, the formation of a strong central writers' organization. Weak from the beginning, after many years of partisan squabbles and fights between groups and factions, the Writers' Union was still unable to control its members or have an impact on Soviet literary life.

The crucial moment in the development of the Union of Writers itself came sometime around 1937 when a number of practical mea-

[7] *Pervi vsesoyuzni s'ezd sovetskiih pisatelj* (stenographic notes), Moscow, Goslitizdat, 1934.

sures were introduced. It must not be forgotten that all this took place in the full swing of the Stalinist era. But regardless of the ideological basis for its organizational centralism, the Soviet Writers' Union would not be what it is today if it had not acquired the right to use the "literary fund." The latter collects ten percent of the income from all new editions of the Russian classics as well as contemporary authors. This power of the purse strings is perhaps the most important source of strength of the Soviet Writers' Union.

About 1960 the Union freed itself from governmental stipends and shortly afterwards was able to return part of its income to the state. Today the Writers' Union is an important item in the state plan of the Soviet Union, and provides its members with such material benefits as housing, "creative travel," rest homes, and honoraria. In fact the honoraria were so high that the Ministry of Finance exerted pressure, at a time of general price increases, to reduce them to levels more in line with the income of other high ranking specialists. In short, membership in the Writers' Union is a privilege which ensures an elevated status to the Soviet writer.

Sometime around 1962, Khrushchev tried to unite all artists into one general union of artists, arguing that the creative problems of socialist realism are the same in all forms of art and that they can therefore be better discussed in a unified organization. It seems that the real reason for this change was the excessive power, or more correctly conservatism, of certain groups, especially the Writers' Union and the Union of Painters and Sculptors. Khrushchev hoped that they could be neutralized in a sea of other artists. The Writers' Union, the Union of Painters and Sculptors and the Film Workers' Union however strongly opposed such fusion and so it was never actually achieved. Khrushchev's fall and the criticism of his mistakes were cleverly exploited as arguments for the continuation of organizational autonomy and the status quo.

The Soviet Writers' Union is a huge establishment, with about 8,000 members and an enormous centralized administrative apparatus. It is very proud of its foreign relations and its well-developed system of medical care which results from the fact that fifty percent of its members are over fifty. It is headed by an administration and secretariat, some of whose members have belonged to the Union for thirty or forty years.[8] Such a picture of organizational power indicates why, irrespective of ideology, the Soviet Writers' Union has for some thirty years been the main influence and unifier of Soviet literary life. Even today its impact is tremendous. It affects the standard of living of all artists, is involved in periodical subvention, supervises the work of publishing houses, and arbitrates aesthetic and ideological questions. The conservative force of the Soviet Writers' Union is thus great.

PROPOSALS FOR REORGANIZATION
OF THE YUGOSLAV WRITERS' UNION

Socialist realism and the Soviet Writers' Union, after which all similar organizations in other countries are modeled, are the two major innovations of socialism in the cultural field. In spite of the fact that Yugoslavia abandoned these "innovations" after a few years, the Soviet twenties provide an object lesson for the understanding of our situation today. Not only is there a historical analogy between the two periods and countries, but what is much more important, it mirrors the openness and dynamism of the Yugoslav literary scene.

Unfortunately these positive aspects of our literary situation have not been sufficiently protected and appreciated during the past fifteen years of Yugoslavia's writers organizations. Even the most elementary reinforcements are lacking. On the contrary, there is a tendency towards the submerging of individuality, and leveling of creativity. There is something stifling, an unsteadiness and insecurity in the very foundations of our literary life. Perhaps it is generated by a basic misunderstanding about the role of literature in society. This factor has a very strong, negative effect on the entire literary atmosphere, and on literature itself.

In 1963–64, regional writers' associations drew attention to the need for a reorganization of literary associations. Unfortunately, however, this call was narrowed down to a change of legal statutes. The 1964 Congress of the Writers' Union held in Titograd was sup-

[8] This information is based on data provided to me in 1965 by the executive secretary of the Soviet Writers' Union, A. Voronkov.

posed to accomplish four tasks of reorganization according to a document released by the Secretariat of the Yugoslav Writers Union. A first proposal by the Serbian Writers Association adopted at the plenary meeting of the Association May 20, 1964 recommends the following changes and additions:

That a secretariat be formed within the Yugoslav Writers' Union, as a permanent executive body for major decision making. The president, vice-president and secretary general of the Union as well as the secretaries general of the regional writers' associations make up the membership of the Secretariat;

That rotation be obligatory in the election of new administrators of the Union. Rotation to affect the president and secretary general, as well as members of the administrative commissions of the Yugoslav Writers Union.

A second proposal by the Croatian Writers Society was adopted at the plenary meeting of that society, June 23, 1964. It recommends the following changes in statutes:

That the wording in the second item of article 2 be changed from "the federal office of the Union is located in Belgrade," to "The Union has no permanent location and will be moved every three years to the offices of one of the regional associations."

That the regional seats of the Union rotate according to the alphabetical order of the names of the republics and that at the end of every three-year period a congress of the federal Union be held in the republic in which the seat was located.

The president and the secretary general be chosen, from regional association members in which the Union will have its seat.

To facilitate international relations, and coordinate relations between the union and the federal government, offices will be maintained in Belgrade. The office will be managed in accordance with administrative directives handed down by union headquarters.

The third proposal by representatives of the Slovenian Writers' Association including Matej Bor, Drago Šega and Jože Šmit suggests:

That the principle outlined in article 4 of the Union Statute stating that the Yugoslav Writers' Union is a federation of regional associations also be applied to the composition and structure of the federal organ.

According to this proposal, the management of the Union would be in the hands of a coordinating committee composed of the presidents, secretaries and one member each of the regional associations, and of the presidents of the literary sections of Voyvodina and Kosovo-Metohije.

This coordinating committee will choose the secretary of the union while the president of the union will be chosen by the congress. Another possibility envisages the president to be chosen by the coordinating committee, provided that he is one of the most distinguished writers of this country. Future congresses of the Yugoslav Writers' Union instead of being concerned with the organizational tasks could thus devote more time to professional problems of authors. Such organizational changes would facilitate closer coordination among regional associations themselves as well as between them and the federal organs of the union.

THE PROPOSAL TO UNITE
ACCORDING TO LITERARY AFFINITIES

A fourth proposal presented by Dobrica Ćosić on behalf of a group of Serbian writers suggested that:

> In addition to the national-geographical organization, the statutes also affirm the right of writers to organize on different bases according to other similarities and affinities, as long as these are in keeping with the social-ideological tenets of the Yugoslav Writers' Union, that is, the Socialist Union of the Working People of Yugoslavia.[9]

Some sixty writers at the congress from all republics except Slovenia supported this fourth proposal for organizations based on "other similarities and affinities." Signatories to this proposal included Oskar Davičo, Novak Simić, Dobrica Ćosić, Antun Šoljan, Dimitar Solev, and Husein Tahmiščić, as well as me. The names of the signatories indicate it was not an organized group since it would be difficult to imagine on what criteria such a group would have joined. The signatories did not meet or consult, but in the official statements it was rumored that these writers were supporting the

[9] Documents in the archives of the Yugoslav Writers' Union.

proposal because of certain disturbing factors in Yugoslav literary life after 1960. Three things were mentioned:

1. The literary atmosphere is unstimulating and bears signs of confusion and disintegration.

2. Existing economic resources are neither properly defined nor utilized by periodicals, publishing houses, and juries.

3. Yugoslav literature is so decentralized that there is a real need for a more lasting grouping of writers to exchange ideas, and provide for cooperation and real encounters.

The proponents and adherents of the proposal stressed at the congress that their fundamental aim was to encourage the development of interest groups. Such groups would provide something entirely new, something which would be distinct from the Western literary salons based on economic necessity. On the other hand these groups would not be anarchical like the Soviet literary groups of the twenties. Finally, they felt that the Yugoslav Union does not and should not resemble the Soviet Writers' Union which is all-encompassing. Yugoslavia's literary organization guarantees minimum social security, pensions, subsidies for some basic work and otherwise leaves room for individual initiative.

I concluded my presentation at the congress with the following words:

We must understand the persistence of old reflexes, especially among older writers. There are other justifiable fears, and I myself have them. It is still not clear to me how this group will actually function within the framework of the Writers' Union. I am thinking in particular about administrative questions, the sending of representatives from these groups to congresses and juries, the founding of periodicals, changes in publishing houses and similar problems. Then there are questions concerning medical care, insurance, distribution of housing, stipends and study abroad.

But I have come to the decision that change in the literary organization itself is desirable and believe that rejuvenation may have to be forced. In any case, we should be concerned with other more essential things than social security alone.[10]

This proposal however raised a tempest and became the central

[10] "Organizacija i stvaralaštvo," *Politika*, October 11, 1964.

debating point of the congress. In the brisk and emotional polemic which followed counter arguments made little sense. Yet, unquestionably those who were against this proposal were extremely strong.

In the end, nothing was settled at the congress itself. A stalemate ensued, complicated by the controversies surrounding the election of the new union president and secretary general. The vote on the new statutes was postponed until the next extraordinary congress of the Yugoslav Writers' Union in 1965, even at the risk of provoking a scandal. It was suggested that the proposal, and in particular the proposal of "Dobrica Ćosić's group" be explained more clearly and be discussed at the plenary meetings of the regional associations.

In the weeks immediately following the congress more detailed and better explanations of the proposal were published in interviews and articles. They all stressed two points. First of all they criticized the fact that the only function of the writers' associations has been to solve trade union type questions, while aesthetic matters were left to the writers themselves. Only exceptional writers of genius are, in fact, able to make such decisions, while others need the proper climate, support, and some mutual understanding from the group.

Explanations noted secondly that the existing organization of literary life in the republics, especially the regional associations, have been supporting a trend toward centralization. Various functions in fact have been turned over to them which are beyond their scope of competence. They slowly, almost imperceptibly, but inexorably, move from housing questions into aesthetics. This is Zhdanovism on a small, regional scale. Adding to this trend is another complicating phenomenon, namely, the transfer of too great a portion of governmental cultural responsibilities directly to the associations. Under the guise of professional concern, the associations are eager to widen their competencies, thus revealing their ultimate goal of programming art and creativity. This danger is worth pointing out.

It thus becomes appropriate to ask whether the republican associations can better represent the writer than some group which he would join voluntarily and on the basis of "affinity." Such affinities could be aesthetic or social concerning the writer's role and the role of the written word in socialism, or based on opinions about literature and communication. Writers might also form groups on generational lines. Such groupings have not been administratively ruled out in Yugoslavia, yet they have also not been explored by writers. Those who did write were always limited by such historical categories as modernists and realists, or differences in age. Such divisions are old-fashioned and outdated in our present literary situation, hindering its further development.

It almost seems as though Yugoslav writers have become accustomed to having privileges handed to them on a silver platter. Consequently, they also expect to be given a charter delimiting freedom of literary expression. The new statute might provide such a charter, and force writers to move out of their old groupings. A single group, without the help of the union, could not organize itself independently under the present circumstances, nor could it obtain the financial means for a journal. The new statute would legalize new writer groups and thus liquidate the practice of granting "good will and material support" to selected people only.

We are not for a Writers' Union as a ruler of literature, we are for a more stimulating creative literary atmosphere. Literature need not accept our "historic conditions" which divide, nor sanction the traditional differences which exist between our peoples and which have recently been played up. In principle, a writer as communicator can bridge gaps and differences between peoples through his art. Yet, such ideas are threatening to many persons, which probably explains the reason for their antipathy to and campaign against association according to affinity. Our proposal was therefore treated as the suspicious meddling of former modernists and some other "intellectual" troublemakers. Three points, taken out of context, were particularly under attack:

1. Yugoslavism — as a politically damaging concept.
2. The poorly defined practical results of such an organization which supposedly shows a lack of concern for the majority of union members.
3. The definition of "closer affinities" which were interpreted as a screen hiding an aristocratic desire of a minority of authors to separate themselves from the "mass" of writers.

Since it was impossible to discuss the proposal rationally, its supporters retreated and ceased being interested. Only Dobrica Ćosić and Oskar Davičo resigned from the Serbian Writers' Association as a sign of protest.[11] Under these circumstances it was not difficult to turn the 1964–65 plenary sessions of the regional associations into plebiscites which emphatically rejected groupings based on common literary interests.

THE NEW FEDERAL STATUTE OF THE
YUGOSLAV WRITERS' UNION

A closer look at the statute adopted in 1965 shows that its basic formulations are even more absurd than the initial statutes. It pushed the principle of regionalism almost to the extreme. Here are some of the essential articles of the new statutes:

Article 1. The Yugoslav Writers' Union is a voluntary federation of regional writers societies and associations.

Article 2. The influence of the Union extends over the entire territory of the Federal Socialist Republic of Yugoslavia. The seat of the Union is in the capital of the FSRY or in the capital of one of the socialist republics. The Coordinating Committee will decide on the location of the seat at its first meeting.

Article 8. All members of regional societies and associations can attend the assembly of the Union, but only delegations have the right to vote. The assembly is in session if four delegations from at least four societies and associations are present. Each association or society is to have one vote. Revisions and amendments must be unanimous. The assembly is headed by a working body selected by the assembly.

Article 10. The Coordinating Committee is composed of representative delegations from societies and associations which in turn include the president, secretary and one elected member from each society and association. The presidents of the literary sections of Voyvodina and Kosovo-Metohije are members of the delegation of the Serbian Writers' Association.

Article 15. Voting is public in the Coordinating Committee, and according to the representational system.[12]

---

[11] Dobrica Ćosić, "O modernizmu i realizmu, potom," *Student*, December 24, 1965; "O Savezu književnika i drugom," *Vjesnik*, December 28, 1965.

[12] Document in the archives of the Yugoslav Writers' Union.

Borislav Mihajlović was the only one who described things accurately when he said that the new Statute legalized the principle of federation for the first time in our supposedly federal nation.[13] Once again a small fictitious organization thus grappled with a problem troubling all of Yugoslav society. It even anticipated some solutions which will inevitably be used on a higher level in the future. As far as literary life is concerned the defeat of the proposal meant another failure in the attempt to organize our writers in a more tightly knit and involved way. Its fate is a significant symptom of the state of Yugoslav society as a whole.

[13] Stenographic notes in the archives of the Yugoslav Writers' Union.

8. THE LITERARY PUBLIC

TYPES OF MASS CULTURE

IT IS GENERALLY assumed that art helps man realize his potentialities to become a free and complete individual.[1] Yet, if we assess this function realistically it appears that modern man spends only a small portion of his leisure time attending to art. Instead of lamenting this fact, we should be aware that all of us are continuously surrounded by beautiful things which are not necessarily art in the traditional sense. Art is therefore not the only means of humanizing man's leisure time nor his life in general.[2]

Undoubtedly serious art should occupy some of contemporary man's leisure time. The question is not however the amount of time he spends on it, but rather whether the presence of art makes itself felt. After all, the French poet Henri Michaux said "sometimes one tapestry is sufficient to fulfill a man's entire life." This is what we have in mind when we say that each one of us has a favorite book to which he returns frequently, or a certain play or film which he enjoys retelling and which he goes to see over and over again.

All of this is well known. What is not well known and rarely studied is what we do with the rest of our time. Since the relationship between leisure and working time, and the way in which spare time is used varies from one social milieu to another, and changes within these milieus, a strictly quantitative inquiry raises new and very complex issues. For our purposes it must therefore suffice to

---

[1] Henri Lefebvre, *Kritika svakidašnjeg života* (translation), Zagreb, Naprijed, 1959, pp. 147–62.

[2] *Umetnost i kriterijumi*, "Estetička perspektiva čoveka, života i sveta," excerpt, pp. 25–39.

consider only Yugoslav society and its possibilities. Even without statistics and scientific precision such a delineation helps to orient our discussion.

First, of all, when we use the term "leisure," we do not include in it remunerative work or regular work executed during spare time. We also exclude the pursuit of high or serious art. Our leisure time is thus mainly occupied with the following: love, family, friendship and acquaintances, sports events, the coffee house and so on. At the end of the list come the "lighter" forms of culture whose main purpose is entertainment and distraction.

Such culture is primarily purveyed by the media including the press, radio, television, and the popular stage whose programs and repertoires are largely filled with entertainment. This is, of course, only part of mass culture. By definition, mass culture is "everything which is widely distributed, has a uniform format and reaches large audiences simultaneously."[3] We avoid the term "masses" because of its misuse, and the fact that in Yugoslavia between 1945 and 1950 it was equated with the slogan "Culture for the Masses! Culture to the Masses!"

That slogan implied that culture needed to be brought to the larger public. The slogan also served to introduce and popularize various other cultural genres such as choruses and folklore, as well as such things as authentic folk music. In addition folk poetry has been fostered and given very serious attention. Both amateur and highly professional ensembles demonstrated the folk origins of artistic creations at that time. During these early years when there was little other entertainment in our country these genres fulfilled the need for "light" entertainment. It is obvious that both the style and approach were imported from the Soviet Union.

Immediately after the liberation, choruses and folk lore threatened to usurp the entire field of mass culture. Yet in spite of administrative prohibitions and suppression other forms of purely entertaining mass culture crept in after 1950. This change in the content of popular culture was opposed by angry letters to the editor

[3] Antonina Kloskowska, *Kultura masowa*, Warsaw, PWN, 1964, p. 476.

of *Borba* and other newspapers criticizing cowboy films, comic strips, and detective stories. Yet it was impossible to stop the trend.

THE EFFECTS OF MASS CULTURE

Research on mass culture is hindered by the fact that it is difficult to pinpoint all of its manifestations.[4] First of all, how do you delineate the phenomenon and the nature of its effects? These are always intertwined and associated with other forms of spiritual activity. Consider, for example, the fact that mass culture is difficult to isolate from "serious" or "high" art. It would be interesting to study their interrelationship throughout history. Without doubt, between the Renaissance and Symbolism, a "lighter" element had regularly become a part of works of art. Today, the situation is somewhat different. Mass culture is separated from traditional forms of culture because of a proliferation of genres, the division of labor, and commercialization. In spite of this however people today confuse the two. It may even be the case that mass culture is growing and developing at the expense of higher culture. For these reasons artists and critics alike sharply differentiate the two, considering mass culture valueless.[5]

What are these "lighter" forms of art and where are they to be found? Many of them are found in the popular press which writes not about art but about artists, emphasizing more titillating biographical details. The popular press also offers articles purporting to be literature. This rather third rate romantic type of writing on a schoolboy level is full of descriptions of nature, quasi-dramatic plots and artificial dialogue. Examples are accounts of events in Yugoslavia preceding World War II.

There is, in addition, detective literature of various kinds. Artistically this form of mass culture is relatively interesting since it offers proper writing, dramatic action, often sharp observations, and normal dialogue. We also have humorous anecdotes and caricatures which are artistically relevant. Finally there is an enormous pro-

[4] Cf. Georges Friedmann, *Enseignement et culture de masse*, Paris, 1962, p. 3.
[5] Antonina Kloskowska, *op. cit.*, p. 476.

duction of popular literature in the Sunday supplements; they include serialized novels and the cheap "green" and "black" libraries. These deal primarily with adventure, crime, and science fiction.

Films and television in addition to the press are undoubtedly the main media distributing mass culture. They purvey all of the same genres mentioned above. Yet musical reviews and light comedies must be especially mentioned. All of these forms of culture propagate a special philosophy of life. The basic ingredient in this philosophy is the rejection of complex meanings and the superficial acceptance of a hedonistic form of life, such as the enjoyment of luxury and sensuality. The music hall was finally, until television's appearance, the most potent and influential form of mass culture. It too repeats the genres already mentioned.

Judging by the enumeration of different forms of popular culture, it is evident that all genres are to be found in all media. Contemporary mass culture is therefore a complex phenomenon mixing ideological, intellectual and purely entertainment features.[6] While entertainment was subordinated to artistic elements in classical art, in today's mass culture entertainment is on a par with other elements. This hybrid nature makes mass culture artistically weak. Mass culture therefore produces primarily works of minor value. Its appeal to mass tastes is one of the reasons for its enormous popularity. Such an appeal requires uniformity, that the products of mass culture be turned out on an assembly line with the author merely innovating small changes.

Cowboy films present an example of such a modal approach. In them, the black/white struggle between good and evil is expressed in the struggle between a positive and a negative hero; the latter comes to a just and happy end following a number of exploits in which some pretty girl must always participate. Popular music too shows such a stereotyped style. During the last fifteen years in the eastern regions of our country new folk music has been produced in this same style.

What are the benefits and drawbacks of mass culture? First of all, according to some critics, it goes against the unwritten rule that

---

[6] Antonina Kloskowska, *op. cit.*, p. 478.

art should not be propagandistic. Yet, historically, suggestion and propaganda have not been taboo in high art provided that they have a basis in reality. This means that the advocacy of certain life styles (such as in American musicals) cannot be blatant or heavy-handed, and they have to be offered in conjunction with other artistic satisfactions. In general, the West does this more cleverly and ably than the East.

However, those who worry about this influence of mass culture on our mass audience are wrong. Many people exposed to mass culture are immune to its ideological effects and are in fact above it. I believe this to be an indisputable fact which we should stress and develop in dealing realistically with the role of mass culture in contemporary life. I believe therefore that the influence of mass culture in our society is practically nil. It is used and "enjoyed" in order to pass the time. Such diversion offers considerable pleasure, it strengthens psychic functions and it affords recreation. Afterwards, man can resume his normal work with greater enjoyment.

Yet this admission does not overlook the fact that mass culture has sanctioned and encouraged the superficiality of contemporary man, though it has not actually caused it. On the other hand it is equally important to emphasize that mass culture is much less influential than is usually assumed. Knowing about its superficiality leaves us with the question of ways in which its influence can be counteracted. Instead of trying to stamp it out we should probably try to neutralize its most rigid, literal, and damaging ideological influences. An effort must be made, in other words, to render mass culture harmless, to make it more of a source of amusement, which is, after all, its basic function.[7]

In practice, we should support those art forms which I call pure, such as cabaret, a more popular Brechtian type of national theater with current themes, and American musicals. Such pure entertainment genres are better than today's hybrids. Unfortunately there is little discussion of these serious questions, discussion in fact is inversely related to the prevalence and importance of mass forms of entertainment. All of us, ideologues, artists, and those who man-

[7] Antonina Kloskowska, *op. cit.*, pp. 480–81.

age the mass media, are letting things go as they are instead of taking action on sober reflection.

PUBLIC INTEREST IN SERIOUS ART

The foregoing demonstrates that mass culture does not exhaust the spiritual interest of the general public. As a matter of fact it fails to satisfy this interest. Consequently, at least in principle, the path to greater appreciation of serious art is wide open. Yet such interest has not developed. On the contrary, public attention has been drawn to pure entertainment. When did this happen? At various times during this discussion I have suggested that public attention was diverted after 1950, during the period of liberation from dogmatism when our culture became differentiated. During that period serious art was strictly segregated from entertainment and sports and when the public finally had a choice between the two around 1954–56 it went for the entertainment which suited its particular inclinations.

This process coincided with the emergence of a new literary generation. In other words when this generation started writing, the broader public, for the first time since the liberation, openly turned its back on serious art. Even later these authors who experimented with new style and content were not accepted. When we therefore say that they are writers without a public, it means that they lack a universally established public. Even if it is limited in size, that public should be known. Between the two wars, Krleža found his readers and followers on "the left side of reality." It seems that after the war Oskar Davičo acquired such a circle composed of students, high school students, and members of the League of Communist Youth. Branko Ćopić accomplished the same thing in a different way, of course. But in the case of Ćosić we have to stop and think who constitutes his public, even though his books have a large circulation. The books of the younger generation have only a professional audience, limited to writers and artists. One can almost say, that they are both their own public and their own critics.

In my *Estetička čitanka* I concluded that our literary audience can be diagrammed very simply.[8] Its inner circle is composed of artists and writers, in short, professionals. They are surrounded by a thin layer of several thousand snobs, who, although they are useful as indirect transmitters of modern ideas, are more intent upon what is "behind" or "around" these ideas. The next layer, those genuine, faithful amateurs who try to keep in touch with artistic events and with literature, is not much bigger.

Then, there is the mass of potential consumers of literature and art. These are people who read occasionally and consider it worthwhile, time permitting, to "catch" something else from the realm of art, most frequently the cinema. This public, comprised of the working intelligentsia and the higher echelons of workers and tradesmen, is the only one which can be termed "broader." Yet unfortunately they are only potentially so. Finally, there is the overwhelming majority of Yugoslavs, the "thickest layer" composed of all classes, who are not really interested in art and literature in the foreseeable future.

In reverse order of interest we have an art audience divided into: (1) the broadest masses, (2) potential consumers, (3) "amateurs," (4) snobs, and (5) professional artists.

The various literary genres can be classified as follows:

1. Popular, light literature (humoristic, detective, folklore)
2. Propaganda (social, religious, technical)
3. Classical literature (from the Greek to the beginning of this century)
4. Fantastic, black humor, which must be separated from the preceding
5. Modern, more strictly called essayistic, intellectual and cerebral
6. All current experiments in expression and style, the "avant-garde"

When audience level and literary genres are combined we may conclude that each layer of the public prefers a particular level of literature. Professional artists for instance are most interested in modern, avant-garde art, while amateurs are interested in the classics though they too try to keep up with new literature. The two largest

[8] *Estetička čitanka*, pp. 29–30.

groups, which are first in order of magnitude, refuse to consider either modern or experimental literature.

Factual evidence on the Yugoslav cultural market substantiating our conclusions was collected by the Center for Public Opinion Research of the Institute of Social Studies during its annual Belgrade poll of May, 1966. One of the questions asked was "Do you have time to read books?" This is how the citizens of Yugoslavia answered that question: [9]

	Percentage
Have no time to read books	48
Find time to read books	36
Do not read (cause: illiteracy, or inability to read well)	16

When we add the number that do not have time to read to those who are illiterate we get a total of 64 percent of our population, roughly two-thirds who do not read books.

The regional breakdown of those who do not read books is as follows:

	Percentage
Macedonia	72
Bosnia and Hercegovina	72
Serbia	68
Kosovo-Metohija	67
Croatia	61
Voyvodina	60
Slovenia	46

The breakdown of those who do read, according to profession, is:

	Percentage
Students (secondary and university)	77
Employees with intermediate training	75
Employees with high and higher training	65
Pensioners and invalids	57
Employees with minimal training	52

Those who read least are wives of agricultural workers (16%) and

[9] *Jugoslovensko javno mnenje 1966*, (serija A) "Izveštaji o rezultatima anketnih istraživanja," Belgrade, Institute for Social Studies, 1967, pp. 142–46.

TABLE 4
Do you have time to read books?

	Yugoslavia	Slovenia	Croatia	Voyvodina	Serbia	Bosnia-Hercegovina	Montenegro	Macedonia	Kosovo-Metohija
				PERCENTAGES					
I find time to read	36	54	39	40	32	28	38	26	32
I do not have time to read	48	44	52	57	45	42	41	50	46
I am illiterate (unable to read well)	16	2	9	3	23	30	21	24	22

TABLE 5
Do you have time to read books?

	Highly skilled and skilled workers	Semi-skilled and un-skilled workers	Highly qualified employees	Moderately qualified employees	Less qualified employees	Agricultural workers (self-employed)	Other (self-employed)	Pensioners, invalids, etc.	Students	Housewives (agricultural)	Housewives (non-agricultural)
					PERCENTAGES						
I find time to read	47	21	65	75	52	15	34	57	77	16	30
I do not have time to read	53	69	35	25	48	63	61	31	23	50	40
I am illiterate (unable to read)	0	10	0	0	0	22	5	12	0	34	30

independent farmers (15%). Highly skilled and skilled workers read more (47%) than semiskilled and unskilled workers (21%).

To summarize the statistical results we find that few of our citizens read. More than half have stated that they do not read. Yugoslavs from the most developed milieus read the most, and those from the less developed read the least. Those belonging to educated and skilled socioprofessional groups have expressed a greater interest in books than those with lesser skills and education (compare Tables 4 and 5).

Taken as a whole, then, there is not much interest in reading in Yugoslavia. Though a more detailed conclusion is impossible to draw from the data, they indicate in part that our inhabitants are temporarily more interested in the problems of living than in art and literature. These facts also show that books, for reasons which are more objective than subjective, have not reached more of our population.[10]

Another interesting question presented to the Yugoslav public was "Which Yugoslav artists (painters, sculptors, writers, musicians, actors, singers, etc.) do you respect and like the most?" The following were the answers given.[11]

Miodrag Petrović Čkalja, actor	664	Djordje Marjanović, singer	65
		Lola Djukić, film director	56
Ivo Andrić, writer	382	Viktor Starčić, actor	51
Safet Isović, singer	223	Zaim Imamović, singer	51
Lola Novaković, singer	152	France Prešern, writer	49
Ivan Meštrović, sculptor	127	Dobrica Ćosić, writer	46
Miroslav Čangalović, singer	117	Vaska Ilijeva, singer	45
Mija Aleksić, actor	112	Miroslav Krleža, writer	42
Branko Ćopić, writer	92	Dušan Jakšić, singer	40
Ivo Robić, singer	89	Olivera Vučo, actress	40
Arsen Dedić, singer	88	Mira Stupica, actress	36
Cune Gojković, singer	83	Dragan Stojnić, singer	36
Vice Vukov, singer	70	Ljuba Tadić, actor	31

[10] See Radomir Smiljanić, "Koliko se čita u Jugoslaviji, NIN, October 15, 1967.

[11] Radomir Smiljanić, "Ko je najpopularniji umetnik," NIN, November 26, 1967.

Ivica Šerfezi, singer	31	Božidar Jakač, painter	18
Antun Augustinčić, sculptor	30	Nela Eržišnik, actress	17
Petar Lubarda, painter	30	Petre Prličko, actor	16
Radojka Živković, musician	30	Relja Bašić, actor	14
Olivera Marković, actress	29	Milivoje Živanović, actor	14
P. P. Njegoš, writer	28	Zdenka Vučković, singer	14
Ivan Cankar, writer	27	Tine Živković, musician	13
Nada Mamula, singer	23	Tereza Kesovija, singer	13
Ismet Mujezinović, painter	21	Boris Kalin, sculptor	13
Marija Crnobori, actress	21	Marijana Deržaj, singer	13
Lado Leskovar, singer	19	Milo Milunović, painter	12
Ružica Sokić, actress	19	Oskar Davičo, writer	11
Bojan Adamić, musician	18	Aleksandar Gavrić, actor	10
Franc Finžgar, writer	18		

THE BOOK MARKET IN YUGOSLAVIA

Yugoslav literature presents a specific challenge to the cultural market place. Though it is inherently rich and varied, we are talking about a relatively modest production in three national languages with two alphabets (excluding a certain number of works in the languages of "national minorities"), in a country of six republics with a population of scarcely twenty million. No wonder then that internal literary production and distribution is not very large. In addition, contemporary Yugoslav belles lettres have to compete with three other sources of literature. These are contemporary world literature which is widely translated and in great demand in Yugoslavia, and Yugoslav as well as world classics. A significant number of amateurs and the majority of the potential literary public are attracted by the "lighter" forms of literature, such as popular novels (detective, historical, melodramatic), some science fiction, and of course the popular and commercial press.

Only those books written by the most distinguished or the most popular "national" writers are printed in more than two or three thousand copies. I do not personally consider this a negative fact. It must be viewed in the larger context of the increasing complexity and richness of our life, more precisely taking the differentiation of interests and needs in our society into account. Can reading be encouraged? Publishing policies and propaganda could be designed to bring the public in contact with contemporary literature. But such contact will be useful only to the extent that a work has intrinsic artistic and communicational value. Lately there have been signs of improvement in this direction.

In 1965 in Belgrade some older well-known and well-liked authors such as Miloš Crnjanski and Ranko Marinković were published. After them came several prominent books of literary criticism and essays written by members of the generation which started its work immediately after 1950. I am thinking here of the work not only of Petar Džadžić and Nikola Milošević, but also of Predag Palavestra's analysis, *Young Bosnia*. Finally, a wave of new prose appeared, published by Prosveta in a uniform collection which was well publicized. This included some ten works, mainly by young authors such as Danilo Kiš, Borislav Pekić, Filip David, Branimir Sćepanović, and Mirko Kovač. All of these are entertaining and solid works. Each is fresh and novel in its genre, if not for our entire literature. What is exceptional in this phenomenon is the fact that the majority of these works acquired an immediate public which was far larger than any of our books had previously had.[12]

[12] Compare Sveta Lukić, "Šta se čita u Beogradu" (in Russian), *Literaturnaya gazeta*, February 15, 1966.

9. SOME ADDITIONAL ASPECTS

OF LITERARY LIFE

LITERARY JOURNALS, NEWSPAPERS,

THE STATUS OF THE WRITER

AN EVALUATION OF CULTURAL
ARTICLES IN THE PRESS

THE FINAL elements of literary life which we must consider are the mass media, literary periodicals, publishing houses, literary prizes, translations abroad, and the question of the social status of Yugoslav writers and their own interpretation of their responsibilities. Though these factors may not play a decisive role in literary life, they undoubtedly have an influence which is worth considering. The relationship between literature and the mass media is so complex that we can only consider one aspect here and ask one question: How does the serious press represent serious literature? Let us deal first with cultural columns and literary supplements in the major daily and weekly papers.[1]

The press, as is generally known, is a complex institution made up of writers, ideologues, journalists — in short all of those who write for it who are influential, as well as the regular editorial and publishing staff. To evaluate the literary press one must therefore consider all of these influences as well as their mutual interdependencies. It is generally expected that the press provides a sensitive

---

[1] See Sveta Lukić, "Ozbiljna književnost u ozbiljnoj štampi," *Borba*, August 22, 1965.

dynamic and immediate channel of communication between literature and society as a whole. It bridges the gap between literature
and the public, literature and other activities, as well as literature
and the authorities.

Ostensibly, this is the case and everything is in order. Our serious
press values literature highly. It devotes considerable space to it,
particularly in comparison with other branches of art and science.
Its treatment of literary events is serious, it rarely stoops to the sensationalism of the tabloids. It provides a vast amount of good and
accurate information, and routinely follows literary life. Finally,
on ceremonial occasions it is fair in evaluating authors and their
contributions.

But outward appearances are deceiving. There are two reasons
for this. First, the controversial and essential problems of contemporary literature are seldom presented and discussed in literary
columns. Second, journalists have a tendency to speak only "positively" or "well" about practically every writer who has attained a
certain immunity, distinction, or position in society, and in particular about those writers who are older and "more neutral."

The cultural sections, in short, have until now been grey, and
dead. Naturally, the press serves neither literature nor society by
adopting such an "academic" stance. No one has tried to find out
whether cultural rubrics are read, who reads them, what is learned
from them and why. In journalistic circles the "cultural pages" are
considered a necessary evil. As a consequence, since the press has
had to make profits to survive, space for cultural matters has diminished considerably. A drastic example of such cutting is *Borba*,
which in 1966 changed its format to become financially solvent at
all costs.

Quite aside from the question of how much literary information
is communicated, the press is also remiss in its reaction to the stormy
process of development and expansion of our literature. It does not
see its function as providing an open forum of discussion. The press
is uninformed about contemporary literary phenomena and works
of art. It is particularly worrisome that the main dynamic of our
literary life is not reflected in the press. And what is more, all attempts to interpret this dynamic to the press have failed.

Though it is not necessary to review the entire period from 1945 to the present, certain points stand out. In the period following the liberation the dogmatic belief that literature played an important ideological and political role in society set the tone and eventually dictated the attitude of the press towards literature. The press therefore adopted a "vigilant" reaction to various new literary appearances, especially those which were "suspicious" or "problematic," by discussing who and what would be printed. The press at the time also sanctioned the dogmatic unification of literature, which in its own way suited the imperatives of that literary moment regardless of what we might think of it today.

However, this particular kind of conservatism persisted well beyond this initial period. During the fifties literary diversity was reflected primarily in periodicals and literary papers, which became the organs of various groups, cliques and camps. How did such diversification affect our press? It remained objective in principle, yet in fact, the press wrote less and less about the excesses or problems arising in our literary life. The reasons for this silence and neutrality were partly ideological.

It was feared for example that criticisms in the press might be considered Zhdanovite attempts to limit the freedom of expression. But this was not the only problem. During the fifties a number of important questions failed to be discussed in the serious press, because our literary groups and camps did not wish to bring them out into the open.

The growing independence of various areas of our cultural and literary life also widened the gulf between the press and literature. It was probably at that time that the press's earlier dogmatism and later reservations were transformed into demagoguery. Economics and the need for subscribers were not the main concern of the editors. They were, in fact, indignant at the acrimony and lack of principles in literary discussions. Such criticism, instead of being published, was once again hidden under a cloak of objectivity and superiority.

By now the press has grown strong and is one of the few forces which can affect our society. Our most serious daily and weekly papers have "arrived" and are self-assured. Consequently they do not wish to take risks or to open up new areas of debate. It is as if culture were a pure luxury and the newspapers the property of those working for them. There is no sensationalism in the serious press today, as in the popular tabloids, but let us not forget that tabloids are published by serious newspaper publishers.

When the press writes about literature it remains aloof, yet sometimes it can play a dirty game. The blame for this cannot be laid at the feet of the editors and collaborators alone. A much more general phenomenon accounts for some of our problems. These have arisen from the fact that our press as a whole has not been fully democratized. It continues to be unnecessarily torn between remnants of dogmatism and the new economics; between the need for ideas and simple arithmetic.

In evaluating cultural rubrics today, we have to ask ourselves: "Can the press become an open forum for many-sided discussions about literature and culture?"[2] A positive answer to this question assumes a desire, a feeling of responsibility as well as available talent on the part of journalists and their collaborators, not to mention the organizational skill of their superiors. Yet these abilities must be evaluated in relation to the general ability of our society to accept and support an open forum.

THE UNIFORMITY OF CONTENT IN LITERARY MAGAZINES

In Yugoslavia, magazines are the most common type of literary periodical. They are more numerous and have been published longer than either the weekly or biweekly literary papers. Since World War II, literary life has unfolded in and around these magazines. During the first phase after 1945, magazines published both the older generation authors who were permitted to appear in print, and the younger ones who were just beginning. They tried to include writing from all republics stressing the unity of all Yugoslav writers in this way.

But this orientation was unfortunately quickly lost. Those maga-

[2] *Periodika u SR Srbiji* (material prepared for internal distribution), Belgrade, 1967.

zines which look beyond republican borders today are an anachronism and bypassed by contemporary literary trends. After 1950, new magazines became centers of literary life in the six republics. These attracted writers of a similar bent and thus encouraged the bifurcation in Yugoslav literature: between modern/classical, avantgarde/traditional, modernism/realism, and so on. Though these magazines are the dependent organs of dependent organizations, they did initiate some very important topics, and at times discussed what Dušan Matić calls the leading questions of the day. Interestingly, in the fifties writers were more closely tied to their town, their republic, and their national literature than previously. Within this ambivalent framework some bitter polemics and duels developed, many of which turned into excesses.

Sometime between 1958 and 1960 the intensity of these conflicts increased and finally exploded. Magazines as well as wider literary circles rejected the empty dichotomy between modern and traditional which had ruled and stultified literary development so long. Today magazines are no longer exclusive about who collaborates and they have also begun to be more tolerant about accepting works from writers outside their own group and camp. Magazines have thus become increasingly representative of all styles of writing and literary philosophies. A comparison with the immediate postwar years indicates, however, that they were intensely committed tribunes in those days while their current representativeness is merely academic.

Yugoslav magazines today resemble one another like peas in a pod. They are stereotyped, out of date, falsely superior, and lacking any serious programs. Not one of them attracts and molds writers into a group. With no political issues at stake, collaboration is loose. Their directors, if they write, prefer to write outside their own magazines. Besides, almost as if by agreement, the major editors of current magazines have limited abilities. They have left no imprint on their magazines, and are unable to stimulate those writers capable of leaving a mark. There is no effort editorially to teach younger, talented writers. Lack of selectivity has caused the magazines, which seem to be edited by the whim of the mailbox, to become hollow and empty. In short, presently magazines are not the scene of action or the focus of literary politics and creativity. Some people have complained that there are too many literary magazines. There are in fact not very many. Yet, an inadequate division of labor gives the impression of confusion and superfluity. We need a variety of magazines to discuss and elucidate the role of culture in Yugoslavia.

We have earlier observed a decrease in the subject matter of cultural columns found in the press. Most of what we find is descriptive information augmented by titillating anecdotes and intrigues about writers. Real literary problems remain outside the framework of the press and therefore outside the framework of the mass media. If these problems are not discussed in the magazines, where else can they be clarified? The proliferation of Yugoslav literature has affected magazines insofar as new writers do not fit into traditional modes and existing literary organization. These new generations therefore have no magazine to turn to.

Yugoslav magazines should be shouldering a series of new tasks. Our country, which is also wide open to new artistic influences and pressures must help young writers express themselves and needs a definition of the role of culture. Writers and intellectuals should be the "conscience of their times" and provide solutions. They should also comment on and evaluate foreign literature, especially modern literature which has appeared in the Yugoslav literary marketplace, and dominates it. Such comments are often presented to the reader without any serious preparation in the press.

Literary magazines can only perform these and similar functions if they become the voice of dynamic, active groups of writers, gathered together for diverse literary, philosophical, and stylistic reasons. Even groups based on age would be a step in the right direction, encouraging variety in our present situation. Such groupings would develop a common value structure enabling some writers to work together over a longer period of time.

The static situation of Yugoslav magazines is well known. Material prepared for a 1967 symposium on periodicals in Serbia provides tangible proof of conflicting opinions as to whether a magazine should be an open forum or the organ of a particular group. This dilemma is still unsolved, because there are too many disagreements about alternative ways of organizing writers groups. Should they be based on geography, age, literary affinities? The press cannot at times discuss these matters freely because of international and domestic reasons.

Magazines would become more influential if they were the voice of a coherent assemblage of writers. Though everyone agrees with this assessment, the character of our magazines does not change. Currently this vacuum is being more frequently filled by a preventive ideology which discourages the publication of "unfriendly" thoughts. But in the absence of public discussion, it is difficult to make any judgments whatsoever, good or bad, friendly or unfriendly.

As a result the status quo is maintained to the satisfaction of the more conservative Yugoslav ideological elements such as the cultural apparatus and possibly the literary public itself. As presently constituted, literary magazines do not cause any except financial worries. If finances become more stringent, however, magazines may be threatened more directly with cessation of publication, mergers and other organizational means.

The problems of magazines are inextricably intertwined with the organization of the publishing houses where they are printed and which provide the funds for their publication. Let us only look at the makeup of their editorial boards, for instance. These continue to be selected on the principle of equilibrium, between factions. Every publisher in Belgrade has a few "modernist" and a few "realist" editors, to which are added a few "neutrals" whose task it is to bring the two polarized groups closer together or at least to normalize the atmosphere. Such an organizational makeup is disfunctional because it makes it impossible for publishers to select good native manuscripts. There is always someone who will recommend the book and just about anything is published which is offered by an author who has had any recognition. Libraries of our contemporary literature for the same reason lack a more defined physiognomy. Rarely is a book published for quality considerations alone and wider distribution of contemporary native writing through livelier publicity and propaganda is also nearly unheard of.[3]

[3] The discussion between Mijalko Todorović and the delegation from the Yugoslav Publishers' and Booksellers' Association further elucidates the problems of publishing in Yugoslavia.

LITERARY PRIZES DO NOT
REINFORCE QUALITY

Quality discrimination is also not stimulated by literary prizes. Not enough prizes have been given to works of a similar nature so as to acquire distinguishing characteristics. It is difficult for instance to differentiate between the July 7th and October prizes given in Serbia. More specialized awards for particular areas in literature, or in painting, do not seem to lessen the existing confusion. In fact, where more than one prize is awarded annually,[4] this confusion increases. Prizes can be categorized by type of art, by date, and by amount. Aside from that, they all reward those works of art which everyone can agree upon, those utilizing a representative style.

In such a situation the jury's role is extremely thankless. It is composed of members creating in different styles and with different artistic points of view. When such a mixed jury has to make awards, a compromise is unavoidable. Lists of literary awards, therefore, have the following characteristics:

First: the same, well-known names appear in all six republics. They belong usually to members of the middle aged and older generation. Consequently, since the liberation all good books written by authors belonging to these generations have been awarded prizes.

Second: literary-political interests as well as special interest groups, generations, or the marketplace, frequently push through compromises which are weak and unimpressive and then claim to have discovered some new values.

Third: moving from the middle to the younger generation, the number of works receiving prizes diminishes, so that it can be said that few young writers receive literary prizes.

Finally: closer to the present, awards become even more confusing, because the criteria of the juries seem to be in continual flux.

Such prizes awarded on the basis of "protocol" and "reconciliation" are old-fashioned. There is, in other words, no public recognition of the diverse currents in our native art. Prizes as they are awarded today fail to reinforce the fruitful differentiation in our art which

[4] Since 1960, there have been numerous discussions in the press concerning prizes and awards.

has taken place in the past twenty-five years. No one has dared establish prizes for revolutionary literature, the experimental novel, a work of great communicational value, or for traditional literature. Such changes would imply other changes which would affect far more important and crucial features of our society. Therefore these changes come only slowly and with compromises.

THE INTERNATIONAL LITERARY MARKET PLACE AND ITS EFFECT ON YUGOSLAVIA

Today, America and Western Europe represent the main literary markets. No wonder then that this area determines and sets standards for the evaluation of literary works all over the world. It is well known that this market primarily demands novels or collections of stories with a strong internal unity, and that such works are therefore sought after. No other forms of writing are acceptable, least of all "transitional" styles, although during this century countless writers from the Soviet Union, from France, and from other countries have created a large number of hybrid works combining prose and poetry. Literary essays and poetry are completely out of the picture. They are an unmarketable commodity all over the world.

Needless to say such a market exerts a certain pressure on literature. This pressure is even more obvious in the case of Yugoslav literature. Only a certain type of Yugoslav literature has "export" value. It must be "Balkan," "oriental," "peasant," and must include dark motives, killings and primitivism. If such "exotic" coloration remains on the surface, as in Andrić, all the better.[5] Urban and intellectual works and those dealing with the revolution and with contemporary life have undeservedly remained in the shadow. Even novels written in the standard way by Yugoslavs are difficult to place.

Of course Yugoslav literature is not the only literature to be adversely affected by the world market. Historical prejudices, which go beyond national boundaries, affect a literary work more than a

---

[5] Alain Bosquet, *Savremena jugoslovenska književnost* (translation), *NIN*, September 13; Jean Cassou's introduction to an anthology of Yugoslav prose (in French), Paris, Pierre Seghers, 1959.

musical composition or a painting. Politics is not alone to blame for this. Assumptions change from environment to environment and there is also the question of literary "manners." This is well documented by critiques of Yugoslav works published abroad. Zygmunt Stoberski, for example, regularly reports on the impact of our literature in Poland.[6] Even Stoberski's estimations and evaluations of Yugoslav works, however, are not convincing because there are visible signs of a superficial reading on his part. It seems that compliments are a necessity of good manners provided they cost nothing. Krleža spoke about this not too long ago after receiving the Njegoš prize.[7]

In other words, the literature of all the Slavs, with the exception of the Russians, is underrated in the world market. After World War II, however, the lesser Slav literatures have produced more significant works on the whole than the Russians, and yet Russian writers are internationally better known and translated. To make matters even worse, not only are the Slav and Balkan literatures generally underrated, they also underrate each other. Look at our own literary market which in twenty years has translated and introduced no other Balkan or Slav literature except the Polish.

Acceptance of literary works from other socialist countries, even Russia in the last ten years, follows what may be called the "five minute rule." When a socialist country begins to liberate itself from Stalinist bureaucracy and dogmatism, interest in this country and in its literature rises in the world market. But this interest soon passes like any fashion. Though internal developmental processes have contributed to the emergence of socialist-literary trends, political considerations alone dictated their vogue abroad. Yet, these capricious needs unfortunately influence the course of literary life and creativity in these socialist countries themselves.

It is unnecessary to reiterate the assertion that non-European literatures are underrepresented and underestimated in the world market. The cultures of Asia, Africa, and Latin America share the same fate. Though our century has unearthed evidence for the unity

---

[6] Zygmunt Stoberski, *Literatura Jugoslavije u Poljskoj* (in manuscript).
[7] "Literatura je nedeljiva" interview with M. Krleža, *NIN*, October 29, 1966.

and universality of civilization, as in Malraux's *Les Voix du Silence* and Toynbee's *A Study of History*, cultural self-centeredness has not been stamped out.[8] In practice Western European and American — and to a lesser extent Russian literary and cultural imperialism continue to dominate the world. In spite of the fact that the exchange of culture and art is livelier than ever before, this exchange flows primarily in one direction, from Europe to Yugoslavia. Such a pattern of flow has two incidental effects. On the one hand, some writers, like Miodrag Bulatović, have one reputation abroad and another at home. On the other, it has elicited a tendency among some young authors to write "for export." Take for instance Grozdana Olujić, whom some of the critics have reevaluated because her novels have been translated abroad.

THE SOCIAL STATUS OF THE YUGOSLAV WRITER

Our analyses so far indicate that the social status of the Yugoslav writer is very high theoretically, but in reality worthless. More precisely, his status is paradoxical. Let us first investigate his economic situation. The first generations of writers after the liberation had practically no public and therefore no income from their books. Consequently a majority of them took refuge in outside jobs which afford them reasonably decent working conditions. Such pseudo-professionalism as we have seen has embarrassing consequences. Periodicals and publishing houses, for instance, seem unable to select manuscripts on quality considerations.

There are other sources of income. Radio critiques are regularly published in the press without any changes. An author may also serialize his books in magazines and newspapers. Unfortunately only a small number of writers have not published every line they have written, and only a few remember that not everything which they write needs to be published.

Such economic security has made Yugoslav writers today relatively passive and conformist. They expect society, or rather the

---

[8] André Malraux, *Les Voix du Silence*, Paris, Gallimard, 1951; A. Toynbee, *A Study of History* (French translation), Paris, Gallimard, 1951.

party, to guarantee them the maximum of creative freedom rather than themselves fight for the extension of that freedom. Few are ready to go to jail for their writing or to die for their books. In the literary community one often hears excuses that a writer is waiting for the right opportunity to take a stand and to make the supreme sacrifice. This is indirect proof that a genuine readiness for creative risk is generally lacking. If it were otherwise, the voice of the writers could have been heard on numerous occasions, such as the reorganization of the Writers' Union or the general questions of political democratization.

The Yugoslav writer does not see himself as having a public role. If he is involved, this usually means in politics and occurs rarely. He may also be involved in his own narrow domain of professional literary preoccupations. In both cases he is not a social force. He therefore only occasionally as an artist and a cultural zealot makes public statements about various social issues. Contemporary Yugoslav writers are not even socially engaged when it comes to the content of their writing. The latter ignore subject matter such as the situation in our villages, except for sentimental and touristic impressions, the problems of urban workers, or even the plight of the modern intellectual. The consequences are twofold. First, contemporary Yugoslav literature is not written for the general public and second, writers do not dare to speak out about the problems besetting contemporary life in Yugoslavia.

It is worth studying this interesting phenomenon and understanding how aspects of literary life are refracted in the writer's work. Many past reflexes still persist in our culture and art today, irrespective of the changes in theoretical outlook and the liberalizations of creative expression which have taken place. What I am referring to here are mechanical reactions which occur despite an individual's best intentions. All of these reflexes indicate that the purpose of high culture is not well defined, permanent or stable.

Certain factors are obvious. We have, for instance, gone beyond dogmatism in art and culture. This attitude was strongest in Yugoslavia's critical prewar situation and immediately after the liberation. Antidogmatism is much more characteristic of our cultural context today, yet it at times manifests itself in a dogmatic way.

It is obvious that art today, and especially the art of words may cause political consequences, just as previously art was directly determined by politics.

Fearing Stalinism our antidogmatism sometimes tries to deny art any social relevance at all. It is obvious that there are historical deficiencies in the Balkan cultural milieu to support this trend. We have to struggle today with two old-fashioned prejudices about the function of art in society. The first views art as symbols, similar to village tombstones, which save us from oblivion and transitoriness.[9] The other overemphasizes the pedagogical role of art in a country whose populace needs to be lifted out of backwardness.[10]

Another historical tradition views us as a cultural and spiritual province of either the West or the East. At best we resemble ambassadors who are peddling Western culture to the East, or vice versa. This opinion, which has been updated, views our artistic progress, whether in literature or in anything else, as narrowing the gap between ourselves and the great cultures. According to its protagonists, we were fifty years behind the world in the past but have caught up to within fifteen years of what the others are doing. Though this view of our cultural inferiority is more often applied to the fine arts, its influence is pervasive.[11]

Though this assessment is not true, of course, our artists frequently behave as if it were. What is lacking is a sense of proportion, of reasonable expectations which can have drastic results. Since our culture lacks many preconditions for world acceptance, creative artists become impatient and fanatical, particularly if they cannot create these preconditions. Every opportunity is then viewed as the last chance on which our fate hinges.

We assume that this emergence beyond our frontiers implies a step up in some hierarchical ladder of cultural values. We should become aware that entering the world cultural market has nothing to do with the quality of our literary production. We need instead

[9] *Estetička čitanka*, p. 123.
[10] Jovan Skerlić, *Obnova naše rodoljubive poezije* (1908), *Collected Works*, Belgrade, Prosveta, 1964, vol. V, pp. 98–99.
[11] Borislav Mihajlović, "Književni razgovori" (1952), reprinted in *Od istog čitaoca*, Belgrade, Nolit, 1956, pp. 164–67.

to concentrate on the role and quality of art in our own country. But in this respect the situation is chaotic. In the past few years unfortunately this confusion has been fed by the press, which in all but two cases claimed that our artists attained exceptional success abroad.

THE SOCIAL RESPONSIBILITY
OF THE ARTIST

In discussing "responsibility" and "involvement," terms which have lost much of their original meaning, we wish to focus on the ethical dimension of the artistic task and the work of art. Both "involvement'" and "responsibility" it turns out are relatively new terms, having been first formulated before World War II,[12] and coming into use primarily in socialist countries. Socialist realism added a series of rules and norms about the responsibility of the artist and so did existentialism. But in addition to these there are a number of other interesting formulations of the terms in Camus, Pilnyak and Leonov.[13] Unfortunately these formulations are less well known and less discussed. None of them help in unraveling the tangled discussion. Current solutions are abstract and murky. The universal nature of "involvement" and "responsibility" are sometimes taken as an excuse for the compromises that a writer makes, for his complacency and conformity.[14]

The most valuable aspect of the newer formulations of "responsibility" is that they emphasize the writer's responsibility to the work of art itself and do not restrict responsibility merely to the artist's involvement in political and cultural life. Yet, such a concept of involvement and responsibility stresses the importance of individual artistic ethics. The view that art reflects eternal and absolute

[12] Jean-Paul Sartre, "Angažovana književnost," in *O književnosti i piscima* (translation), Belgrade, Kultura, 1962, pp. 3–4.

[13] Albert Camus, *Leto* (translation), Belgrade, Nolit, 1955; Leonid Leonov, in a speech at the 1st Congress of Soviet Writers, 1934, published in *Literatura i vremya*, Moscow, 1967, pp. 37–38; Boris Pilnyak, *Čitav život* (translation), Belgrade, Nolit, 1956.

[14] The case of Leonov is particularly characteristic for the period 1934 to the present.

moral norms belongs to the past as does the illusion that art transforms people's lives. In order to evaluate realistically the ethical functions of art we must take social and political conditions into account as providing the foundation of morality. This is the essence of the change.[15] We see then that different contexts require different kinds of responsibilities.[16]

I think that the responsibility of poets, writers and artists in socialism is quite different from that in other societies. Socialism assumes that all men are equally valuable. Though it may be unable to eliminate all inequalities between men in actual fact, such a society expects a new attitude on the part of the artist. Much of history shows writers criticizing the society of which they are a part. In socialism this is theoretically different. The writer's task is both positive and negative.

Objectively, for the first time in history the writer is living in a society to which he can say "yes."[17] But this does not mean that he should exclude the portrayal of the dark and negative side of reality from his work. Once again critical elements and the criticism of society must be possible. What form should this criticism take and how can it be constructive and still remain artistic? Will it be understood and to what extent will it be accepted?[18]

All of these unsolved questions have made the position of the writer in socialism contradictory, even paradoxical. Critical love seems to be a contradition in terms. Oskar Davičo once characterized the position of the writer toward socialism as that of a dishonest lover.[19] Our situation is particularly complicated since some of our writers were involved in creating and carrying out the socialist revolution which changed our country. With the passing years, they have developed a kind of defensiveness about this revo-

---

[15] Ernst Bloch, *Das Prinzip Hoffnung*.

[16] This is how the topic for the symposium "Struške večere poezije" was formulated.

[17] Presented by Veljko Vlahović as a seminar on "The Independent Society and Culture," *Politika*, February 14, 1968.

[18] *Umetnost i kriterijumi*, p. 194; see also "Književnost u socijalizmu, *Encyclopaedia moderna*, 1967, nos. 5–6.

[19] Oskar Davičo, *Poezija i otpori*, Belgrade, Nopok, 1952 (cited in *Savremena poezija*, p. 112).

lution, not permitting themselves or others to probe existing social problems seriously. Some of our older colleagues have not gone beyond a touching attempt at this "critical love." In spite of being unsuccessful they have at least raised the issue. One can ask no more of them.

In all socialist countries this serious creative task of criticism is waiting for a younger generation of writers. This is the generation which began its work around 1950 or 1955; in other words, my generation. At the 1965 Ohrid meeting of poets and critics, I spoke about our critical responsibilities:

> Our generation entered art barehanded, counting on the artistic word as the main weapon. We participated in the overthrow of Stalinism and dogmatism in our society and in our culture. More specifically our work, our literary creations represent a criticism of the official doctrine of "socialist realism" unmasking it as Stalinism in the literary field. We introduced new themes and advocated a more complex humanistic approach to man's destiny.
>
> Furthermore our work has exploded the rigid patterns of classical poetics. We have shattered established concepts about genres and varieties of literature. In fighting for art we have enriched the expressive apparatus and each one of us has a respectable general culture. We have also renewed the interest in avant-garde literature created after World War II.
>
> We are different from our colleagues and contemporaries in other socialist countries. But I do not wish to dwell on these differences now. It is sufficient to say that we vacillate between stoginess and intellectualism.
>
> Our basic problem has been that with a few exceptions, we have not created great works. Instead of great works we have had great literary activity. Instead of being personalities we are phenomena. It seems to me that we are tailored to the specifications of permissible freedom rather than having conquered freedom completely. Most of us have agreed that the liberation of poetry, culture and society should proceed step by step. We are, however, much more dependent on circumstances than we like to admit.
>
> Instead of being the avant-garde of the de-Stalinization process, it may be legitimately asked whether the literary work of our generation does not trail this process. What is more, some of us, who are most well known for our anti-Stalin activities, live parasitically off this recognition and profit

from it at this very moment. I don't believe that we have grasped what is essential. I hope that we have not spent all our energies on merely being present at a historic moment, between 1955 and 1960.[20]

In short, the question of responsibility is a different one for our generation. Above all it is a question of fundamental responsibility toward what we do. It is the responsibility to create a serious literary work. Such a view of responsibility is inevitable for us as a generation at this point in time. What we have accomplished as a result of historical responsibility should now culminate in an artistic responsibility. We should pass from an ethical to an aesthetic plane. Because I am a practitioner of art as well as a critic or theoretician of culture, I do not like to instruct or to give advice. What I have said is not to be taken as creating literary norms, it is not even to be understood as a warning to my generation. I am simply trying to see where we stand.

[20] The responsibility of a "generation" (from historic to artistic responsibility), *Borba*, September 5, 1965.

PART III. CONCLUSION

10. LITERARY LIFE AND LITERARY STANDARDS

AT THE BEGINNING of this study we stated that literary life is a complicated set of interrelationships between literature and society and literature and its epoch. The discussion itself amplified this statement to arrive at a better definition of literary life. First the general review, then the analysis of each individual element of literary life in postwar Yugoslavia provided insight into the total network of connections. Far from being a passive transmitter, literary life, through the interweaving of all its elements, actively influences and even determines the course of literature, literary phenomena, and writers and their output.

What exactly are these effects of literary life and where do they have the greatest impact? This study began with the assumption, and now finds it justified, that literary life has its strongest influence on literary criteria. These criteria have shaped Yugoslav literature from 1950 onwards. Our study shows more precisely which elements of literary life were most influential in the past period and have therefore most strongly affected the formation of literary standards.

First there is the party in its position as the avant-garde of social change in Yugoslavia. It initiated the struggle for national liberation and guided the revolution toward socialism. Historical facts alone are sufficient to validate this point, yet the analysis itself offers proof to what extent the other elements of literary life were dependent on the party, its ideology and its cultural politics. Ideology, as our chapter on literary politics indicates, is probably the most influential component of literary life.

Second, we have to mention the fact that writers grouped themselves spontaneously into varied and distinctive literary currents, trends, and programs. These groupings did not occur as a result of a common aesthetic outlook, but once they were formed they had a practical impact on literary life. Finally, there is a literary criticism which passively accepted ideological impulses and then zealously transferred them to literature. When literary criticism became independent, it overemphasized the "artistic" aspect of art and became aesthetic, as well as aestheticizing. These three elements are the main factors determining the atmosphere in the Yugoslav literary community since World War II. From their interrelationship emerged criteria for evaluating literary works.

Various other elements such as the literary public, the market and writers organizations are components of literary life whose impact is secondary. The literary public is not an active element affecting literary criteria because it has not been differentiated in Yugoslavia. No wonder then that its desires, its tastes and its demands are ignored in contemporary Yugoslav literature. Other evidence suggests that a wider segment of the public which follows our literature periodically requires a new type of content. Possibly this content should be presented in a traditional way or transposed into "lighter" forms bordering on mass culture. Yugoslav writers have not catered to this need.

The marketplace, too, is not an active factor in setting value standards because it responds passively and only to selected provocative phenomena. A writer's book is often sold not for its intrinsic value, but because there has been a scandal in the author's life. Finally, in the past few years writers' organizations have been more fiction than fact in governing literary life. They did however reinforce the tendency to screen contemporary life and subject matter out of contemporary literature.

Though many may assume that I am overstressing the case, I am not exaggerating when I say that contemporary life itself is not reflected in Yugoslav literature. The absence of certain literary criteria, it appears, makes this very difficult. The first criterion to be neglected is the criterium of contemporaneity. Contemporaneity in a literary work is that which most corresponds to our personal experience, and to the experiences of our contemporaries. It refers to how we see the world and how we would approach life itself. Naturally such contemporaneity is not the ultimate criterion of literary value. It is merely one of many, but among these I consider it the final and perhaps the crowning one. Overemphasizing this criterion however presents another set of problems since it would lead to a preference for contemporary literature over classical, which would also be stultifying.

The rejection of contemporaneity along with other elements of literary life in postwar Yugoslav literature has resulted in the emergence of a set of new standards which are a form of aestheticism. I have called this "socialist aestheticism" and have for years tried to describe and analyze it. This essay has demonstrated the important point that aestheticism is a system of literary criteria evolving out of the special characteristics of our literary life during the past fifteen to twenty years. I have also noted that Yugoslav socialist aestheticism has a number of special characteristics.

First of all, our criteria were developed within the framework of socialism, in an attempt to redefine the role of art and the artist in this type of society. Theoretically, as we have seen, the position of the artist in socialism is unique since the artist can for the first time be positively related and say "yes" to his society. Yet, as a result of this agreement he must not abrogate criticism and merely glorify the new society in his literary work. To find the proper balance between these extremes presents the greatest difficulty for art in socialist countries. By neglecting the criterion of contemporaneity, we have buried this problem and put off its solution.

Second, it must be kept in mind that our criteria emerged as a counterstance to socialist realism, which represents the first defined system of literary standards in a socialist society. They negate socialist realism or Stalinism in culture and art on the grounds that the latter limit free artistic creation, subjugate art to daily politics, and elevate cheap and false propaganda to historic and artistic truth.

Furthermore, our literary criteria are a response to modern world art and Yugoslav art after 1950. The interrelationship between world and local art, in other words modified the nature of our literary standards. Postwar Yugoslav exposure to modern art was not particularly broad. It started as an echo to Yugoslav prewar modernism, and surrealism and then developed under the influence of the Western avant-garde. Soviet modern art of the decade following the October Revolution came to us even later, more as a confirmation than as an inspiration. Except for Mayakovsky, it has had no direct influence on our contemporary literature.

Other influences on our literary standards include aesthetic theory, and the historical situation in which Yugoslavia found itself after World War II. Among aesthetic theories three points of view were most influential. These include the classical and metaphysical aesthetics of Goethe and Hegel, as well as the aesthetic aspects of the theory of alienation propounded by the young Marx. Our writers and aestheticians most frequently quote these authors, or their views as represented in the writings of Lukacs, Lefebvre, and others.

Finally there is the historical situation itself in which our literary criteria developed as described in the section on literary politics. The evolution of the new Yugoslav society was extremely complicated, and riddled with breaks and shocks. In 1945, from the war to the election of the assembly, there was uncertainty. In 1948 came the break with Stalin and the Informbureau. Then in 1953 there were further problems of internal development and so on. Since all of these were politically sensitive issues, it was dangerous to interpret them in a literary work, and the right to interpretation was granted to politicians only. Literature had no "diplomatic immunity" to enter this foreign sphere. To this must be added the fact that culture is not yet recognized as an important and independent component of society and social life. The role of art has therefore up to now been viewed either in terms of political, pedagogical, or "educationist" involvement to some quasi-aristocratic formula of art-for-art's sake and aestheticism.

The above discussion of the elements of literary life contains an indirect description of literary criteria in Yugoslavia. According to these criteria a good work must have its own sphere of reality, and be organized according to its own indigenous principles. These criteria are, however, extremely aesthetic or more precisely aestheticizing, and generally applicable to high art only. Yet at present we apply these criteria indiscriminately. We noted early in the discussion that Yugoslav literature is historically condemned to being average and yet we have paid no attention to developing criteria which are able to judge great as well as average art.

Introducing the criteria of "contemporaneity" and "completeness" would fulfill such a function. They would unify content and form. The first criterion of contemporaneity ensures the uniqueness of a work of art, while completeness evaluates the extent to which this uniqueness is structured. These two criteria should not, however, replace the criteria of style, language and means of expression.

Coming back to the problem of evaluating average works of art, we need to first classify different kinds of literary production. Starting at the bottom we find first of all "kitsch" and "schund," and other light literature, which are all products of "mass" culture. On the second level are the large number of works of art which make up what may be called the "golden mean." This category is particularly interesting because it highlights the two extremes, great art and kitsch. The large domain of the "golden mean" consists of three categories: works of merit and current production, plus the less successful works of great artists.

We have then the following three-part schema to classify literary productions:

I. Works of genius — complete works judged to be classics

II. "Golden mean" works, consisting of

a) creations by an outstanding writer

b) above average, solid, works of merit

c) current productions such as melodramas, commercial art and so on

III. "Schund" works

a) kitsch — as a positively defined, nonvalue

b) dilletantism — absence of any positive definition.

In my *Umetnost i kriterjumi* and in *Merila književne osredjenosti* I further concluded that a work belongs to the domain of the golden mean if it has some of the following five characteristics, three of which are negative and two positive:

a) no internal cohesion and historical permanence

b) no impact beyond its own individual borders

c) limitation to a narrow ethical or social milieu

d) autonomous structure

e) belonging to a definite "type" within a genre.

One important aspect of average literatures such as ours consisting of works belonging to the golden mean is that such a literature can be prescribed, or at least influenced. And yet after 1950, during the fight against socialist realism, prescribing artistic production was the focus of attack. We thought at the time that the abolition of this type of prescription would ensure Yugoslav freedom in art and society. But what has actually happened? Just as Yugoslav society was unaware that it often fought Stalinism with Stalinist methods, Yugoslav writers were unaware that seemingly neutral, objective standards amounted to a new form of negative prescription.

This kind of prescription differs, however, from that prevailing in the West. American theater and film too is typed by a prescribed set of norms. Here the rules of the game skillfully utilize the "free space" left by government regulation and industry censorship. Such a system covers everything including the time permitted to suggest the sexual act, moderate propaganda for the American way of life, and a definite way of mixing opposites in order to achieve maximum dramatic conflict. These practical "production" principles, when consistently enforced, have positive effects, they insure a certain artistic level. The best evidence for this is serialized American art, such as television shows, short stories, or musicals, which are at times enviably sound.

Prescription in America and in other capitalist countries, as Vanja Sutlić has pointed out, is undertaken by industry itself because culture is viewed as part of its domain. In socialism on the other hand, culture has been considered a part of ideology. Yugoslav prescription as we have seen is ideological, but different from the kind imposed by socialist realism. It offers an antiprogram or an indirect program for artistic creation. Earlier I formulated the situation in the following way: "In Soviet dogmatism the bureaucracy orders artists to do something in a prescribed way, whereas in Yugoslav society, in the persons of politicans and ideologues, it reaches an agreement with the artists or advises them not to do something."

When direct intervention in art was rejected, the political determination of aesthetics and other utilitarian demands on art were negated as well. Yugoslav literary critics stressed that art has no ulterior, nonartistic functions, it does not serve interior, momentary needs and interests. Such an absolute denial of utilitarian purposes is a reductio ad absurdum because it logically implies that art has no content at all. In literary practice such an attitude led to what we have called socialist aestheticism, a treatment of content which rejects current, relevant, and contemporary themes. Our art and literature consequently withdrew almost entirely from a modern, critical approach to life.

The very neutrality of many contemporary works led me to conclude that aestheticism created works which suit our bureaucracy even though they need not like them. If we were to develop the social analysis further we would find that such art in fact expresses the essence of this kind of bureaucracy. Socialist aestheticism has thus functioned negatively as a program for a politically loyal, neutral, aestheticizing, literature which lacks a larger public. Its positive justification lies in the fact that it has produced some works of merit.

In my essay "Književnost u socializmu" I viewed aestheticism from a more general point of view and concluded that socialist realism is a well-rounded literary theory, with a set of criteria, a definite program, and a well-defined practice. It lasted as long as the Stalinist epoch, beginning with the first Five Year Plan and ending with Stalin's death, or the twentieth Soviet Party Congress.

Criticism of socialist realism in Poland and among the intellectual left of the West, particularly in Sartre's magazine Les Temps Modernes did not start until 1956 long after such criticism had begun in Yugoslavia. Other socialist countries like Rumania, Hungary, and Czechoslovakia did not come to it till the sixties. Today, socialist realism no longer dominates the literature of the socialist countries, which are now entering a new phase. Seen from the outside there is greater tolerance and freedom of creativity. But internally, literature is still not dealing with reality in a critical way. There is an exaggerated emphasis on the autonomy of the work of art, its structure and its meaning. In short, we find in other countries the same characteristics which we called socialist aestheticism in Yugoslavia.

Socialist aestheticism turns out to be the next legitimate phase in the literary development of socialist countries as they free themselves from Stalinism. Yet, it too is only a temporary phase which will be outgrown as literary freedom of expression increases and literary life changes. In Yugoslavia there are already signs of a third epoch. To reach it and expand artistic variety, literature must face and deal positively with the demand of contemporaneity. More precisely, it must approach contemporary reality critically. This is the main problem now facing writers and literature under socialism.

11. EPILOGUE

A QUARTER of a century has elapsed since Yugoslavia's postwar literature first emerged, and a half a decade since the period described in this book. What has happened since then to the relationship between literary life and literary criteria? To begin with, what was the fate of this book itself? Its publication triggered heated debates, fifty reviews, and numerous discussions in Yugoslavia itself and abroad. Some of these carried such sensational titles as "the most attacked book of the decade," "literary and historical color-blindness," "synthesis attempted," "what does Sveta Lukić really want?," and "an unusual book of ill-conceived axioms."

The preface to this American edition places some of these reactions into perspective. Let me reiterate here that the intent of the book was theoretical: to investigate the impact of literary life on literary criteria and thus to set up a provisional typology describing Yugoslav literary development. Unfortunately, many of the theoretical insights were lost in the disproportionate attention paid to the book's presentation of historical facts. This is not surprising since there is a crying need for a history of contemporary Yugoslav literature which is yet to be written. Even Slavic literary scholars mistook the book for a history. Compared to a serious history of literature, this book is, however, no more than an introduction, something that students prefer to skip, sketching the social and historical background of literary activity in our epoch.

Another criticism, on which much ink was wasted, was the book's use of the term "Yugoslav literature." This seems to stem from a basic misconception about the differences between various national literatures. In defense of his usage, the author must point out that the social conditions throughout the period of administrative socialism, which is the primary focus of the book, were the same all over the country. Since these conditions are the determinants of literary life, a unified analysis of all Yugoslav literatures is justified.

In addition, it must be noted that, though the author is opposed to all forms of provincialism, he has never advocated a forced integration of different Yugoslav literary traditions. Nor did he attempt to decide whether contemporary Yugoslav literatures are more "Yugoslav" than before. The term "Yugoslav literature" merely refers to the close geographic proximity of different literary centers in the same way that the terms "Balkan" or "Danube literature" might be used to draw attention to Krleža's connection with Hungarian writers.

Finally, there is the criticism that the book pays an inordinate amount of attention to the Belgrade literary scene to the detriment of other literary centers throughout Yugoslavia. This was done for theoretical, not chauvinistic, reasons. It is methodologically easier to develop hypotheses in a limited, more familiar, context and then to test them in a broader setting. This is what the author has attempted to do. He feels that such a strategy is justifiable even if it leads to a "Belgrade interpretation," because this center is not only an important component in the total literary scene but the cradle of "socialist aestheticism" as well.

In many discussions, all of these arguments were overlooked, and the author was attacked for his neglect of the specific nature of national literatures in Yugoslavia. The bitterest critics even claimed that the book promulgated "bureaucratic statism." It seems as though the term "Yugoslav" in the title immediately turned certain critics off and thus blinded them to the central argument. Many of these are contemporaries and classmates of the author and some of them are even close friends. Their critiques cannot, therefore, be interpreted as malicious or personal. These critics are, it seems, victims of a state of mind exemplified by such Zagreb writers as Branimir Donat, Duško Car, Vlatko Pavletić, and maybe more insidiously, Vlatko Gotovać.

How did writers get that way? I believe that the explanation can be found in the secondary role of literature in modern society. While literature is not of central concern anywhere in the world, it is even more marginal in Yugoslavia due to a generally low cultural niveau and the development of aestheticism. A writer, therefore, cannot gain recognition except in the narrower milieu of his own republic. This milieu is not, however, primarily interested in literature. It is concerned with politics, economics, and national problems. For many years, the government and party admonished writers, "aesthetics belongs to you, leave politics to us politicians." No wonder then that writers today naively confuse literature with politics, politics with economics, and republics with nations. Little by little we modern writers and intellectuals seem to be thrown back into an ancient Pannonic and Balkan swamp along with all other conservatives, narrow minded nationalists, aimless politicians, etc.

Such a development is not interesting in itself but as a symptom of changes which have occurred in Yugoslav society since 1965. Five of these changes are most important for an understanding of what goes on in our literary scene today. There is, first of all, the 1965 economic reform designed to bring about economic stabilization, convertibility of the dinar, and democratization of social life in general. Unfortunately, this reform was launched at a moment of growing tension between the republics and lacking adequate preparation. Then, in the following year, the vice-president and secret police chief Ranković was ousted by the Central Committee. In Yugoslavia, this move was hastily interpreted as the demise of those conservative, bureaucratic, and statist functionaries who were allied with Serbian nationalist groups. Two years later, in June of 1968, a student revolt erupted in Belgrade, criticizing Yugoslav social conditions. The participants were influenced by the European and American New Left and lacked a clear program. The spontaneous movement, full of inconsistent and heterogeneous ideas, collapsed easily under government pressure, leaving no visible trace.

To make matters worse, instead of improving, the country's economic difficulties multiplied culminating in the dinar devaluation of 1971. Finally, there has been sharpening of nationalist feelings in various regions of Yugoslavia. These are paving the way for a constitutional reform which will convert the country from a unified federal state into a federation of states. The boundaries of these new states are to be determined on the basis of nationalities in spite of the fact that there are no clearly identifiable regions of sufficient size to make up viable units.

Yugoslavia today is, therefore, in the midst of a serious crisis. Some observers believe that her national problems are caused by economic; others, that her economic problems are the result of nationalist issues. In any case, national and socioeconomic problems are the focal points of this crisis. From the national point of view, the notion of "Yugoslavism" is under attack as a form of forced "unitarism" referring to the fear that the largest nation, Serbia, intends to gobble up the smaller ones. Critics of Yugoslavia and "Yugoslavism," seeing this danger, are literally so obsessed with this fear that they are unable to perceive certain other implications of the notion they are tearing down.

To comprehend these implications, we must go back to the definition of a "nation." In recent European history, a number of definitions prevailed, among these the Stalinist. For Stalin, a "nation" and "nationalism" are aberrations of the capitalist system. Such a definition implies that the problem will automatically disappear with a change in political system. During the administrative period of socialism when centralized controls prevail, however, such a definition paves the way for the idea of a supernation. This Stalinist interpretation was revived in Yugoslavia immediately after the war when the demands for "brotherhood" and "unity" psychologically reinforced a new "Yugoslav" romanticism, which is still powerful today. This new romanticism was an ambiguous mix of two contradictory notions: the nineteenth century ideas of south Slav unity as well as the ideas from King Alexander's dictatorship during which "Yugoslavism" meant Serbian domination.

With progressive decentralization during the past ten years, the nationalities problem has erupted once more in Yugoslavia. This time it cannot be ignored. Wartime and postwar Yugoslav romantics consider the mere reopening of the question a sacrilege, hoping to solve the problem by partisan style "unity" and "brotherhood" slogans. Those subscribing to a nationalist point of view deny any similarities between the various Yugoslav peoples and consider *any* unifying perspective a bad omen. Without rational and historical basis, the Yugoslav nationalists (who are in the majority today) remain provincial, regional, and local. They lack a broader horizon permitting them to see the Yugoslav problem in a world context. No wonder, then, that the two factions fight each other so primitively, creating an ideological vicious circle of false consciousness from which there is no escape.

The sharpening nationalities crisis has had an overwhelming impact on literary life as witnessed by the need for this epilogue. Among these effects were the "Declaration on the name and existence of a Croatian literary language," coming out of Zagreb in 1967. Although officially condemned by politicians, this declaration has acquired increased momentum with time. Cooperation, for instance, on a Serbo-Croatian dictionary, part of which had already been published by Matica Hrvatska and Matica Srpska, has stopped. In addition, the postulates of the declaration have now infiltrated the schools and the press.*

A group of Belgrade writers retorted with a "Proposal for reconsideration," stressing literary unity and correctly predicting some of the illogical consequences yet to be felt. Their statement has, however, been interpreted as the Serbian equivalent of the original declaration and attacked as the "flag of Serbian nationalism." In the subsequent period, there have been demands that the various national literatures be clearly delineated, a task which is almost impossible in a country where each republic contains amalgams of traditions. Our discussion of the Writers' Union noted that Yugoslavia and "Yugoslavism" can no longer mediate between the various national literatures. Art and culture in Yugoslavia today are, therefore, without a unifying perspective. The ridiculous consequences of such a position are clearly discernible from a Yugoslav news agency report of March 1971 entitled "World Anthology without a Yugoslav Novel," which requires no further comment.

A year ago a Brazilian institute announced the publication of a world novel anthology for which Yugoslavia, with a literary Nobel prize winner, was eligible. The Brazilian editor asked for the sub-

* They amount to changes in spelling between the Croatian and Serbian versions of a word and the restriction of literary history to local and regional writers. — Ed.

mission of Yugoslavia's five best novels, neither period, theme, or genre being specified, from which the institute reserved the right to select one. According to the TANJUG* report, however, the Yugoslav Writers' Union objected to leaving the final choice in foreign hands on the grounds that "there is no such thing as a 'Yugoslav' literature which could be represented by a single writer. . . . The literatures of our peoples and nationalities should instead be represented by a novel each, since each of these literatures has authors of world renown." The letter, it seemed, neglected to reveal the names of eligible authors. Instead the union suggested that they make a subsidy available to the Brazilian institute so that the novels of *all* the Yugoslav nationalities may be included in the anthology.

After the 1968 Belgrade University riots and the Warsaw Pact invasion of Czechoslovakia, new forms of interference reappeared in Yugoslav literary life. Harassment has taken three forms. First, extreme ideological accusations have been leveled against cultural and scientific creativity by party functionaries and cultural boards. Then, there have been formal bans of texts either by the courts or by various arts councils which constitute the organs of social control. Finally, there is the renewed imposition of preventative censorship, which is widespread in the press, theater, film, and television.

Although these phenomena are less severe than during the first postwar period, their number and frequency have drastically increased. In Belgrade and Serbia, for instance, there were about forty cases of interventions of one type or another in the eighteen-month period between June 1968 and December 1969. In spite of the diversity of causes and reasons given, the mere existence of such a long list in a relatively short time span is very worrysome. Even in the twenty-year postwar period when Yugoslavia and Yugoslav literature underwent some drastic crises such as the Informbureau and Djilas affairs, there were not as many cases of censorship as today.

A number of examples will illustrate the new techniques. Gluš-ćević's anti-Soviet article in *Književne novine* entitled "Variations on a Prague Spring," which appeared on the anniversary of the Czech invasion, was banned and nearly landed the author in jail. Not a

* Yugoslavia's national news agency. — *Ed.*

single protest against converting this literary event into a court case was heard. It did, however, immediately trigger the press and other media of information to increase preventative censorship without an explicit blacklist of people and topics; whatever a writer might have to say about contemporary political events might lead to undesirable consequences, and was, therefore, safer in the wastebasket.

Another case of censorship has to do with a group of Belgrade writers including Dragoslav Mihailović, Vidosav Stevanović, and Milisav Savić, as well as Živojin Pavlović and Bora Ćosić. Their interest in contemporary themes, in spite of some exaggerations, is crucially important for the normalization of the Yugoslav literary atmosphere, after the stifling aestheticist period. Precisely because they are not afraid to portray the darker sides of life, their writing has been viciously attacked. These were neither ideological nor aesthetic, but politically motivated.

Then, there is the attack on Mihailović's dramatization of the book *When the Pumpkins Blossomed* because it sympathized with some of the victims of the post-Cominform purge of Yugoslav Stalinists. After various groups including President Tito had registered their displeasure with the book, the Yugoslav Drama Theatre decided to discontinue this production which promised to have a long run to full houses. Needless to say, the political criticism of the play should not have led to its discontinuation. An "indefinite postponement" occurred as well to Alexsandor Popović's play *Second Door to the Left* where the *Atelier's 212* self-governing council of actors voted for discontinuation. In theory, this group could have left the play on the bill had they been willing to act independently from the social pressures surrounding them.

Film production, too, is unfortunately witnessing its share of intervention just as it began to blossom after twenty years of stagnation. It all started with Saša Petrović's *Collapse of the World* and the introduction of the term "black series" to describe this and other contemporary films. Critics trying to do away with them are suggesting that their international recognition stems from the fact that they criticize and paint Yugoslav society in dark and sombre tones. In fact, these films received their awards because of superior quality.

Late in 1969, the Serbian Philosophical Society discussed the renewed imposition of censorship at two public meetings on "Society and Culture" which attracted a large crowd of people. Most political and party forums immediately condemned these discussions, launching an irrational campaign full of innuendos lasting several months. It seemed at first that not always were the critics party functionaries, nor were they all voicing the same criticisms. Shortly afterwards it became clear, however, that the real leaders were bureaucrats who were mounting a public media campaign blending financial with ideological threats.

In the last two or three years, when a number of novels, dramas, and films were finally growing away from the sterile "socialist aestheticism" described throughout this book, politicians once again resorted to censorship to discourage authors. The portrayal of our contemporary society in these works is direct, understandable, and somewhat critical. Problems are interestingly discussed and the authors pose relevant questions, though they are by no means against socialism. It is, therefore, absurd to subjugate them to condemnations, bans, and preventative censorship as enemies of the state. Unfortunately, this absurdity is, however, happening and we already feel its consequences. New ideas and currents, which were about to appear, are strangled and the progress of Yugoslav postwar literature is once again threatened.

BIOGRAPHICAL NOTES

ON CONTEMPORARY YUGOSLAV WRITERS

In these notes the republic or autonomous province (in parentheses) gives a clue to the language the author uses and to the national literature to which he belongs. [Where no parentheses appear, the republic is assumed to be Serbia. — *Ed.*]

Abadžijev, Georgi (1910–63). Prose writer (Macedonia). Collections of short stories: *Zora, Poslednji susret, Priče.* Novels: *Aramijsko gnjezdo* and *Pustoš.*

Ač, Karolj (1928 –). Poet and translator (Voyvodina). Collections of poetry (in Hungarian): *Ruka na kvaci, Pesnik u inkognitu, Pesma umesto tišne.* Editor of anthology: *Sto godina srpske i hrvatske lirike.*

Andrejevski, Petre (1934 –). Poet (Macedonia). Collections of poetry: *Jazli, i na nebu i na zemlji, Gluvo doba*; and short stories: *Sedmi dan.*

Andrić, Ivo (1892 –). Began by writing poetry and lyrical prose, translations, articles and critiques. Later he turned to short stories and novels. His main works include *Ex ponto* (prose poems, 1918); *Nemiri* (poems, 1920); *Pripovetke* (short stories, 1924, 1931, 1936); *Na Drini ćuprija, Travnička hronika* and *Gospodjica* (1945); *Prokleta avlija* (novels). His works have been translated into almost all European languages and in Asia and Africa as well. He received the Nobel Prize for literature in 1961. [Books available in English translation: *The Bridge on the Drina*, New York, Macmillan, 1959; *The Vizier's Elephant*, New York, Harcourt, Brace and World, 1962; *Bosnian Chronicle*, New York, Knopf, 1963; *The Woman from Sarajevo*, New York, Knopf, 1965; *The Pascha's Concubine and Other Tales*, New York, Knopf, 1968.]

Antić, Aleksandar (1923 –). Writer of children's prose and plays, author and producer of children's TV serials.

Antić, Miroslav (1932 –). Poet. Author of radio dramas and screenplays.

Poems: *Ispričano za proleća, Plavo nebo, Roždestvo tvoje, Psovke nežnosti, Boje i reči, Koncert za 1001 bubanj*. Poems for children: *Poslednja bajka* and *Plavi čuperak*. Radio dramas: *Otužni marš* and *Povečerje*.

Arsovski, Tome (1928 –). Poet (Macedonia). Writer of radio and TV plays. Poetry: *Pregršt smeha, Neprebol*. Plays: *Aleksandra, Diogenov paradoks*. TV plays: *Pregršt sreće, Stoti korak*.

Asanović, Sreten (1931 –). Prose writer and journalist. Short stories: *Dugi trenuci, Ne gledaj u sunce, Igra vatrom*.

Bajsić, Zvonimir (1923 –). Radio and TV producer, dramatist and novelist. Radio dramas: *Laku noć, Leno*; *Mekana proljetnja zemlja, Varalice, Tice iza stakla*. Received the award of the City of Zagreb in 1964 for his TV production of Isaac Babel's play *Sumrak* ("Dusk").

Bandić, Miloš (1930 –). Literary critic and essayist. Works: *Vreme romana, Ivo Andrić: Zagonetka vedrine*; *Mihailo Lalić: Povest o ljudskoj hrabrosti*.

Banjević, Mirko (1905–69). Poet. Collections of poetry: *Sutjeska, Šuma, Zvijezdani voz, Do iskapi, Zavjet*.

Barković, Josip (1918 –). Prose writer (Croatia). Novels: *Dolina detinjstva, Alma, Podjimo časak umrijeti*. Collections of short stories: *Tri smrti, Na rubu noći, Zeleni dječak*.

Bećković, Matija (1939 –). Poet. Poetry: *Vera Pavladoljska, Metak lutalica, Tako je govorio Matija* (two editions).

Bevk, France (1890 –). (Slovenia). Major works: *Kapetan Martin Čedermac, Čovek protiv čoveka, Crna braća i sestre, U noći Sv. Jovana (Kresna noć), Krvavi jahači, Gvozdena zmija, Ljudi pod Osojnikom, Izmedju dva rata, Put u slobodu*.

Bihalji-Merin, Oto (1934 –). Essayist, art critic and prose writer. Travel and topical books: *Osvajanje neba, Španija izmedju smrti i radjanja*. Critiques and essays: *Misli i boje, Susreti sa mojim vremenom, Savremena nemačka umetnost, Jugoslovenska skulptura 20 og veka, Prodori moderne umetnosti, Graditelji moderne misli*. Novels: *Do vidjenja u oktobru*. Some of his works have been translated into French, English, German, Dutch and Swedish.

Blagojević, Desimir (1905 –). Poet. Collected poetry: *Šaputanja s mostova, Karneval andjela, Dolazak medj cvrčke, Tri kantate, Vreme bezazlenih, Ptice nemilice, Rodoslov*, and *Zemaljska trpeza*.

Bogdanović, Milan (1892–1964). Literary critic. Translated Romain Roland's *Colas Breugnon*. Monographs, essays and critiques: *Stari i novi*

I–IV, Vuk Karadžić: njegov život i kulturno-revolucionarni rad, Njegoš, Djura Jakšić, Dečja poezija Zmajeva, and others.

Bor, Matej (pen name of Vladimir Pavšič, 1913 –). Slovenian author and translator (French and German). Collected poems: *Previharimo viharje* (published clandestinely in Ljubljana), *Pesme, Bršljan nad jezerom, Trag naših senki, U letnjoj travi.* Novel: *Daljine.* Critiques and essays; plays: *Gospodin Lisjak, Odrpanci, Povratak Blažonovih, Točkovi tame.*

Boškovski, Jovan (1920–68). (Macedonia). Prose writer and critic. Short stories: *Streljanje, Begunci, Ljudi i ptice.* Novel: *Solunski atentatori.* Collection of drama criticisms: *Oplemenjena igra.* Film scenarios: *Solunski atentatori* and *Pod istim nebom.*

Božić, Mirko (1919). (Croatia). Plays: *Most, Devet gomolja, Povlačenja, Skretnica, Ljuljačka u tužnoj vrbi, Pravednik, Novele.* Novels: *Kurlani, Neisplakani, Svilene papucice.* Film scenario: *Djevojka i hrast.*

Božić, Petar (1932 –). (Slovenia). Novels: *Čovek i senka, Izvan, I–II,* Plays: *Vojnika Jošta nema, Kažnjenici.*

Bulatović, Miodrag (1930 –). One of the most widely translated Yugoslav writers in Western Europe. Short stories: *Djavoli dolaze, Vuk i zvono.* Novels: *Crveni petao leti prema nebu* and *Heroj na magarcu.* Play: *Godo je došao.* [Available in English translation: *The Red Cockerel,* London, Weidenfeld and Nicholson, 1962.]

Bulatović, Vladimir Vib (1931 –). Satirist, columnist, and children's author. Books: *Budilnik* (satiric collage adapted for the theater) and *Menjačnica ideala.*

Čašule, Kole (1921 –). (Macedonia). Collected short stories: *Prvi dani* and *Priča.* Plays: *Vejka na vetru, Brazda, Crnila, Socijalistička Eva.*

Cesarić, Dobriša (1902 –). Poet, essayist, scholar. Poetry: *Lirika, Spasena svijetla, Izabrani stihovi, Pjesme, Osvijetljeni put, Goli časovi, Izabrane pjesme.* Has published numerous translations of poetry and prose, especially from German.

Čingo, Živko (1936 –). Storyteller and journalist (Macedonia). Selected writings: *Paskvelija, Nova Paskvelija.*

Čolanović, Vojislav (1922 –). Author and translator (English). Short stories: *Osedlati mećavu.* Novel: *Druga polovina neba.*

Ćopić, Branko (1915 –). Prose writer and poet. Major works: Novels: *Prolom, Gluvi barut, Ne tuguj bronzana stražo, Osma ofanziva.* Short stories: *Pod Grmečom, Bojovnici i bjegunci, Rosa na bajonetima, Doživljaji Nikoletine Bursaća, Gorki med.* Poetry: *Ognjeno radjanje do-*

movine, Ratnikovo proljeće. Children's books: *Priče partizanke, Orlovi rano lete, Priče mačka Toše.* Has written plays and scenarios.

Ćosić, Bora (1932 –). Prose writer, essayist and translator. Novels: *Kuća lopova, Svi smrtni, Andjeo je došao po svoje.* Essays: *Vidljivi i nevidljivi čovek, Sodoma i Gomora.* Translator of Mayakovski.

Ćosić, Dobrica (1921 –). Author and journalist. Novels: *Daleko je sunce, Koreni, Deobe, Bajka.* Collection of articles: *Akcija.* Report: *Sedam dana u Budimpešti.* [Available in English translation: *Far Away Is the Sun,* Belgrade, Yugoslavia Publishing House, 1963.]

Crnčević, Brana (1935 –). Satirist, TV and children's writer. Major works: Aphorisms: *Govori kao što ćutiš.* Children's poetry: *Bosonogi i nebo.* Satirical play: *Kafanica, sudnica i ludnica.* TV plays: *Cipelice od krokodilske kože, Devojka sa tri oca.*

Crnjanski, Miloš (1893 –). Poet, novelist, and dramatist. Poetry: *Lirika Itake.* Short stories: *Priče o muškom.* Plays: *Maska, Konak, Nikola Tesla.* Novels: *Dnevnik o Čarnojeviću, Seobe, Druga knjiga Seobe.* Travels: *Pisma iz Pariza, Ljubav u Toskani, Knjiga o Nemačkoj, Naša nebesa.* (Has translated Chinese and Japanese poetry.)

Danojlić, Milovan (1937 –). Poet. Collections: *Urodjenički psalmi, Nedelja, Noćno proleće, Balade.* Children's poetry: *Kako spavaju tramvaji.*

Davičo, Oskar (1909 –). Poet and novelist. Major works: *Višnja za zidom, Hana, Flora, Nastanjene oči.* Poetry: *Zrenjanin, Čovekov čovek.* Novels: *Pesma, Beton i svici, Radni naslov beskraja, Generalbas, Ćutnje, Gladi, Tajne, Bekstva.* Essays: *Poezija i otpori, Pred podne.* Has written several film scenarios. [Available in English translation: *The Poem,* 1959.]

David, Filip (1940 –). Has written for the theater and TV. Collection of short stories: *Bunar u tamnoj šumi.* Play: *Balada o Dobrim Ljudima.*

Dedinac, Milan (1902–66). Poet and drama critic. Works: *Javna ptica, Jedan čovek na prozoru, Pesme iz dnevnika zarobljenika broj 60211, Od nemila do nedraga, Pozorišne hronike.*

Desnica, Vladan (1905–67). Writer, translator and essayist. Novels: *Zimsko letovanje, Proleća Ivana Galeba.* Stories: *Olupine na suncu, Proljeće u Badrovcu, Tu odmah pored nas, Fratar sa zelenom bradom.* Poetry: *Slijepac na žalu.* Essays: *Priča o tipičnome.*

Direnbah, Zora (1929 –). Playwright and scenarist. Radio dramas: *Alkimonova jabuka, Sestre Brsali* and *Posle petnaest godina.* Film scenario: *Deveti krug.*

Dizdar, Mak (1917 –). Poet (Bosnia-Hercegovina). Collections of poetry: *Vidovpoljska noć, Okontnosti kruga, Koljena za Madonu, Kameni spavač, Plivačica* and *Povratak.*

Djerćeku, Enver (1928 –). Poet (Macedonia). *Tragovi života* and *Zenice čeznje.*

Djilas, Milovan (1914 –). Journalist, writer and ideologue. Author of *Legenda o Njegošu,* numerous political pamphlets and articles. His later political writings, such as *Nova klasa, Razgovori sa Staljinom* and *Srce Naroda,* were translated and published abroad. Translated Milton's *Paradise Lost* into Serbo-Croatian. [Books available in English: *Land without Justice,* New York, Harcourt, Brace and World, 1958; *Anatomy of a Moral,* New York, Praeger, 1959; *The New Class,* New York, Praeger, 1957; *Conversations with Stalin,* New York, Harcourt, Brace and World; *Montenegro,* New York, Harcourt, Brace and World, 1962; *Njegoš: Poet, Prince, Bishop,* New York, Harcourt, Brace and World; *The Imperfect Society: Beyond the New Class,* New York, Harcourt, Brace and World, 1969; *Under the Colors,* New York: Harcourt, Brace, Jovanovich, 1971.]

Djurčinov, Milan (1928 –). Literary critic (Macedonia). Has done extensive research on Chekov and Dostoyevsky. Books: *Vreme i izraz,* and *Prisutnosti* (collections of critiques and reviews) and an anthology of contemporary Macedonian prose and poetry.

Djurdjević, Miodrag (1920 –). Prose writer and playwright. *Senke nad Beogradom* (chronicle). Short stories: *Pesnik i slava.* Radio-dramas: *Povratak, Dogadjaj u noći, Tragična sudbina, Doručak u motelu.*

Djuzel, Bogomil (1939 –). Poet (Macedonia) and translator of French and English literature. Collections of poems: *Medovina, Alhemijska ruza, Nebo, zemija i sunce.*

Dragojević, Daniel (1934 –). Poet, essayist, biographer. Main works: *Kornjača i drugi predjeli, U tvom stvarnom tjelu, Kosta Angeli Radovani* and *Albert Kinert.*

Drainac, Rade (pen name of Radojko Jovanović) (1899–1943). Writer and journalist. Collected poems: *Modri smeh, Erotikon, Lirske minijature, Dah zemlje.* Novel: *Španski zid.* Short stories: *Srce na pazaru.*

Drakul, Simon (1930 –). Prose writer and dramatist (Macedonia). Short stories: *Planina i daljine, Vitli vo porojot.* Novels: *Zvezde padaju same, Bela dolina.* Plays: *Nemirna rudina, Stubovi na nebu.*

Džadžić, Petar (1929 –). Literary critic and essayist, author of numerous reviews and critiques. Has published monographs on Ivo Andrić and Branko Miljković plus a collection of criticism, *Iz dana u dan.*

Egerić, Miroslav (1934 –). Critic and essayist. Books: *Portreti i pamfleti* (collection of literary criticism) and *Molitva na Čegru* (essays).

Feher, Ferenc (1928 –). Poet (Voyvodina). Collected poems (in Hungarian): *Unuci kmetova, Snovi pokraj seoskih puteva, Do pojasa u zemlju zakopan, Ljubavlju punom nade*. Writer of children's poetry. Has compiled a collection of Yugoslav poetry for young people, *Igra oblaka*.

Fetahagić, Sead (1935 –). Collected short stories: *Četvrtak poslije petka*. Drama and literary critic, has written TV plays.

Finci, Eli (1911 –). Literary and drama critic, translator of Roger Martin du Gard, Emile Zola, Stendhal, Jules Laforgue and Marcel Proust. Works: biography of Diderot, monographs on Krleža, Cesarić, Jovan Skerlić, Djordje Jovanović, Branimir Ćosić and others. Collection of drama criticisms: *Više i manje od života* (4 volumes).

Finžgar, Frančišek Saleški (1871–1962). Writer (Slovenia). Short stories: *Prerokovana, Borbe*. Novels: *Pod slobodnim suncem, Iz modernog sveta*. Popular plays: *Lovokradica, Razvalina života, Lanac*. Memoirs: *Godine mog putovanja*.

Franičević, Marin (1911 –). Poet and essayist. Major works: Collected poems: *Na pojih i putih* and *Govorenje Mikule Trudnega, Zvijezda nad planinom, Luke bez sidrišta, Nastanjene uvale*. Essays and dialogues: *Pisci i problemi, Književnost jučer i danas, Književne interpretacije*.

Franičević-Pločar, Jure (1918 –). Poet, novelist, dramatist. *Preko rovova, Oganj zemlje, Konjik na proplanku, Stope na kamenu, Nagnuta neba*. Novels: *Gluha zvona, Raspukline, Zvoni na nebo*. Poetry: *Sunčana*. Play: *Na otoku* (with his brother M. Franičević).

Gal, Laslo (1902 –). Poet, storyteller and humorist (Voyvodina). Poetry (in Hungarian): *Pesme, 57 Pesama, Pesma o sirotom ribaru, Cveće na strnjici, Pripovetke*. Humorous pieces: *Vesela knjiga*.

Ganza, Mate (1936 –). Poet. Collected poems: *Pjesme strpljenja*.

Gavrilović, Zoran (1926 –). Literary critic and essayist. Works: *Kritika i kritičari, Od Vojislava do Disa, Antologija srpskog rodoljubivog pesništva*, and *Antologija srpskog ljubavnog pesništva*.

Georgijevski, Taško (1935 –). (Macedonia). Short stories: *Mi iza napisa*. Novels: *Ljudi i vuci, Zidovi*. Radio-drama: *Pepeo na mom ognjištu*.

Gligorić, Velibor (1899 –). Literary and drama critic, president of the Serbian Academy of Arts and Sciences. Works: *Kritike, Lica i maske, Matoš-Dis-Ujević, Pozorišne kritike, Srpski realisti, Ogledi i studije, U vihoru, Branislav Nušić*.

Gluščević, Zoran (1926 –). Critic, essayist, and translator (German). Works: *Kako se posmatra književno delo, Putevi humaniteta, Perom u raboš.*

Golija, Pavel (1887–1959). Poet and dramatist (Slovenia). Works: *Pesme o ženama sa zlatnom kosom, Večernja pesmarica, Izabrane pesme, Knjiga dramskih dela za mladež.* Translator of works by Maxim Gorky.

Golob, Zvonimir (1927 –). Poet and popularizer of primitive poetry. Anthology: *Ptica u oku sunca.* Poetry: *Afrika, Okovane oči, Nema sna, Glas koji odjekuje hodnicima.*

Gotovac, Vlado (1930 –). Poet and essayist. Poetry: *Pjesme od uvijek, Opasni prostor, Osjećanje mjesta, Zastire se zemlja.* Essays: *Princip djela.*

Gradnik, Alojz (1882–1967). Poet and translator (Slovenia). Poetry: *Zvezde padalice, Put bolesti, De profundis, Svetle samoće, Večiti izvori, Zlatne lestvice, Pesme o Maji, Krv što peva* and others. Has translated Dante, Michelangelo and Leopardi as well as Italian, Chinese and contemporary Spanish poetry. Has also translated *Gorski Vijenac* by Njegoš and *Smrt Smail-age Čengića* by Mažuranić (from the Serbo-Croatian).

Gunga, Fahredin (1936 –). Poet (Kosmet*). Collection of poems: *Jutarnja šaputanja.*

Hasani, Sinan (1922 –). Novelist (Kosmet). *Grožđje je počelo da zri, Jedna tmurna noć, Gde se razidje reka.*

Hing, Andrej (1925 –). Writer and producer (Slovenia). Collection of short stories: *Presudna ivica, Visoravan, Samoće* (in Serbo-Croatian).

Horvatić, Dubravko (1939 –). Poet and art critic. Collection of poetry: *Groznica, Zla vojna.*

Hristić, Jovan (1933 –). Poet, essayist and dramatist. Plays: *Čiste ruke, Orest, Savonarola i njegovi prijatelji.* Poetry: *Dnevnik o Ulisu, Pesme, Aleksandrijska škola.* Collected essays: *Poezija i kritika poezije* and *Poezija i filozofija.*

Humo, Hamza (1895 –). Writer. Poetry: *Nutarnji život, Grad rima i ritmova, Nova saznanja, Izabrane pjesme.* Novels: *Grozdanin kikot, Zgrada na ruševinama, Adem Čabrić.* Play: *Srebrenova pobjeda.* Short stories: *Pod zvrnjem vremena, Hadžijin mač.*

Isaković, Antonije (1923 –). Short story writer, whose stories *Velika deca* and *Paprat i vatra* have been made into films.

Isaku, Murat (1928 –). Poet and prose writer (Kosovo-Metohija). Col-

* "Kosmet" and "Kosovo-Metohija" are used interchangeably. —*Trans.*

lections of poems: *Glas iz planine* and *Nasmejano podne*. Novel: *Sunce zna svoj put*.

Ivanac, Ivan (1936 –). Dramatist. Plays (stage): *Zašto plačes, tata; Život pod reflektorom*. Radio plays: *On i ona, Ponoćno sanjarenje, Krik*. TV plays: *I odrasti se mora, Na plesu, Čovek i njegova žena*.

Ivanov, Blagoja (1931 –). Prose writer (Macedonia). Collections of short stories: *Sedam umiranja, Noć bez počinka, Crveni rondo*.

Ivanović, Vasko (1928 –). Reporter and dramatist. Collection of articles: *Ratnici, klinci i ostali*. Play: *Ko puca, otvoriće mu se*.

Ivanovski, Gogo (1925 –). Poet (Macedonia). Poetry: *Za novo proleće, Senka daljina*. Lyric prose: *Ljudi na putu* and *Ulica Koja je bila život*. Has translated Jakšić, Šantić and Preradović from Serbo-Croatian and Lermontov from Russian into Macedonian.

Ivanovski, Srbo (1928 –). Poet (Macedonia). Writer of children's verse, prose and radio plays. Main works: Poetry: *Lirika, Želje i medje, Susreti i rastanci, Beli krikovi*. Short stories:*Žena na prozoru*. Novel: *Usamljenici*.

Janevski, Slavko (1920 –). Writer and scholar (Macedonia), occasional work with films. His works are: Poetry: *Krvava niska, Pesme, Lirika, Hleb i kamen*. Short stories: *Klovnovi i ljudi, Ulica*. Travelogue: *Gorke legende*. Novels: *Selo iza sedam jasenova, Dve Marije; I bol i bes*.

Janjušević, Gojko (1936 –). Collections of poetry: *Mravi odlaze neprimjetno, Greben, Očajno sunce*.

Jelić, Vojin (1921 –). Prose writer and journalist (Croatia). Major works: Short stories: *Djukin djerdan, Ljudi kamenjara, Lete slijepi miševi*. Novels: *Andjeli lijepo pjevaju, Nebo nema obala, Trka slijepih konja, Trči mali život*.

Jeremić, Dragan (1925 –). Writer and aestheticist. Has written on aesthetics, philosophy and literary criticism. Works: *Prsti nevernog Tome* and *Kritičar i estetski ideal*.

Jocić, Ljubiša (1910 –). Writer and film producer. Poetry: *San ili biljka, Sumorna pitanja, Ogledalo; Krilato korenje*. Collection of allegories: *U zemlji Arastrata*. Drama: *Na rubu noći*. Novels: *I s tobom sama, Polomljena kola, Draga Mašin*, and others.

Kalan, Filip (pen name of Filip Kumbatović) (1910 –). (Slovenia). Short stories: *Pustolovi* and *Dete*. Essays: *Beleške o slovenačkoj književnosti, Život i delo Iga Grudena, Beleške o partizanskom pozorištu* and *Pregled istorije pozorišta kod Slovenaca; Veseli vetar; Eseji o pozorištu* (in French).

Kaleb, Vjekoslav (1905 –). Short stories: *Na kamenju, Izvan stvari, Brigada, Samrtni zvuci.* Novels: *Ponižene ulice, Divota prašine, Bijeli kamen, Nagao vetar.* [Available in English translation: *Glorious Dust,* Belgrade, Yugoslavia Publishing House, 1960.]

Kaštelan, Jure (1919 –). Poet, dramatist, essayist. Has translated Macedonian, French, Italian, Spanish and Russian poetry. Poetry: *Crveni konj, Pijetao na krovu, Biti ili ne, Malo kamena i puno snova.* Play: *Pijesak i pjena.* Short stories: *Čudo i smrt.* Monograph on the poetry of A. G. Matoš.

Kelmendi, Ramiz (1930 –). Collection of short stories: *Bore i ožiljci, Dve ispovesti, Ispovest jedne studentkinje.*

Kermauner, Taras (1930 –). Literary critic and sociologist (Slovenia). Theatrical producer who has also worked in radio and television. Has written numerous aesthetic discussions and polemics about criteria and contemporary Slovenian literature and art.

Kiš, Danilo (1935 –). Writer and translator of French and Hungarian works. Novels: *Mansarda, Psalam 44* and *Bašta, pepeo.*

Kmecl, Matijaž (1934 –). Dramatist (Slovenia). Radio-drama: *Samoća velikog teatra, Nova škola Sent Frenku, Automobil, Odlučujući dan u mačijoj istoriji* (for young people). TV play: *Kraj opere.*

Kocbek, Edvard (1904 –). Poet and short story writer (Slovenia). Poetry: *Zemlja* (1934) and *Užas* (1963). Partisan diary: *Medju drugovima.* Short stories: *Strah i srčanost.* Has translated Maupassant and St. Exupéry.

Kolar, Slavko (1891–1963). Prose writer and dramatist. Main works: Plays: *Sedmorica u podrumu* and *Svoga tela gospodar* (also film version). Satire: *Natrag u naftalin.* Short stories: *Nasmijane pripovijesti, Perom i drljačom, Mi smo za pravicu.*

Kolundžija, Dragan (1938 –). Poet. Collections of poetry: *Zatvorenik u ruži, Čuvari svetlosti.*

Koneski, Blaže (1921 –). Writer and philologist, president of the Macedonian Academy of Arts and Sciences. Poems: *Zemlja i ljubav, Pesme, Vezilja.* Short stories: *Vinograd.* Studies: *O makedonskom književnom jeziku, Makedonski udžbenici u XIX veku, Gramatika makedonskog književnog jezika, Istorija makedonskog jezika.* Translated Njegoš's *Gorski Venac* and Heinrich Heine.

Konstantinović, Radomir (1928 –). Poet, novelist and essayist. Works: Poetry: *Kuća bez krova.* Novels: *Daj nam danas, Mišolovka, Čisti i prljavi, Izlazak, Ahasver.* Radio plays: *Saobraćajna nesreća, Euridika, Ikarov let, Liptonov čaj.* Essays on Vuk Karadžić and Stanislav Vinaver.

Koš, Erih (1913 –). Prose writer. Major works: Novels: *Veliki Mak, Il tifo, Sneg i led, Vrapci Van Pea, Imena.* Short stories: *Vreme: ratno, Najlepše godine, Kao vuci, Prvo lice jednine.* Has translated *Peter Schlemihl* and Goethe's *Dichtung und Wahrheit.* [Available in English translation: *Names,* New York, Harcourt, Brace and World, 1966; *The Strange Story of the Great Whale, Also Known as Big Mac,* New York, Harcourt, Brace and World, 1962.]

Kos, Janko (1931 –). Essayist and critic (Slovenia). Has written about contemporary Slovenian poetry, the problems of Slovenian literature, drama and criticism.

Kosmač, Ciril (1910 –). Prose writer (Slovenia). Short stories: *Sreća i hleb, Iz moje doline.* Novels: *Prolećni dan* and *Balada o trubi i oblaku.* [Available in English translation: *A Day in Spring,* London, Lincolns Praeger Ltd., 1959.]

Kostić, Dušan (1917 –). Poet and journalist. Major works: *Pjesme, Zemlji voljenoj, Proljeće nad rovom, Govor zemlje, Zov lišća, Mreže, Povratak u Zelengoru, Zaboravljeni snjegovi, Tiha žetva, Dnevi izmedju nas.*

Kovač, Mirko (1938 –). Novels: *Gubilište* and *Moja sestra Elida.*

Kovačić, Lojze (1928 –). Prose writer (Slovenia). Short stories: *Razglednice* and *Dogadjaji u gradu Rič-Rač* (for children). Novel: *Dečak i smrt.*

Ković, Kajetan (1931 –). Poet (Slovenia). Works: *Prerani dan, Korenje vetra, Čas savesti.*

Kozak, Juš (1892 –). Writer of novels, short stories and essays. Novels: *Maske, Šentpeter, Drvena kašika.* Collected essays: *Lutanja.*

Kozak, Primož (1929 –). Literary critic and dramatist (Slovenia). Plays: *Afera* and *Dijalozi.*

Krakar, Lojze (1926 –). Poet (Slovenia). Has translated extensively, especially Polish poetry and prose. Collected poems: *U usponu mladosti, Cvet pelina, Medju tragačima bisera, Umrite mrtvi, Sunce u knjizi* (children's poems).

Kralj, Vladimir (1901 –). Theater critic and theoretician (Slovenia). Short stories: *Čovek koji je strigao ušima.* Essays: *Pogledi na dramu* and *Dramaturški vademecum.*

Kranjec, Miško (1908 –). Prose writer (Slovenia). Has published some twenty-five books. His major works are: Short stories: *Male su ove stvari, Proleće, Mrtva priroda i pejzaži.* Novels: *Kapitanovi, Osovina*

BIOGRAPHICAL NOTES   195

života, Mesto na suncu, Povest o dobrim ljudima, Do poslednjih granica, Parohija sv. Ivana, Zemlja se okreće s nama. Collection of articles: *Nešto bih hteo da vam kažem.*

Krasnići, Mark (1920 –). Writer, ethnologist and geographer (Kosovo-Metohija). Has written articles and essays about contemporary Shiptar (Albanian) literature. Children's stories: *Dedine priče, Prva svetlost.* Collected poems: *Preporučena pošta.* Monographs: *Savremene društveno-geografske promene na Kosovu i Metohiji.*

Kreft, Bratko (1905 –). Writer (Slovenia). Plays: *Celjski grofovi, Velika buna, Tugomer, Balada o poručniku i Marjutki, Kreature, Kranjski komedijaši.* Novels: *Čovek mrtvačke lubanje.* Short stories: *Priče iz davnih dana, Kalvarija za Vasju.* Essays: *Poslanstvo slovenačkog pozorišta, Pozorište i revolucija, Portreti.*

Krklec, Gustav (1899 –). Writer of poetry, essays, travel books, reviews. Translator (Russian, Czech, and German). Works: *Lirika, Srebrna cesta, Nove pjesme, Izlet u nebo, San pod brezom, Tamnica vremena.* Newspaper serials: *Lica i krajolica* and *Pisma Martina Lipnjaka iz provincije.*

Krleža, Miroslav (1893 –). Works: Poetry: *Pan* (1917), *Tri simfonije* (1917), *Pjesme* (I, II, and III, 1918–1919), *Hrvatska rapsodija* (1919), *Lirika* (1919). Prose: *Tri kavalira Gospodjice Melanije* (1920). Short stories: *Hrvatski bog Mars* (1921), *Vražiji otok* (1924). Travels: *Izlet u Rusiju* (1926). Plays: *Golgota* (1922), *Gospoda Glembajevi, U agoniji* (1928, 1958), *U logoru* (1922, 1934), *Vučjak* (1923), *Leda* (1932), *Aretej* (1963). Essays: *Eseji I* (1932), *Evropa danas* (1935), *Deset krvavih godina* (1937), *Eppur si muove* (1938), *Knjiga studija i putopisa* (1939), *O smrti slikara Josipa Račića* (1947). Novels: *Povratak Filipa Latinovića* (1932), *Na rubu pameti* (1938), *Banket u Blitvi* (knj. I, 1938, knj. II, 1939), *Zastave* (1964). Satires and polemics: *Dijalektički Anti-Barbarus* (1939); *Moj obračun s njima* (1932). Croatian songs: *Balade Petrice Kerempuha* (1936). [Available in English translation: *The Return of Philip Latinovitz,* Belgrade, Yugoslavia Publishing House, 1959.]

Krmpotić, Vesna (1932 –). Poet. Translator (English). Poetry: *Plamen i svijeća, Jama bića.* Travel essays: *Pisma iz Indije.*

Krnjević, Vuk (1935 –). Poet and critic. Poetry: *Zaboravljanje kućnog reda, Dva brata uboga, Pejzaži mrtvih* and *Pridvidjenja gospodina Proteja.*

Kulenović, Skender (1910 –). Writer. Poetry: *Stojanka majka Knežpoljka, Ševa.* Plays: *Večera, Djelidba, Svjetlo na drugom spratu.*

Kuzmanović, Vojislav (1930 –). Prose writer and dramatist. Short stories: *Petar na pijesku.* Radio dramas: *Spasitelj, Ubio sam Petra, Sezona lova.* Has received several prizes for his radio dramas.

Lalić, Ivan (1931 –). Poet and translator. Poetry: *Bivši dečak, Vetrovito proleće, Velika vrata mora, Melisa, Argonauti i druge pesme, Vreme, vatre, vrtovi* and *Čin.* Verse play: *Majstor Hanuš.* Translated an anthology of modern French poetry.

Lalić, Mihailo (1914 –). Novelist and short story writer. Collected short stories: *Izvidnica, Prvi snijeg, Na mjesečini.* Novels: *Zlo proljeće, Raskid, Hajka, Lelejska gora.* [Available in English translation: *The Wailing Mountain,* New York, Harcourt Brace and World, 1965.]

Lebović, Djordje (1928 –). Dramatist. Plays: *Nebeski odred* (film version with A. Obrenović), *Haleluja.* Radio plays: *Svetlosti i senke, Hiljadita noć, Crni kovčeg, Svetionik, Snežna padina, Do videnja druže Gal, Sahrana počinje obično po podne.*

Leovac, Slavko (1929 –). Critic. Collected essays: *Mit i poezija, Drama poezije.* Monographs: *Metamorfoze* and *Helenska tragedija i srpska književnost XX veka.*

Leskovac, Mladen (1904 –). Poet and essayist. Works: Anthologies: *Srpsko gradjansko pesništvo XVIII veka, Članci i eseji, Na našoj postojbini, Bećarac, Antologija starije srpske poezije.* Translations from French and Hungarian.

Lukić, Dragan (1928 –). Children's author. Books: *Iz jednog džepa, Dečaci, devojčice i odrasli, Ovde stanuju pesme, Vagon prve klase, Moj pra-pra-ded i ja.*

Lukić, Velimir (1936 –). Poet and dramatist. Verse play: *Okamenjeno more.* Other plays: *Bertove kočije ili Sibila, Dugi život kralja Osvalda, Valpurgijska noć* (some have been produced abroad). Collected poetry: *Poziv godine, Leto, Čudesni predeo, Madrigali i druge pesme.*

Madjer, Miroslav Slavko (1929 –). Poet. Collection of poetry: *Mislim na sunce, Raskršće vjetra, Utaman, U čovjeku.* Has written short stories, essays and articles.

Majdak, Zvonimir (1938 –). Poet, prose writer. Collected poems: *Tip na zelenoj livadi, Ukleti motociklisti.* Novels: *Bolest* and *Mladić.*

Majetić, Alojz (1938 –). Poet and prose writer. Poems: *Djete s brkovima priča, Otimam.* Novel: *Čangi.*

Major, Nandor (1931 –). Hungarian prose writer (Voyvodina). Collected short stories: *Prozor na dvorište, Poraz* (also published in Serbo-Croatian). For children: *Konjici od krompira.*

Makarović, Svetlana (1940 –). Slovenian poet of the youngest generation.

Makavejev, Dušan (1932 –). Essayist and film producer. Essays: *Poljubac za drugaricu parolu,* and on contemporary cinema. Producer of short films and art films based on his own scenarios: *Pečat, Antonijevo razbijeno ogledalo, Osmeh 1961, Parada, Čovek nije tica, Ljubavni slučaj.*

Maksimović, Desanka (1898 –). Poet and beloved children's writer. Has also written short stories and novels. Poems: *Zeleni vitez, Pesnik i zavičaj, Otadžbino, tu sam; Miris zemlje, Tražim pomilovanje.*

Maleski, Vlado (1919 –). Prose writer (Macedonia). Collection of short stories: *Crvena Georgina, Talasanja.* Novel: *Ono što beše nebo.* Film scenario: *Frosina.*

Manojlović, Ljubiša (1913 –). Prose writer, satirist, and journalist. Works: *Na času istorije* (on the massacre at Kragujevac). Monograph: *Svetozar Marković.* Satirical stories: *Vetar* and *Hijavatin čvor.* Novel: *Meteor sa žutom mašnom.*

Marinković, Ranko (1913 –). Prose writer and essayist. Plays: *Albatros* and *Glorija.* Collected short stories: *Proze, Ruke, Pod balkonima, Poniženje Sokrata.* Novel: *Kiklop.* Essays: *Geste i grimase.*

Marković, Slobodan (1928 –). Poet and journalist. Has published some twenty books of poetry including children's verse and prose poems. Translator of Sergei Yesenin. More important works: *Pesma o dečaku Izvoru, Mornar na konju, Vedri utopljenik,Crni cvet, Ikra, Svirač u lišću, Posetilac tamnog čela, Umiljati apostol, Sedefaste dveri.*

Markovski, Venko (pen name of Venijamin Tošev, 1915 –). Poet (Macedonia). Poetry: *Ilinden, Nas dvanaest; Klime, Priča o rezbaru; Partizani.* Play: *Goce.*

Matevski, Mateja (1929 –). Poet (Macedonia). Collected poems: *Kiša* and *Ravnodnevica.* Translated into many languages.

Matić, Dušan (1898 –). Poet and essayist. More important works: Collected poems: *Bagdala, Budjenje Materije, Laža i paralaža noći.* Verse prose: *Ruža vetrova.* Novels: *Kocka je bačena, Gluvo doba* (with A. Vučo). Essays: *Jedan vid francuske književnosti, Anina balska haljina, Na tapet dana.*

Matković, Marijan (1915 –). Prose writer and dramatist. Plays: *Slučaj Maturanta Vagnera, Igra oko smrti, Vašar snova, Heraklo, Ahilova baština, Ranjena ptica.* Collections of poems: *Iz mraka u svjetlo.* Essays: *Dramaturske studije.*

Mekuli, Esad (1916 –). Poet, essayist and journalist (Kosmet). Poetry: *Pesme gorke i ponosne, Za tebe.* Has published a large number of essays and articles. Has translated works by Njegoš, Mažuranić, Voranc, Zmaj, Goran, Kočić, Domanović and Sijarić from Serbo-Croatian into Shiptar. Also translates contemporary Shiptar poetry and prose into Serbo-Croatian.

Mekuli, Hasan (1929 –). Critic and literary historian (Kosmet). Has published *Utisci i razmatranja* and translates from Serbo-Croatian and Albanian.

Melvinger, Jasna (1940 –). Poet and translator of French poetry. Works: *Vodeni cvet, Sve što diše.*

Mihailović, Dragoslav (1930 –). Prose writer. Short stories: *Frede, laku noć.* Novel: *Kad su cvetale tikve.*

Mihajlović, Borislav Mihiz (1922 –). Critic and dramatist. Major works: Book of critiques: *Ogledi, Od istog čitaoca.* Plays: *Banović Strahinja, Komandant Sajler.* Stage adaptations: *Stradija* by Radoje Domanović and *Autobiografija* by Nušić. Compiled an anthology of Serbian poets between the two wars and collaborated on the scenarios for the art films *Saša* and *Dve noći u jednom danu.*

Mihalić, Slavko (1928 –). Poet. Works: *Komorna muzika, Put u nepostojanje, Početak zaborava, Darežljivo progonstvo, Godišnja doba, Ljubav za stvarnu zemlju, Prognana balada.*

Milićević, Nikola (1922 –). Poet and translator (Croatia). Major works: Poetry: *Obečanja žute zore, Snijeg i crna ptica, Pod ravnodušnim zvijezdama* (with S. Novak and V. Pavletić). Has compiled anthologies of Croatian poets between the two wars, modern Spanish poetry, modern Latin American poetry and Latin poetry.

Miljković, Branko (1934–61). Poet. Works: *Uzalud je budim, Poreklo nade, Vatra i ništa, Smrću protiv smrti* (with Blaže Šćepanović). Translated a large number of poems in an anthology of modern Russian poetry as well as French avant-garde poets. Has written monographs on poetry and poetry criticism.

Milošević, Nikola (1930 –). Philosopher and essayist. Works: *Antropološke eseje, Negativni junak u literaturi*, plus a series of articles.

Minati, Ivan (1924 –). Poet (Slovenia). Translates from Serbian and Macedonian. Collections of poems: *S puta, Doći će mladost, Nekoga moraš voleti, Bolest nedoživljenog.*

Minderović, Čedomir (1912–66). Poetry: *Cveće gladi, Mladost bez sunca, Koraci tutnje, Iznad ponora, Gorke godine, Ogrlica za Nailu.* Short stories: *Uska ulica.* Novel: *Poslednji koktel.* Partisan diary: *Za Titom.* Chronicle: *Oblaci nad Tarom.* Selected prose: *Film u tri epohe.*

Mirković, Milosav (1932 –). Critic and political writer. Has published a collection of essays on poetry: *O estetici, o etici, o tici.*

Mišić, Zoran (1921 –). Critic and essayist. Books of essays: *Reč i vreme.* Compiled an anthology of Serbian poetry and an anthology of Serbian literary criticism. He has published anthologies of contemporary Yugoslav prose and poetry in French.

Mitrev, Dimitar (1919 –). Critic and journalist (Macedonia). Major works: Essays and articles: *Vapčarov, Kriterijum i dogma, Prošlost i literatura.* An anthology of postwar Macedonian poetry.

Mladenović, Tanasije (1913 –). Poet. Major poetic works: *Pesme, Kamen i akordi, Pod pepelom zvezda, Vetar vremena* (selected with an introduction by Z. Glušćević).

Momirovski, Tome (1927 –). Prose writer (Macedonia). Short stories: *Koraci.* Novel: *Grešna nedelja.* Travels: *Strehe i pesak.*

Nikolić, Nebojša (1928 –). Prose and children's writer. Awarded the 1961 Prix Italia for his radio play *M'sje Žozef.*

Novak, Slobodan (1924 –). Writer (Croatia). Poetry: *Glasnice u oluji, Iza lukobrana* (with N. Milićević and V. Pavletić). Short stories: *Izgubljeni zavičaj, Tvrdi grad.* Radio dramas: *Strašno je znati, Trofeji.* TV drama: *Dolutali metak.*

Obrenović, Aleksandar (1928 –). Dramatist and film producer. Plays: *Nebeski odred* and *Cirkus* (with D. Lebović), *Varijacije* (Prix Italia). Radio plays: *Povratak Don Žuana, Subota uveče.* Has also written TV scripts.

Ocvirk, Vasja (1920 –). Prose writer (Slovenia). Radio plays: *Kad bi pali oživeli, Srećno ljudi, Mati na zgarištu.* Novels: *Majka, Suncu se ne može verovati, U novu zimu.*

Oljača, Mladen (1926 –). Prose writer. Novels: *Molitva za moju braću, Crne sekire, Nadja, Kozara.* Collected short stories: *Šapat borova.* History: *Herojska odbrana Beograda.*

Olujić, Grozdana (1934 –). Novels: *Izlet u nebo, Glasam za ljubav, Ne budi zaspale pse* and *Divlje seme.* Collection of interviews: *Pisci o sebi.*

Palavestra, Predrag (1930 –). Critic. Collected essays: *Književne teme, Odbrana kritike.* Monograph: *Književnost Mlade Bosne.* Anthology of postwar Serbian poetry 1945–55. Anthology of twentieth-century Serbian and Croatian poetry.

Parun, Vesna (1922 –). Poet. Collected poetry: *Zore i vihori, Pjesme, Crna maslina, Vidrama vjerna, Ropstvo, Pusti da otpočinem, Koralj vraćen moru, Ti i nikad.* Children's books: *Zec mudrijan, Patka zlatka, Tuga i radost šume.* Plays: *Marija i mornar.*

Pavletić, Vlatko (1930 –). Literary critic and poet. Collected poems: *Pjesme.* Essays and critiques: *Kako su stvarali književnici, Sudbina automata, Hrvatski književni kritičari, Trenutak sadašnjosti.*

Pavlović, Živojin (1933 –). Author and film producer; has written extensively on cinematography. Main works: Short stories: *Krivudava reka, Dve večeri u jesen.* Novel: *Lutke.* Articles: *Film u školskim klupama,* plus numerous essays. Films: *Neprijatelj, Povratak, Budjenje pacova.*

Pavlovski, Radovan (1937 –). Poet (Macedonia). Poetry: *Suša, svadba, selidba* and *Suša.*

Pekić, Borislav (1930 –). Novel: *Vreme čuda.* Scenario: *Dan četrnaesti* and others.

Pervić, Muharem (1934 –). Literary and drama critic, long-time editor of the journal *Delo.* Writes about the problems of contemporary Yugoslav literature and the theater.

Petrović, Boško (1915 –). Poet, short story writer and translator. Poems: *Ljubavni soneti, Zemlja i more, Ruj.* Short stories: *Lagano promiću oblaci.* Novel: *Dnevnik jednog vojnika.* Translates from German.

Petrović, Branislav (1937 –). Poet. Collection of poems: *Moć govora, Gradilište.*

Petrović, Rastko (1898–1949). Poet, prose writer, essayist, one of the most complex and innovative Yugoslav writers of the interwar period. Main works: Poetry: *Otkrovenja.* Story: *Ljudi govore.* Novels: *Burleska gospodina Peruna, boga groma* and *Dan šesti.* Travels: *Afrika.*

Petrović, Svetozar (1931 –). Literary theoretician and essayist. Has also written about Indian literature and culture and translated from Hindi. Works: *Kritika i djelo.*

Petrović, Veljko (1884–1967). Poet, political worker and short story writer. Major works: Poetry: *Rodoljubive pesme, Stihovi.* Short stories: *Bunja i drugi u Ravangradu, Pomerene savesti, Prepelica u ruci, Zemlja, Razgovoru nikad kraja.* Essays: *Vremena i dogadjaji.* Collected Works: Volumes I-VII (1954–1958).

Peza, Murteza (1919 –). Dramatist (Kosmet). Plays (comedies): *Ne ženim se za pare, Izgubljeni raj* and others. Scenarios for art films: *Vuk sa Prokletija.*

Pirjevec, Dušan (1921 –). Essayist and literary historian (Slovenia). Has published numerous essays and monographs, and edited the collected works of Murn and Župančić.

Podbevšek, Anton (1898 –). Poet and journalist (Slovenia). Collected poems: *Čovek sa bombama*. Monographs on the painters Grohar and Jakopić; anthology of Slovenian poetry.

Popa, Vasko (1922 –). Poet. Poetry: *Kora, Nepočinpolje, Uspravna zemlja*. Anthologies: *Od zlata Jabuka* (folk art), *Urnebesnik* (poetic humor in Serbian literature), *Ponoćno sunce* (Serbian fantastic literature).

Popović, Aleksandar (1928 –). Dramatist and children's author. Plays: *Čarapa od sto petlji, Sablja dimiskija, Ljubinko i Desanka*. TV plays: *Nameštena soba*. Children's books: *Sudbina jednog Čarlija; Devojčica u plavoj haljini*, and *Tvrdoglave priče*.

Popović, Jovan (1905–52). Poet, prose writer, journalist and public worker. Poems: *Ples nad prazninom, Lasta u mitraljeskom gnjezdu, Pesme*. Short stories: *Reda mora da bude, Lica u prolazu, Istinite legende*. Has written on social and postwar Yugoslav literature.

Popović, Zoran (1939 –). Children's writer, author of many radio scripts and a collection: *Priče sata Antverpena*.

Popovski, Ante (1931 –). Poet (Macedonia). Collected poems: *Odblesci, Vardar, Nepokor*.

Potrč, Ivan (1913 –). Prose writer (Slovenia). Short stories: *Sin, Svet na Kajžarju*. Novels: *Na selu, Zločin* and *Srečanje*. Dramatic trilogy: *Kreflovo imanje, Lacko i Krefli, Krefli*.

Prica, Čedo (1931 –). Author and journalist (Croatia). Novels: *Nekoga moraš voljeti, Dolazak ljeta, Svijet vidjen na kraju, Izlaz na ista vrata, Dnevnik sumraka*. Collected poems: *Plitvička rapsodija, Zavičaj krvi, Andjeo vatre*.

Pupačić, Josip (1928 –). Poet and essayist. Poetry: *Kiše pjevaju na jablanima, Mladići, Svijet izvan sebe, Oporuka, Ustoličenje*.

Radičević, V. Branko (1925 –). Poet and prose writer. Collected poetry: *Zemlja, Večita pešadija, Vojničke pesme*. Novels: *Bela žena*. Children's books: *Učeni mačak, Poslastičarnica kod veselog čarobnjaka, Čudotvorno oko, Priče o dečacima*. Monograph on rural monuments: *Plava linija života*. Compiled a collection of Gypsy poetry with R. Uhlik.

Radović, Borislav (1936 –). Poet. Received the Belgrade October prize for his translation of St. John Perse's *Amers*. Collected poems: *Poetičnosti, Ostale poetičnosti, Maina*.

Radović, Dušan (1922 –). Children's poet and dramatist, Works: *Pošto-*

vana deco, Smešne reči, Pričam ti priču. Plays: *Tužibaba i još 9 jednočinki, Kapetan Džon Piplfoks.* TV series: *Na slovo, na slovo.*
Raičković, Stevan (1928 —). Poet. Major poetry: *Pesme tišine, Balada o predverčerju, Kasno leto, Kamena uspavanka.* Books for children: *Veliko dvorište, Družina pod suncem, Gurije.* Has translated Shakespeare's sonnets.
Rehar, Voja (1925–56). Critic and journalist. Has written about existentialism and contemporary Yugoslav literature in general. His important 20-volume diary remains in manuscript.
Ribnikar, Jara (pen name of Dušanka Radak, 1912 —). Prose writer, poet and translator of Czechoslovakian. Poetry: *Idu dani, noći, dani.* Short stories: *Largo; Ja, ti, mi.* Novels: *Nedovršen krug, Zašto vam je unakaženo lice, Bakaruša.* Edited an anthology of contemporary Czechoslovak poetry.
Ristić, Marko (1902 —). Essayist, poet. More important collections of essays: *Nacrt za jednu fenomenologiju iracionalnog, Književna politika, Prostor — vreme, Predgovor za nekoliko nenapisanih romana . . . , Tri mrtva pesnika, Ljudi u nevremenu, Istorija i poezija, Hacer tiempo.* Poetry: *Od sreće i od sna, Bez mere, Turpituda, Nox microcosmica.*
Ristović, Aleksandar (1933 —). Prose and prose writer. Collections of poetry: *Sunce jedne sezone, Ime prirode, Drveće i svetlost unaokolo, Venčanje.* Writes for newspapers and periodicals.
Rožman, Smiljan (1927 —). Prose writer (Slovenia). Novels: *Neko, Obala, Družina.* Short stories: *Mesto, Rozalija i vrtlar.* Play: *Vetar.* Author of children's stories.
Ršumović, Ljubivoje (1939 —). Children's author. Coauthor with Miša Brujić of the TV series *Hiljadu zašto.*
Samokovlija, Isak (1889–1955). Writer (Bosnia-Hercegovina), outstanding realist. Major works: *Od proljeća do proljeća, Nosač Samuel, Plava jevreika, Djerdan, Nemiri.*
Sarajlić, Izet (1930 —). Poet (Bosnia-Hercegovina). Poetry: *U susretu, Sivi vikend, Minutu ćutanja, Godine, godine, Ipak elegija.*
Šćepanović, Blažo (1934–66). Poet. Collected verse: *Lobanja u travi, Ivicom zemlje zmija, Smrću protiv smrti* (with Branko Miljković), *Smrt pjesnikova.* Compiled an anthology of Yugoslav revolutionary poetry.
Šćepanović, Branimir (1937 —). Collected short stories: *Pre istine.* Novel: *Sramno leto.* Author of radio, TV and film scripts.
Šegedin, Petar (1909 —). Prose writer and essayist. Novels: *Djeca božja*

and *Osamljenici*. Travels: *Na putu*. Short stories: *Mrtvo more, Orfej u maloj bašti; Eseji*. Has compiled an anthology of Croatian prose.

Sekulić, Isidora (1877–1958). Prose writer. Short stories: *Saputnici, Kronika palanačkog groblja, Zapisi o mome narodu*. Travels: *Pisma iz Norveške*. Essays: *Analitički trenuci i teme, Njegošu, knjiga duboke odanosti, Govor i jezik — kulturna smotra naroda*.

Selenić, Slobodan (1933 –). Drama critic and novelist. Essays: *Angažman u dramskoj formi*. Novel: *Memoari Pere Bogalja*. For many years a historian of the theater.

Selimović, Meša (1910 –). Prose writer and essayist (Bosnia-Hercegovina). Novels: *Tišina, Derviš i smrt*. Short stories: *Prva četa, Tudja zemlja*. Essay: *Za i protiv Vuka*, and others.

Sijarić Ćamil (1913 –). Prose writer (Bosnia-Hercegovina). Major works: Short stories: *Ram-Bulja, Zelen prsten na vodi*. Novels: *Bihorci, Kuću kućom čine lastavice, Moskovačka bitka*.

Simić, Novak (1906 –). Prose writer (Croatia). Major works: Collections of short stories: *Nepoznata Bosna, Iza zavjesa, Zakoni i ognjevi, Proljeće, Ljubav Stjepana Obrdalja*. Novels: *Druga obala, Braća i kumiri, Brkići iz Bara*. Has published poetry and written essays and articles about modern Soviet literature.

Simović, Ljubomir (1935 –). Poetry collections: *Slovenske elegije, Veseli grobovi* and *Poslednja zemlja*. Verse play for radio: *Ključevi sv. Vlaha*.

Šinko, Ervin (1898–1966). Distinguished writer and journalist (Hungarian). Has written poetry, plays, short stories, novels and essays both in Hungarian and Serbo-Croatian. Major works: Novels: *Četrnaest dana* and *Optimist*. Memoirs: *Roman jednog romana, Književne studije*. Essays: *Falanga Antikrista*. Anthology: *Sudbonosna pisma*.

Šita, Vehap (1924 –). Critic and translator (Kosmet). Has published a collection of drama criticism and collaborated on an anthology of prose and poetry by Yugoslav Albanians. Translates from Russian, French and Serbo-Croatian.

Slamnig, Ivan (1930 –). Writer of poetry, novels and essays and translator. Major works: Poetry: *Aleja poslije svečanosti, Odron, Naronska Cesta*. Short stories: *Neprijatelj*. Has translated contemporary British and American poetry.

Slaviček, Milivoj (1929 –). Poetry: *Zaustavljena pregršt, Daleka pokrafina, Modro veće, Predak, Noćni autobus, ili naredni dio cijeline; Izmedju*.

Smiljanić, Radomir (1934—). Prose writer and sociologist. Short story: *Alkarski dan*. Novels: *Martinov izlazak, Vojnikov put, Mirno doba*.

Solev, Dimitar (1930—). Writer (Macedonia). Short stories: *Okopneli snegovi, Niz reku i protiv nje, Ograda, Kraj proleća, Pod užarenim nebom*. Novel: *Kratko proleće Mona Samonikova*.

Šoljan, Antun (1932—). Prose writer, critic, poet and translator (English and Russian). Collection of poems: *Na rubu svijeta, Izvan fokusa*. Books of short stories: *Specijalni izaslanici, Deset priča za moju generaciju*. Novels: *Izdajice, Kratki izlet*. Radio plays: *Lice i Brdo*. TV plays: *Slava*. Articles: *Trogodišnja kronika poezije hrvatske i srpske*.

Šopov, Aco (1923—). Poet, essayist, and translator (Macedonia). Has translated Yugoslav authors such as Jovan Jovanović Zmaj, Gustav Krklec and Oton Zupančić into Macedonian. Also translates from Russian. Collected poetry: *Pesme, pruga, mladosti* (with S. Janevski), *Našim rukama, Stihovi za muku i radost, Slej se sa tišinom, Na Gramom, Vetar nosi lepo vreme, Nepostajanje*.

Spasov, Aleksandar (1925—). Critic and literary historian (Macedonia). Has written numerous works on the history of Macedonian literature; edited the collected works of Koča Racin, and published a book of articles and critiques *Putevi ka reci* and an anthology of contemporary Macedonian literature.

Stardelov, Gorgi (1930—). Critic and essayist (Macedonia). Essays: *Moderno i modernizam*. Anthology: Macedonian postwar prose.

Stefanović, Mirjana (1939—). Poet, essayist, children's writer. Poems: *Voleti*. Prose: *Odlomci izmišljenog dnevnika*. Children's book: *Vlatko Pidžula*.

Strniša, Gregor (1930—). Poet (Slovenia). Collected poems: *Mozaici, Odisej*. Verse play: *Mavričina krila, Inorog*.

Sulejmani, Hivzi (1912—). Prose writer (Kosmet). Short stories: *Vetar i kolona*. Play: *U džepu miš*.

Šujica, Božidar (1936—). Poetry: *Prestupne noći, Vreme i temelji*.

Tadijanović, Dragutin (1905—). Poet, essayist, literary historian and translator. Collected poems: *Lirika, Sunce nad oranicama, Pepeo srca, Dani djetinjstva, Tuga zemlje, Pjesme, Blagdan žetve, Prsten*. Translates from Czech and German; has published numerous commentaries and introductions for collected and selected works of Croatian authors.

Tahmiščić, Husein (1931—). Poet and essayist. Short stories: *Ljude nisam video*. Essays: *Ponovo osvojen grad* and *Izbor i govor*. Collected verse:

Putnik života, Budna vrteška, Preludij za neimare, Neimari, Kamerno veče poezije, Gde sad zvoni.
Tartalja, Gvido (1899 –). Poet. Major works: *Pesma i grad, Začarani krug, Poema o pruzi, Pesme.* Noted children's writer.
Taufer, Veno (1933 –). Poet (Slovenia). Poetry: *Olovne zvezde, Zarobljenik slobode.* Plays: *Prometej.* Translator of English, Serbo-Croatian and Macedonian literature.
Timotijević, Božidar (1932 –). Poetry: *Veliki spavač, Slovo ljubve, Srebrno brdo, Dan se radja, Večernje.*
Tišma, Aleksandar (1924 –). Poet, short story writer and translator. Collected poetry: *Naseljeni svet, Krčma.* Collected short stories: *Krivice* and *Naselje.*
Todorović, Gordana (1933 –). Poet. Collections: *Gimnazijski trenutak, Sunce.*
Todorovski, Gane (1929 –). Poet (Macedonia). Poetry: *Zvuci nemira, Spokojni korak, Duga.* Has written adaptations of Yugoslav, English and Russian poetry.
Tomičić, Zlatko (1930 –). Writer of travel books and poetry, translator of Slavic poetry. Collected poetry: *Četvrtoga ne razumijem, Vode pod ledinom, Dosegnuti ja, Balada uspravnog čovjeka.* Travels: *Nestrpljivi život, Otkrivanje Čehoslovačke.*
Torkar, Igor (pen name of Boris Fakin, 1913 –). Poet and dramatist (Slovenia). Plays: *Bajka o smehu, Porobljeni ljudi, Delirij, Šarena lopta.* Collected poems: *Ludi Kronos, Kurent,* and others.
Tošović, Risto (1923 –). Poetry: *Stihovi sa Košura, Cvijet na zgarištu, Nespokojni prozori, Pohvala mirnom letu.* Essays and articles on contemporary Yugoslav literature.
Trifunović, Duško (1933 –). Poet (Bosnia-Hercegovina). Collections: *Zlatni kuršum, Babova rdjava baština, Jetke pripovetke.*
Udovič, Jože (1912 –). Poet (Slovenia). Translator of Spanish and French poetry. Collected poetry: *Ogledalo snova.*
Ugrinov, Pavle (pen name of Vasilije Popović, radio and TV producer, 1926 –). Prose writer and dramatist. Poetry: *Bačka zapevka.* Novel: *Odlazak u zoru.* Short stories: *Kopno, Ishodište.* Radio plays: *Siluete, Zlatni prsti, Začarani krug.*
Ujević, Augustin-Tin (1891–1955). Poet, essayist, and translator. Poetry: *Lelek sebra, Kolajna, Auto na korzu, Ojadjeno zvono, Pesme, Rukovet, Žedan kamen na studencu, Odabrane pjesme.* Collections of articles, polemics and critiques: *Nedjela maloljetnih, Dva velika bogumila* (Tol-

stoy and Ghandi), *Ljudi za vratima gostionice, Skalpel kaosa*. Has translated Proust, Maupassant, Verhaeren and Poe.

Urošević, Vlada (1934 –). Poet, short story writer and essayist. Collected poems: *Jedan drugi grad, Nevidelica*. Collection of short stories: *Znaci*.

Vasić, Dragiša (1885–1945). Author and journalist. Novel: *Crvene magle, Devetstotreća*. Short stories: *Resimić dobošar* and *U gostima*.

Vaupotić, Miroslav (1925 –). Critic and literary historian. Monographs on Croatian literary journals, (1914–26), Croatian prose between the two wars, and the Croatian authors Mihovil Kombol, A. B. Šimić and Miroslav Krleža.

Velmar-Janković, Svetlana (1933 –). Essays on modern Yugoslav literature. Novel: *Savremenici*. Radio dramas: *Ožiljak, Vetar* and *Tunel*.

Vidmar, Josip (1895 –). Critic, essayist, journalist. Monographs on Župančić, Prešern, Levstik, and Cankar. Author of numerous drama critiques and essays, also a translator of French, Russian and English works. Major books: *Kulturni problemi slovenstva, Literarne kritike, Meditacije, Dramaturški zapisi*. Is currently president of the Slovenian Academy of Arts and Sciences.

Vinaver, Stanislav (1891–1955). Writer, expressionistic poet, journalist, and distinguished translator. Poetry: *Mjeća, Varoš zlih volšebnika, Gromobran svemira, Evropska noć*. Essays: *Goč gori, Jezik naš nasušni, Pantologija novije srpske pelengirike*. Has translated the works of Andersen, Poe, Rabelais, Villon and Bloch and *Tristram Shandy* and *Clochemerle*.

Vipotnik, Cene (1914 –). Poet (Slovenia). Collection of poems: *Drvo u samoći*.

Vodnik, Anton (1901 –). Author of several collections of poetry (Slovenia): *Žalosne ruke, Vigilije, Kroz vrtove, Srebrni rog, Zlatni krugovi, Glas tišine*.

Vodušek, Božo (1905 –). Poet, essayist (Slovenia). Poetry: *Odčarani svet*. Monograph on Oton Župančić. Translator of Goethe.

Vrkljan, Irena (1930 –). Poet and translator. Collections: *Krik je samo tišina, Paralele, Soba taj strašni vrt*. Radio drama: *Opasno poslepodne* and others.

Vučetić, Šime (1909 –). Writer and essayist (Croatia). Poetry: *Pjesme Ilije Labana, Kniga pjesama, Na svome, Rude na ogledalu, Putnik*. Essays: *Krležino književno djelo, Hrvatska književnost 1914–1941, Granice*.

Vučo, Aleksandar (1897 –). Poet and prose writer. Poetry: *Krov nad prozorom, Nemenikuće, Mastodonti.* Children's poetry: *Podvizi Družine pet petlića, San i java hrabrog Koče.* Novels: *Koren vida, Gluvo doba* (with D. Matić), *Raspust, Mrtve javke, Zasluge.* [Available in English translation: *The Holidays,* Belgrade, Yugoslavia Publishing House, 1959.]

Vukmirović, Mirjana (1936–). Poet, essayist, translator (French). Collections of poetry: *Oblakoder* and *Južni Zid.*

Vuletić, Andjelko (1933 –). Poet and writer (Bosnia-Hercegovina). Collected poems: *Gramatika ili progonstvo, Jedina nada.* Novels: *Gorko sunce, Drvo s paklenih vrata.*

Zajc, Dane (1929 –). Poet (Slovenia). Collected poetry: *Sažežena trava, Jezik od zemlje* and *Deca reke* (verse play).

Zidić, Igor (1939 –). Essayist and poet. Poems: *Uhodeći more, Krug s grane, Eseji.*

Ziherl, Boris (1910 –). Politician, journalist and critic (Slovenia). More important works: *Članci i rasprave, Književnost i društvo, O nekim aktuelnim problemima socijalizma,* and *Umetnost i idejnost.*

Zlobec, Ciril (1925 –). Poet and prose writer (Slovenia). Has translated Serbo-Croatian and Italian poetry. Collections of verse: *Pesme četvorice, Odbeglo detinjstvo, Ljubav.* Novel: *Muške godine našeg detinjstva.*

Zogović, Radovan (1907 –). Poet and translator from Russian. Major poetry: *Pjesma o biografiji druga Tita, Prkosne strofe,* and *Artikulisana riječ.*

Zupančič, Beno (1925 –). Writer and politician (Slovenia). Short stories: *Vetar na cesti.* Novels: *Sedmina (Pozdravi Mariju), Izmaglica pod reflektorom.* Travels: *Mrtvo more.*

Župančić, Oton. (1879–1949). Poet (Slovenia). Poetry: *Čaša opojnosti, Pisanice, Preko polja, U svitanje vidova, Zimzelen pod snegon, Duma.* Children's poetry: *Ciciban.* Play: *Veronika Deseniška.* Has translated fifteen of the plays of Shakespeare.

A CHRONOLOGY

OF LITERARY EVENTS IN YUGOSLAVIA, 1945-1965

MANY ALMOST INSOLUBLE problems were connected with the compilation
of the chronology of literary events in Yugoslavia. This is a collection of
literary texts and activities which are most typical for the twenty-year
span covered by Yugoslav literature up to 1965. We have made an effort to
detect data buried in periodicals and magazines and the unreliable memory
of contemporaries.

The chronology would never have acquired its present form without
the conscientiousness and perseverence of Svetsilav Pavičević, its main
editor. The *Bibliography of Yugoslav aesthetic literature, 1945–1965,*
completed by Professor Andrija Stojković was also of considerable help
to the compilers. It is regrettable that it could not be included as a separate addition to this book. Valuable advice and guidance were given to
the compilers by Roksanda Njegus and Taras Kermauner for Slovenian
literature, by Vlado Gotovac for Croatian, by Vuk Krnjević for the literature of Bosnia and Hercegovina, and by Mateja Matevski and Dimitar
Solev for Macedonian writing. The compilers hope that the chronology
fulfills its purpose and will be satisfied if students of contemporary Yugoslav literature find it useful.

The chronology is arranged in sections and the latter are divided according to regional (republic), national and cultural centers. In organizing articles and polemics a chronological order was followed, although
not consistently since the editors kept adding new items, being interested
in completeness rather than organization. Because of linguistic barriers,
the calendar does not contain books, anthologies and articles by the
Hungarians of Voyvodina or by writers of Kosmet, whose work is in
Macedonian.

This deficiency is partly remedied by the fact that the main body of the work surveys these two literatures; and by the bio-bibliographical notes which list numerous representatives of these two literatures and the titles of their books in Serbo-Croatian translation. The first sections of the chronology deal with poetry, prose, and criticism. Only the most important literary prizes are mentioned with the books which received them while others are given only sporadically. The section on literary prizes is the most uneven and incomplete since it was impossible to get complete information.   S.L.

TRANSLATOR'S NOTE

Wherever possible titles of works by foreign authors have been given in the original. When this was not possible, the nature of the work has been indicated.

The following abbreviations of publishers' names are used frequently:

DKH — Društvo književnika Hrvatske

DZS — Državna založba Slovenije

SKZ — Slovenski knjižni zavod

ZDK — Založba društva književnika

1945

POETRY

Ćopić, Branko. *Pjesme*, Kultura, Belgrade.

Maksimović, Desanka. *Oslobodenje Cvete Andrić* (poem), Central Committee of the AFŽ, Belgrade.

Franičević, Marin. *Govorenje Mikule Trudnega* (Prize of the Republic of Croatia).

Župančić, Oton. *Zimzelen pod snegom*, Državna založba Slovenije, Ljubljana (Prize of the Committee for Culture and Art of Yugoslavia).

Janevski, Slavko. *Krvava niza* (lyrical fragments), Kultura, Skopje.

Koneski, Blaže. *Mostot*, Kultura, Skopje.

Markovski, Venko. *Glamji*, Državno knigoizdatelstvo na Makedonija, Skopje.

PROSE

Andrić, Ivo. *Na Drini ćuprija* (novel), Prosveta, Belgrade (Prize of the Committee for Culture and Art of the government of the FNRY).

———. *Travnička hronika* (novel), Državni izdavački zavod Jugoslavija, Belgrade.

———. *Gospodjica* (novel), Svjetlost, Sarajevo.

Krleža, Miroslav. *Glembajevi* I–II (drama and prose), Zora, Zagreb.

Minderović, Čedomir. *Za Titom* (diary), Dizjug, Belgrade.

Dončević, Ivan. *Bezimeni* (short story), Vjesnik, Zagreb (Prize of the government of Croatia).

Nazor, Vladimir. *S partizanima 1943–1944* (diary), Dizjug, Belgrade, Nakladni zavod Hrvatske, Zagreb.

Voranc, Prežihov. *Jamica* (novel), Slovenski knjižni zavod, Ljubljana (Prize of the Committee for Art and Culture of Yugoslavia).

CRITIQUES AND ESSAYS

Gligorić, Velibor. *Kritike*, Prosveta, Belgrade.

TRANSLATIONS OF WORKS BY YUGOSLAV AUTHORS

Zogović, Radovan, *Pjesma o biografiji druga Tita*, Moscow.

TRANSLATIONS OF WORKS BY FOREIGN AUTHORS

Mayakovski, Vladimir. Poems. Kultura, Belgrade.

Sholokhov, Mikhail. *Oni srazhalis za rodinu* (fragments) (no publisher given). Belgrade and Cankarjeva založba, Ljubljana.

―――. *Nauka nenavisti*, Vjesnik, Zagreb.

―――. *Podnataya tselina*, Kultura, Belgrade.

NEW LITERARY PERIODICALS

Mladost. Journal for literature and culture; editor Dušan Kostić, Belgrade, 1945–52.

Republika. Monthly for art, culture, and public life; editors Miroslav Krleža, Vjekoslav Kaleb, Jože Horvat; Zagreb, 1945 –.

Književnik. Published by the Cultural Workers Club of Croatia; editors Vjekoslav Kaleb, Ivo Frol, Petar Lasta, Marin Franičević; Zagreb, 1945 (ceased publication with no. 1, 1945).

Izvor. Journal of self-activist writers; editor-in-chief Ivo Ćaće; Zagreb, 1945 –.

Novi den. Journal of art, science and current problems; editor-in-chief Vlado Maleski; Skopje, 1945–50.

ARTICLES AND POLEMICS

Krleža, Miroslav. "Književnost danas," *Republika*, no. 1–2.

―――. "Krokodilina ili Razgovor o istini," *Republika*, no. 3.

Barac, Antun. "Mrak na svijetlim stazama," *Republika*, no. 1–2 (life and work of I. G. Kovačić).

M. "O kulturnoj strani omladinskih listova," *Mladost*, no. 1.

Alečković, Mira. "Oni su ponos domovine," *Mladost*, no. 1 (review of the book *Oni su ponos omladine*).

Seferović, Nusret. "Kako se ne smije praviti zbirka recitacija," *Mladost*, no. 1.

Soldić, Luka. "Jedna generacija i jedna knjiga," *Mladost*, no. 2 (on the novel of N. Ostrovski *Kako se kalio čelik*).

Koneski, Blaže. "Problemi na makedonskata literatura," *Novi den*, no. 1.

1946

POETRY

Nazor, Vladimir. *Djela*, I–III (epics, epic poems), Nakladni zavod Hrvatske, Zagreb.

Franičević-Pločar, Jure. *Oganj zemlje*, Naprijed, Zagreb.

Bor, Matej. *Pesmi*, Slovenski knjižni zavod, Ljubljana.

Šopov; Koneski; Janevski; Ivanovski; Karovski. *Pesni,* Glavniot odbor na NO Makedonije, Skopje.

Markovski, Venko. *Robii* (Macedonian epic), Državno knigoizdatelstvo, Skopje.

Janevski, Slavko. *Raspeani bukvi* (poems for children), Državno knigoizdatelstvo, Skopje (prize of the Committee for Art and Culture of Yugoslavia).

Kulenović, Skender. *Stojanka majka Knežpoljka* (poem), Svjetlost, Sarajevo.

Banjević, Mirko. *Sutjeska* (poem), Pobjeda, Cetinje (13th of July Award of Montenegro for the 4th edition, 1955).

PROSE

Šegedin, Petar. *Djeca božja* (novel), Matica hrvatska, Zagreb.

Kaleb, Vjekoslav. *Novele,* Nakladni zavod Hrvatske, Zagreb.

Simić, Novak. *Iza zavjesa* (short stories), Matica hrvatska, Zagreb.

Kranjec, Miško. *Pesem gora* (novel), Slovenski knjižni zavod, Ljubljana.

Potrč, Ivan. *Kočarji in druge povesti,* Slovenski knjižni zavod, Ljubljana.

Kreft, Bratko. *Krajnski komedijanti* (comedy), Matica slovenska, Ljubljana.

Bor, Matej. *Raztrganci* and *Teška ura* (plays), SKZ, Ljubljana.

Kosmač, Ciril. *Sreća in kruh* (short stories), Državna založba Slovenije, Ljubljana.

Samokovlija, Isak. *Nosač Samuel* (short stories), Svjetlost, Sarajevo (Prize of the Committee for Culture and Art of Yugoslavia).

CRITIQUES AND ESSAYS

Gligorić, Velibor. *Pozorišne kritike,* Prosveta, Belgrade.

Kozak, Juš. *Blodnje* (essays), Slovenski knjižni zavod, Ljubljana.

TRANSLATIONS OF WORKS BY YUGOSLAV AUTHORS

Zogović, Radovan. *Pjesma o biografiji druga Tita.* Prague.

TRANSLATIONS OF WORKS BY FOREIGN AUTHORS

Sholokhov, Mikhail. *Tikhi Don.* Kultura, Belgrade-Zagreb and Cankarjeva založba, Ljubljana.

———. *Podnataya tselina.* Kultura, Skopje.

Aragon, Louis. *Les Cloches de Bâle.* Kultura, Belgrade-Zagreb.

Brecht, Bertolt. *Mutter Courage.* ZOJHS, Zagreb.

Naša književnost. Monthly; editor-in-chief Čedomir Minderović; Belgrade, 1946 (since July 1947 published as "Književnost").

Pregled. Journal for social problems; editors Todor Kruševac, Skender Kulenović, Nika Miličević; Sarajevo, 1946–49 (resumed publication 1953).

Stvaranje. Journal for literature and culture; published in monthly and bimonthly volumes; editors Mihailo Lalić, Janko Djonović, Mirko Banjević; Cetinje, 1946 –.

Letopis Matice srpske. Founded 1825 in Budapest (publication suspended 1941–46); Novi Sad, 1946 –.

Hid. Monthly journal for literature, science and social problems of the Hungarians of Voyvodina (publication suspended 1939–46); Novi Sad, 1946 –.

First Congress of the Yugoslav Writers Union, Sarajevo, September 17–19. Main report: Radovan Zogović, on the position and tasks of literature today. Speakers: Ivan Ivanović Anisimov and Jean Richard Bloch.

Tito, Josip Broz. "Govor održan književnicima," *Borba*, November 20.

Andrić, Ivo. Report given at the 1st Congress of the Yugoslav Writers' Union, *Naša Književnost*, No. 12.

Bogdanović, Milan. "Prvi Kongres Književnika Jugoslavije," *Politika*, November 14.

Kulenović, Skender. "Smisao kulture i njeni glavni problemi," *Pregled*, No. 1.

Popović, Dušan. "Tri ocene prvih brojeva *Mladosti*," *Mladost*, No. 1–2 (in response to critical articles in *Mladi borac*, *Omladinski borac* and *Omladina*).

Popović, Jovan. "Nekoliko napomena u vezi sa književnim početnicima," *Mladost*, No. 3.

Mišić, Zoran. "Koje teme očekuju naše mlade pisce," *Mladost*, No. 4–5.

Zogović, Radovan. "Osvrt na naše književne prilike i zadatke," *Republika*, No. 11–12 (report on the Writers' Congress).

Matković, Marijan. "O Krležinom ciklusu Glembajevih," *Republika*, No. 4–5.

Popović, Vladimir. "Iza zavjesa," *Republika*, No. 9–10 (review of Novak Simić's book).

1947

POETRY

Ćopić, Branko. *Ratnikovo proljeće* (poems), Nopok, Belgrade-Zagreb (Prize of the Committee for Art & Culture of Yugoslavia).

Zogović, Radovan. *Prkosne strofe*, Kultura, Belgrade (Prize of the Committee for Art and Culture of Yugoslavia).

Djonović, Janko. *Gorski tokovi*, Prosveta, Belgrade (Prize of the Committee for Art and Culture of Yugoslavia).

Kostić, Dušan. *Pjesme*, Prosveta, Belgrade.

Krklec, Gustav. *Izabrane pjesme*, Nakladni zavod Hrvatske, Zagreb.

Parun, Vesna. *Zore i vihori*, Društvo književnika Hrvatske, Zagreb.

Minati, Ivan. *S poti*, Mladinska knjiga, Ljubljana.

PROSE

Krleža, Miroslav. *Baraka pet b* (short stories), Nopok, Zagreb.

Davičo, Oskar. "Medju Markosovim partizanima" (reportage), *Trideset dana*, Belgrade (Prize of the Committee for Art and Culture of Yugoslavia).

Kulenović, Skender. *Večera* (comedy), Rad, Belgrade (Prize of the Committee for Art and Culture of Yugoslavia).

Minderović, Čedomir. *Oblaci nad Tarom* (account), Prosveta, Belgrade.

Čolaković, Rodoljub. *Kuća oplakana*, Kultura, Belgrade-Zagreb.

Šegedin, Petar. *Osamljenici* (novel), Društvo književnika Hrvatske, Zagreb.

Šinko, Ervin. *Četrnaest dana* (novel), Nakladni zavod Hrvatske, Zagreb (Prize of the Committee for Art and Culture of Yugoslavia).

Kaleb, Vjekoslav. *Brigada* (short stories), Nakladni zavod Hrvatske, Zagreb (Prize of the Committee for Art and Culture of Yugoslavia).

Horvat, Joža. *Prst pred nosom* (comedy), ZOJSRNH, Zagreb (Prize of the Committee for Art and Culture of Yugoslavia).

Slodnjak, Anton. *Pogine naj pes* (novel), Slovenski knjižni zavod. Ljubljana (Prize of the Committee for Art and Culture of Yugoslavia).

Kreft, Bratko. *Tugomer* (tragedy based on F. Levstik), Slovenski knjižni zavod, Ljubljana (Prešern prize).

Kranjec, Miško. *Fara svetega Ivana* (novel). SKZ, Ljubljana.

Grabeljšek, Karel. *Za svobodo in kruh* (sketches and short stories), SKZ, Ljubljana (Prešern prize).

Boškovski, Jovan. *Rastrel* (short stories), Državno knigoizdatelstvo, Skopje.

CRITIQUES AND ESSAYS

Krleža, Miroslav. *Račić* (monograph). Nakladni zavod Hrvatske, Zagreb.

Ravbar, Stanko Janež-Miroslav. *Zgodovina slovenske književnosti* (2d rev. ed.), Obzorja, Maribor.

COLLECTIONS AND ANTHOLOGIES

Antologija nove čakavske lirike (edited by Ivo Jelenović and Hijacint Petris; 2d enlarged ed.), Nakladni zavod Hrvatske, Zagreb.

TRANSLATIONS OF WORKS BY YUGOSLAV AUTHORS

Andrić, Ivo. *Na Drini ćuprija*, Budapest. *Gospodjica*, Prague.

Zogović, Radovan. *Pjesma o biografiji druga Tita*, Sofia.

Kozak, Juš. *Šentpeter*, Prague.

TRANSLATIONS OF WORKS BY FOREIGN AUTHORS

Shaw, Bernard. *Pygmalion*, Prosveta, Belgrade.

Lukacs, Georg. *Probläme des Realismus*, Kultura, Belgrade.

Steinbeck, John. *Of Mice and Men*, Ateneum, Belgrade.

Aragon, Louis. *Sketches*, SKZ, Ljubljana.

NEW LITERARY JOURNALS AND PERIODICALS

Odjek. Journal of cultural, artistic and literary life; Sarajevo, 1947–51 (publication resumed in 1955).

Lumina. Literary journal of the Rumanians of Voyvodina; editor Vasko Popa, Vršac, 1947–.

ARTICLES AND POLEMICS

Minderović, Čedomir. "O neposrednim zadacima naše književnosti i naših književnih radnika," *Mladost*, no. 12 (from the report of the plenary council of the Yugoslav Writers' Union).

Zogović, Radovan. "Primjer kako ne treba praviti 'Primjere iz književnosti,'" *Borba*, 8 May (on Vica Zaninović's book).

Štambuk, Zdenko. "O našoj književnosti i književnim prilikama," *Republika*, no. 3 (report given at the annual assembly of the Croatian Writers' Association).

Gamulin, Grga. "Umjetnost na zaokretu," *Republika*, no. 4.

Šinko, Ervin. "Umjetnost i publika," *Republika*, no. 5.

Franičević, Marin. "O nekim negativnim pojavama u našoj savremenoj književnosti," *Republika*, no. 7–8 (on Vesna Parun's book of poems *Zore i vihori*).

Krleža, Miroslav. "Prije trideset godina," *Republika*, no. 11.

1948

POETRY

Dedinac, Milan. *Pesme iz dnevnika zarobljenika broj 60211*, Prosveta, Belgrade (Prize of the Government of Serbia; Zmaj award for the 2d ed.).

Mladenović, Tanasije. *Pesme*, Prosveta, Belgrade (Prize of the Government of Serbia).

Kostić, Dušan. *Zemlji voljenoj*, Nopok, Belgrade.

Vučetić, Šime. *Knjiga pjesama* (selection). Matica hrvatska, Zagreb.

Parun, Vesna. *Pjesme*. Matica hrvatska, Zagreb (Prize of the Government of Croatia).

Župančić, Oton. *Veš, poet, svoj dolg* (collection of poems, speeches, and articles, NOB). Društvo slovenskih književnikov, Ljubljana.

Koneski, Blaže. *Zemjata i ljubovta*, Kultura, Skopje.

Janevski, Slavko. *Pesni*, Državno knigoizdatelstvo, Skopje.

PROSE

Andrić, Ivo. *Nove pripovetke*, Kultura, Belgrade (Prize of the Government of Yugoslavia).

Petrović, Veljko. *Prepelica u ruci* (short stories), Matica srpska, Novi Sad (Prize of the Government of Yugoslavia).

Ćopić, Branko. *Surova škola* (short stories), Nopok, Belgrade.

Lalić, Mihailo. *Izvidnica* (short stories), Prosveta, Belgrade (Prize of the Government of Yugoslavia).

Popović, Jovan. *Istinite legende* (short stories), Kultura, Belgrade.

Marinković, Ranko. *Proze*, Matica hrvatska, Zagreb (Prize of the Government of Yugoslavia).

Simić, Novak. *Brkići iz Bara* (novel), Prosvjeta, Zagreb.

Potrč, Ivan. *Svet na Kajžarju* (account), SKZ, Ljubljana.

Kranjec, Miško *Os življenja* (novel), SKZ, Ljubljana.

———. *Pot do zločina* (play), SKZ, Ljubljana.

CRITIQUES AND ESSAYS

Krleža, Miroslav. *Goja* (monograph), Nakladni zavod Hrvatske, Zagreb.
Franičević, Marin. *Pisci i problemi* (critiques), Kultura, Zagreb (Prize of the Government of Croatia).
Koneski, Blaže. *Po povod na najnovijot napad na našiot jezik.* Zemskiot odbor NF na Makedonija, Skopje.

COLLECTIONS AND ANTHOLOGIES

Poezija mladih (edited by Risto Tošović), Nopok, Belgrade.
Proza mladih (Čedo Vuković, Luka Soldić, editors), Nopok, Belgrade.

TRANSLATIONS OF WORKS BY YUGOSLAV AUTHORS

Andrić, Ivo. *Na Drini ćuprija*, Prague.
Destovnik-Kajuh, Karel. *Pesme*, Sofia.

TRANSLATIONS OF WORKS BY FOREIGN AUTHORS

Aragon, Louis. *Quartier residentiel* (novel), Nakladni zavod Hrvatske, Zagreb.
Shaw, George Bernard. *The Devil's Disciple*, Prosveta, Belgrade.
Lukacs, Georg. *Realism in French literature*, SKZ, Ljubljana.

NEW LITERARY JOURNALS AND PERIODICALS

Književne novine. Journal of literature and social problems; organ of the Yugoslav Writers' Union, Belgrade, 1948 — No. 6, 1952; 1954, nos. 1–40; 1955–.
Polet. Young peoples' literary and cultural journal. Editor-in-chief Slavko Vukosavljević, Belgrade, 1948–50.
Izvor. Journal for literature and cultural problems; editor-in-chief Josip Barković, Zagreb, 1948–51.

DECEASED

Igo Gruden, Milan Begović.

ARTICLES AND POLEMICS

Zogović, Radovan. "O jednoj strani borbe za novu socijalističku kulturu i umetnost," *Književne novine*, July 27.
Gligorić, Velibor. "Više savremenosti u *Letopisu Matice srpske*," *Književne novine*, October 19.

Ziherl, Boris. "Dekadentstvo pod vidom borbe protiv malogradjanskih ostatka," *Književne novine*, April 27.

Minderović, Čedomir. "O neprosrednim zadacima naše književnosti i naših književnih radnika," *Republika*, no. 1.

Mitrev, Dimitar. "Socijalnoto i ličnota vo edna stihotvorna zbirka," *Nov den*, no. 7 (on the collection of poems of Gogo Ivanovski).

Spasov, Aleksandar. "Za poemata 'Tikveska legenda' od Lazo Karovski," *Nov den*, no. 10.

Bihalji-Merin, Oto. "Jedan pogled na našu književnu kritiku," *Književne novine*, December 14.

Popović, Jovan. "O problematici satire na domaću reakciju," *Književne novine*, December 9.

"Peti kongres Komunisticke partije Jugoslavije" (Zogović, Djilas), *Književne novine*, July 27.

Popović, Jovan. "Partija i književnost," *Književne novine*, June 29.

Djilas, Milovan. "Ekspoze o razvitku kulturnog života Jugoslavije," *Književne novine*, April 27.

Finci, Eli. "Nekoliko misli o razvojnim tendencijama naše knjizevnosti," *Književne novine*, March 2.

Popović, Jovan. "Pisci pred tematikom oslobodilačkog rata," *Književne novine*, March 9.

"Diskusija povodom tri prve predstave Jugoslovenskog dramskog pozorišta," participants: Stefan Mitrović, Jovan Popović, Milan Bogdanović, Velibor Gligorić, Skender Kulenović, Radovan Zogović, Eli Finci, Veljko Vlahović; *Književne novine*, July 13 (discussion of three Yugoslav plays).

"Odgovor jugoslovenskih književnika sovjetskim književnicima F. Glatkovu, N. Tihonovu i drugim," *Književne novine*, December 27 (in response to the greetings of Soviet writers extended to the people of Yugoslavia via Radio Moscow on the occasion of the Yugoslav national holiday).

1949

POETRY

Davičo, Oskar. *Zrenjanin* (poem), Nopok, Belgrade (Prize of the Government of Yugoslavia).

Kulenovic, Skender. *Zbor derviša* (poem), Politika, Belgrade (Prize of the Government of Yugoslavia).

Alečković, Mira. *Tri proleća*, Prosveta, Belgrade.

Krklec, Gustav. *Tri poeme*, Nakladni zavod Hrvatske, Zagreb (Prize of the Republic of Croatia).

Destovnik-Kajuh, Karel. *Kajuhove pesmi*, SKZ, Ljubljana.

Krakar, Lojze. *V vzponu mladosti*, Mladinska knjiga, Ljubljana.

Humo, Hamza. *Poema o Mostaru*, Svjetlost, Sarajevo.

PROSE

Bihalji-Merin, Oto. *Livnica* (play), Prosveta, Belgrade.

Samokovlija, Isak. *Izabrane pripovijetke* (stories), Prosveta, Belgrade.

Simić, Novak. *Miškovići* (novel), Nopok, Zagreb (Prize of the Republic of Croatia).

Marinković, Ranko. *Ni braća ni rodjaci* (short stories), Nakladni zavod Hrvatske, Zagreb.

Kolar, Slavko. *Sedmorica u podrumu* (play), Glas rada, Zagreb.

Božić, Mirko. *Povlačenje* (play), Glas rada, Zagreb.

Voranc, Prežihov. *Solzice* (short stories), Mladinska knjiga, Ljubljana (Prize of the Government of Yugoslavia).

Kocbek, Edvard. *Tovarišija* (diary), Državna založba, Slovenije, Ljubljana.

Kozak, Juš. *Maske* (2nd enlarged edition), short stories, Državna založba Slovenije, Ljubljana.

CRITIQUES AND ESSAYS

Krleža, Miroslav. *O Marinu Držiću* (essay), Prosveta, Belgrade.

Jovanović, Djordje. *Studije i kritike*, Prosveta, Belgrade.

Matković, Marijan. *Dramaturški eseji*, Matica hrvatska, Zagreb (Prize of the Government of Croatia).

COLLECTIONS AND ANTHOLOGIES

Jugoslovenska poezija (anthology of poetry), Savez književnika Jugoslavije, Belgrade.

Jugoslovenska proza (anthology of prose), Savez književnika Jugoslavije, Belgrade.

TRANSLATIONS OF WORKS BY FOREIGN AUTHORS

Neruda, Pablo. Selected poems, Rad, Belgrade.

Mayakovski, Vladimir. 20 Poems, Nakladni zavod Hrvatske, Zagreb.

Brecht, Bertolt. *Mutter Courage*, Ljudska prosveta Slovenije, Ljubljana.
Shaw, George Bernard. *The Doctor's Dilemma*, Prosveta, Belgrade.

NEW LITERARY JOURNALS AND PERIODICALS

Jeta e re. Bimonthly literary journal of Yugoslav Shiptars, Priština, 1949.

LITERARY CONGRESSES AND PLENARY MEETINGS

2d Congress of the Yugoslav Writers' Union, Zagreb, December 25–28.
Reports:
Minderović, Čedomir. "O razvitku i zadacima naše književnosti."
Gligorić, Velibor. "O našoj savremenoj proznoj književnosti."
Bogdanović, Milan. "O savremenoj jugoslovenskoj poeziji."
Matković, Marijan. "O problemima naše drame."
Šegedin, Petar. "Naša savremena lirika."
Barković, Josip. "Stvaralački problemi naših mladih piscaca."
Leskovac, Mladen. "O položaju i razvoju naših manjinskih literatura."

DECEASED

Rastko Petrović, Vladimir Nazor, Oton Župančić, Janko Leskovar, Slavko
Grum.

ARTICLES AND POLEMICS

Gligorić, Velibor. "O časopisu *Književnost*," *Književne novine*, Febru-
ary 22.
Mišić, Zoran. "Jedan pogled na poeziju mladih," *Književne novine*,
March 1.
Andrić, Ivo. "Nešto povodom razgovora o književnoj tematici," *Zora*,
no. 3–4.
Majstorović, Stevan. "Naši ljudi i naša stvarnost u radovima mladih pisaca,"
Polet, no. 3–4.
Bogdanović, Milan. "O onima koji izneveravaju istinu u književnosti,"
Književne novine, May 31.
"Zaključci savetovanja redakcija omladinskih časopisa," *Književne novine*,
November 22.
"Savetovanje mladih pisaca Jugoslavije," *Književne novine*, November 22.
Tošović, Risto. "O radu sa mladim piscima" (report on advice to young
writers), *Mladost*, no. 12.
Gligorić, Velibor. "Proza mladih," *Književne novine*, May 4.

Davičo, Oskar. "'Argumenti' sile i snaga morala," *Književne novine*, May 10 (on the Informbureau resolution).

"Diskusija o književnoj kritici," *Književne novine*, June 17. Participants: I. Dončević, E. Šinko, M. Jurković, V. Gligorić, B. Drenovac, C. Minderović.

Popović, Jovan. "Za teoretsko izdizanje kulturnih kadrova i povećanje kvaliteta književno-umetničkih dela," *Književne novine*, January 4.

Finci, Eli. "Kruta dogma i stvarnost," *Književne novine*, January 4.

Zogović, Radovan. "K licu čovjeka," *Književne novine*, January 11 (on Djordje Andrejević's painting "Svjedoci Užasa").

Gligorić, Velibor. "*Gorski tokovi* Janka Djonovića," *Književne novine*, November 30.

1950

POETRY

Maksimović, Desanka. *Izabrane pesme*, Zora, Zagreb.

Davičo, Oskar. *Višnja za zidom*, Nopok, Belgrade.

Vukosavljević, Slavko. *Kadinjača* (poems), Zemaljski odbor SBNOR, Novi Sad.

Ujević, Tin. *Rukovet*, Zora, Zagreb.

Kaštelan, Jure. *Pijetao na krovu*, Zora, Zagreb.

Novak, Slobodan. *Glasnice u oluji*, Novo pokoljenje, Zagreb.

Ković, Kajetan. *Kajubova pesem*, Prosvetni servis, Ljubljana.

Ivanovski, Srbo. *Lirika*, Nopok, Skopje.

Župančić, Oton. *Dela*, Cankarjeva založba, Ljubljana.

PROSE

Krleža, Miroslav. *Djela* (1945–50), Zora, Zagreb.

Lalić, Mihailo. *Svadba* (account), Prosveta, Belgrade.

Minderović, Čedomir. *Kupina se rascvetala* (play), Rad, Belgrade.

Desnica, Vladan. *Zimsko ljetovanje* (novel), Zora, Zagreb.

Jelić, Vojin. *Ljudi kamenjara* (short stories), Nopok, Zagreb.

Bor, Matej. *Bele vode* (play), Slovenski knjižni zavod, Ljubljana.

CRITIQUES AND ESSAYS

Matković, Marijan. "Dva eseja iz hrvatske dramaturgije," Zora, Zagreb.

Kisić, Čedo. "O književnom izrazu" (essays), *Polet*, Sarajevo.

COLLECTIONS AND ANTHOLOGIES

Hrvatska književna kritika 1 — od Vraza do Markovića (edited by Antun Barac). Matica hrvatska, Zagreb.

Antologija slovenske poezije (edited by Lino Legiša), Matica srpska, Novi Sad.

TRANSLATIONS OF WORKS BY FOREIGN AUTHORS

García Lorca, Federico. Selected Poems, Zora, Zagreb.

Shaw, George Bernard. *Mrs. Warren's Profession*, Prosveta, Belgrade.

Hemingway, Ernest. *For Whom the Bell Tolls*, Bratstvo-jedinstvo, Novi Sad.

DECEASED

Voranc Prežihov.

ARTICLES AND POLEMICS

Šegedin, Petar. "O kulturi," *Književne novine*, January 17.

Konstantinović, Radomir. "Nekoliko utisaka s Kongresa piscaca," *Mladost*, no. 1.

Gligorić, Velibor. "Kritika i kritikantstvo," *Književne novine*, March 28 (in reply to an article by Radomir Konstantinović).

Konstantinović, Radomir. "Povodom odbrane jedne kritike," *Mladost*, no. 5 (reply to Velibor Gligorić).

Barković, Josip. "Stvaralački problemi naših mladih pisaca," *Književne novine*, January 24.

Bogdanović, Milan. "Književnici u velikom narodnom poslu — izborima," *Književne novine*, March 14.

Gligorić, Velibor. "Kod nas iza reci stoji delo," *Književne novine*, March 14.

Davičo, Oskar. "Za Partiju, Tita," *Književne novine*, March 14.

Komar, Slavko. "Prikazaćemo našu stvarnost pošteno i istinski," *Književne novine*, March 14.

Majstorović, Stevan. "Ka smelijim pothvatima," (contribution to a discussion on young critics), *Mladost*, no. 6.

Matković, Marijan. "Problemi naše savremene drame," *Književne novine*, January 3.

Minderović, Čedomir. "Za socijalistički preobražaj naše zemlje," *Književne novine*, March 21.

Mišić, Zoran. "Dva primera šablonske kritike na poeziju mladih," *Književ-*

nost, no. 10 (in response to a review of Slobodan Galogaža's poems, *Zora nad cestama* — Nasko Aganov, Dušan Puhalo).

Nikolić, R. "Nešto o partijnosti u književnoj kritici," *Književne novine*, March 28.

Petrović, Veljko. "Književnici i izbori za Narodnu skupštinu," *Književne novine*, February 28.

Popović, Dušan. "O slobodi književnog stvaranja," *Književne novine*, November 14.

Matić, Dušan. "Poezija je neprekidna svežina sveta," *Književne novine*, December 26.

Kisić, Čedo. "Estetika pod udarcem revizije marksizma," *Književne novine*, April 11.

Finci, Eli. "Teorija i praksa vulgarizacije u kritici," *Književne novine*, April 18 (in response to an article by V. Gligorić, "Kritika i kritikantstvo").

Gligorić, Velibor. "Odgovornost kritike," *Književne novine*, May 9 (reply to an article by E. Finci, "Teorija i praksa vulgarizacije").

Finci, Eli. "Odgovornost kritike," *Književne novine*, May 16 (reply to V. Gligorić).

Majstorović, Stevan. "Jedna poezija opštih osećanja," *Književne novine*, February 7 (in *Tri proleća*, a collection of poems by Mira Alečković).

1951

POETRY

Maksimović, Desanka. *Otadžbino, tu sam*, Prosveta, Belgrade.

Vučo, Aleksandar. *Mastodonti* (poem), Nopok, Belgrade.

Davičo, Oskar. *Hana*, Zora, Zagreb.

Konstantinović, Radomir. *Kuća bez krova*, Nopok, Belgrade.

Popović, Jovan. *Pesme*, Kultura, Belgrade.

Kostić, Dušan. *Proljeće nad rovom*, Zora, Zagreb.

Banović, Djonović, Kostić, Lalic, Mladenović, Ćopić. *Poezija i proza šestorice*, Prosveta, Belgrade.

Krklec, Gustav. *Lirska petoljetka*, Nopok, Zagreb.

Cesarić, Dobriša. *Pjesme* (selection), Zora, Zagreb.

Tadijanović, Dragutin. *Pjesme* (selection), Zora, Zagreb.

Franičević-Pločar, Jure. *Sunčana*, Mladost, Zagreb.

Pavlović, Bora. *Tišina*, Grafički zavod Hrvatske, Zagreb.

Janevski, Slavko. *Lirika*, Kočo Racin, Skopje.
Todorovski, Gane. *Vo utrinite*, Državno knigoizdatelstvo, Skopje.

PROSE

Ćosić, Dobrica. *Daleko je sunce* (novel), Prosveta, Belgrade.
Manojlović, Ljubiša. *Na času istorije* (chronicle), Prosveta, Belgrade.
Kolar, Slavko. *Pripovijetke* (selection), Zora, Zagreb.
Žerve, Drago. *Karolina Riječka* (comedy).
Kocbek, Edvard. *Strah in pogum* (short stories), Državna založba Slovenije, Ljubljana.
Humo, Hamza. *Tri svijeta* (play), Svjetlost, Sarajevo.

CRITIQUES AND ESSAYS

Sekulić, Isidora. *Njegošu, knjiga duboke odanosti*, SKZ, Belgrade.
Andrić, Ivo. *O Vuku kao piscu, o Vuku kao reformatoru* (essay), Prosveta, Belgrade.
Jovanović, Djordje. *Protiv obmana* (critiques), Prosveta, Belgrade.
Marinković, Ranko. *Geste i grimase* (critiques), Zora, Zagreb.
Vidmar, Josip. *Literarne kritike*, Državna založba Slovenije, Ljubljana.

COLLECTIONS AND ANTHOLOGIES

Hrvatska književna kritika II — Razdoblje realizma (edited by Antun Barac).
Antologija na makedonskata lirika (selected by Dimitar Mitrev, Blaže Koneski), Jugoslovenska knjiga, Belgrade.

TRANSLATIONS OF WORKS BY FOREIGN AUTHORS

Amuleti — Anthology of Primitive Poetry (compiled by Zvonimir Golob and Zvonimir Bajšić), Zagreb.
Sartre, Jean-Paul. *Two Plays*, Matica hrvatska, Zagreb.
Camus, Albert. *L'Étranger* (novel), Zora, Zagreb.
Steinbeck, John. *The Pearl*, Slobodna Voyvodina, Novi Sad.
Mann, Thomas. *Tonio Kröger*, Zora, Zagreb, SKZ, Ljubljana.
Shaw, George Bernard. *Androcles and the Lion*, Zora, Zagreb.
Miller, Arthur. *All My Sons*, Glas rada, Zagreb.
Steinbeck, John. *The Pearl*, Slobodna Vojvodina, Novi Sad.

NEW LITERARY JOURNALS AND PERIODICALS

Beseda. Literary and cultural reviews, Ljubljana, 1951–57.

Mlada literatura. Literary and cultural journal, editor-in-chief Aleksandar Ezov, Skopje, 1951–57.

DECEASED

Louis Adamič, Ljubo Vizner.

ARTICLES AND POLEMICS

Gluščević, Zoran. "Nešto o stvaranju lepog," *Mladost*, no. 5–6 (based on L. I. Timofeyev's *Teorije književnosti*).

Djilas, Milovan. "Ideja i umjetničko djelo," *Književne novine*, October 12.

Davičo, Oskar. "Poezija i otpori," *Mladost*, no. 7–8.

Bogdanović, Milan. "Mladost (poezija bez smisla)," *Književne novine*, December 23, review of *Mladost* no. 7–8 (double issue).

Ristić, Marko. "Velja kruška u grlo zapadne," *Borba*, December 25.

Kos, Janko. "Kultura in profesionalizam," *Beseda*, no. 1.

―――. "Zapiski s svidnikom," *Beseda*, no. 8 and no. 9–10.

Levec, Peter. "Estetski okus in različni interesi," *Beseda*, no. 7.

Gamulin, Grga. "Opča teorija umjetnosti kao teorija socijalističkog realizma," *Zbornik radova Filozofskog fakulteta u Zagrebu*, no. 155–186.

Djilas, Milovan. "Razmišljanja o raznim pitanjima" (brochure), Kultura, Belgrade.

Stojković, Živorad. "O jednom ćutanju u književnosti" (brochure), author's edition in response to "Razmišljanja o raznim pitanjima" (banned), Belgrade.

1952

POETRY

Vinaver, Stanislav. *Evropska noć*, Nopok, Belgrade.

Kulenović, Skender. *Ševa* (poem), Kultura, Belgrade.

Pavlović, Miodrag. *87 pesama*, Nopok, Belgrade (prize of the Serbian Writer's Society).

Mandić, Svetislav. *Kad mlidijah živeti*, Nopok, Belgrade.

Raičković, Stevan. *Pesma tišine*, Prosveta, Belgrade.

Alečković, Mira. *Tragovi bez stopa*, Prosveta, Belgrade.

Čiplić, Bogdan. *Divlje jato*, Matica srpska, Novi Sad.

Vukosavljević, Slavko. *Šta ti kažeš Marija*, Nopok, Belgrade.

Golob, Zvonimir. *Nema sna koji te može zamijeniti*, author's edition, Zagreb.

Markovski, Venko. *Stihovi,* Kočo Racin, Skopje.

PROSE

Krleža, Miroslav. *Djetinjstvo u Agramu god 1902–1903* (from his diary), Zora, Zagreb.

———. *Pijana noć 1918* (from his diary), Zora, Zagreb.

Davičo, Oskar. *Pesma* (novel), Nopok, Belgrade (Prize of the Yugoslav Writers' Union).

Ćopić, Branko. *Prolom* (novel), Prosveta, Belgrade.

Simić, Novak. *Druga obala* (novel), Mladost, Zagreb.

Desnica, Vladan. *Olupine na suncu* (short stories), Matica hrvatska, Zagreb (Prize of the Yugoslav Writers' Union).

Božić, Mirko. *Kurlani gornji i donji* (novel), Mladost, Zagreb.

Matković, Marijan. *Prometej* (play), Glas rada, Zagreb.

Jelić, Vojin. *Limeni pijetao* (short stories), Zora, Zagreb.

Markovski, Venko. *Goce* (play), Kočo Racin, Skopje.

Janevski, Slavko. *Selo za sedumte jaseni* (novel), Kočo Racin, Skopje.

CRITIQUES AND ESSAYS

Krleža, Miroslav. "Govor na Kongresu književnika," Zora, Zagreb.

Djilas, Milovan. *Legenda o Njegošu* (essay), Kultura, Belgrade.

Davičo, Oskar. *Poezija i otpori,* Nopok, Belgrade.

Ristić, Marko. *Književna politika* (essays), Prosveta, Belgrade.

———. *Prostor-vreme* (essays), Zora, Zagreb.

Matić, Dušan. *Jedan vid francuske književnosti* (essays), Prosveta, Belgrade.

PROBLEMS OF LITERARY LANGUAGE

Belić, Aleksandar. *Pravopis srpskohrvatskog jezika* (new, enlarged and corrected edition), Prosveta, Belgrade.

Koneski, Blaže. *Gramatika na makedonskiot literaturen jezik,* Državno knigoizdatelstvo, Skopje.

TRANSLATIONS OF WORKS BY FOREIGN AUTHORS

Baudelaire, Charles. *Les Fleurs du Mal,* Zora, Zagreb.

———. *Spleen de Paris,* Mladost, Zagreb.

Joyce, James. *Portrait of the Artist as a Young man,* Zora, Zagreb.

Sartre, Jean-Paul. *La Nausée,* Zora, Zagreb.

Camus, Albert. *La Peste,* Zora, Zagreb.

Proust, Marcel. *A la recherche du temps perdu* (volumes 1, 2, 3), Zora Zagreb.

Faulkner, William. *Light in August*, Cankarjeva založba, Ljubljana.

Lukacs, Georg. *Probläme des Realismus*, Cankarjeva založba, Ljubljana.

Gide, André. *Les Faux Monnayeurs*, Bratstvo-jedinstvo, Novi Sad.

Mann, Thomas. *Der Tod in Venedig*, Matica srpska, Novi Sad.

Shaw, George Bernard. *A Career*, Matica srpska, Novi Sad.

Hemingway, Ernest. *A Farewell to Arms*, Mladost, Zagreb.

———. *For Whom the Bell Tolls*, Bratstvo-jedinstvo, Novi Sad.

———. *The Old Man and the Sea*, Seljačka sloga, Zagreb.

Steinbeck, John. *Of Mice and Men*, SKZ, Ljubljana.

———. *The Moon Is Down*, Glas rada, Zagreb.

———. *In Dubious Battle*, Slovenski poročevalec, Ljubljana.

NEW LITERARY JOURNALS AND PERIODICALS

Svedočanstva. Literature, art, science, politics, social problems; editor Aleksandar Vučo, Belgrade 1952. Ceased publication with no. 17, 1952.

Revija. Review of literature, theater, music, films, fine arts; editor-in-chief Dušan Timotijević, Belgrade 1952–53 (last issue no. 20, 1953).

Zapisi. Literature and culture of the young, editor Emil E. Pavelkić, Belgrade 1952. One issue only.

Mlada kultura. Editor-in-chief Slavko Vukosavljević, Belgrade 1952–57 (ceased publication with no. 16, 1957).

Krugovi. Literary and cultural monthly; editor-in-chief Vlatko Pavletic, Zagreb 1952–58 (ceased publication with no. 10, 1958).

Medjutim. Literary monthly; editor-in-chief Zlatko Tomičić, Zagreb, 1952–53.

Naši razgledi. Fortnightly review of politics, government and culture. Ljubljana, 1952.

Sovremenost. Journal of literature, art and general problems. Skopje, 1952–.

Život. Literary and cultural monthly; editor Marko Marković, Sarajevo, 1952–.

CONGRESSES AND PLENARY MEETINGS OF WRITERS

3rd Congress of the Yugoslav Writers' Union, September 5–7.

Reports:

Vučo, Aleksandar. "Položaj književnika u našem društvu i stanje domaće savremene knjige."

Krleža, Miroslav. "O slobodi kulture."

LITERARY FESTIVAL

First Yugoslav Poetry Festival, Lake Plitvice.

DECEASED

Jovan Popović, Pero Ljubić, Antun Debeljak.

ARTICLES AND POLEMICS

Bogdanović, Milan. "Otpozdrav na pismo," *Borba*, January 6, 1952 (on Marko Ristić's article "Velja kruška u grlo zapadne").
Mišić, Zoran. "O smislu i besmislu, o lirici mekog i nežnog štimunga, o jednoj čežnji i jednom govoru na svim jezicima sveta," *Mladost*, no. 2–3 (on M. Bogdanović's "Poezija bez smisla").
Finci, Eli. "Duh i slava tradicije," *Svedočanstva*, March 22.
Ristić, Marko. "Nije jednostavno," *Svedočanstva*, April 5.
Finci, Eli. "Pravo smeha i pravo na smeh," *Svedočanstva*, April 19 (on the removal of the *Thieves' Carnival* from the repertoire of the Belgrade Theater).
Drenovac, Bora. "Da ne ostane bez odgovora," *Književne novine*, June 24 (on Eli Finci's article "Pravo smeha . . .").
Finci, Eli. "Još jednom o pravu smeha," *Svedočanstva*, July 12 (reply to Bora Drenovac).
Mitrović, Mitra. "Povodom diskusije o skidanju 'Bala lopova' sa repertoara Beogradskog dramskog pozorišta," *Svedočanstva*, September 6.
Mičić, Zoran. "Ipak se kreće," *Svedočanstva*, no. 9 (on the new periodicals *Krugovi*, *Tribina* and *Zapisi*).
Gavrilović, Zoran. "Kritika i kritizerstvo," *Književne novine*, August 16 (in response to Zoran Mišić's article above).
Mišić, Zoran. "Nekoliko 'nehajnih' asocijacija o Branku Ćopiću, realizmu, tradicionalizmu, modernistima i ostalim 'vukodlacima' a u vidu odgovora Zoranu Gavriloviću," *Svedočanstva*, September 6 (in response to Z. Gavrilović's "Kritika i kritizerstvo").
Gavrilovic, Zoran. "Još jedan 'branilac' realizma," *Književne novine*, September 14 (on Zoran Mišić as a critic).
Kulenović, Skender. "Avec un petit souris," *Književne novine*, September 14 (in reply to Z. Mišić's "Nekoliko 'nehajnih' asocijacija . . .").
Mladenović, Tanasije. "Otvoreno i bez uvijanja," *Svedočanstva*, September 6.

230   CONTEMPORARY YUGOSLAV LITERATURE

Bogdanović, M.; Kulenović, S.; Drenovac, B. "Izjava," *Književne novine,* September 14 (in response to T. Mladenović's "Otvoreno i bez uvijanja").

Finci, Eli. "Dobra volja i 'zla volja'," *Svedočanstva,* no. 9.

Bogdanović, Milan. "Ne, ni zlovoljno, ni prozvoljno," *Književne novine,* July 6 (reply to Eli Finci's article "Dobra volja i 'zla volja' ").

"Osnovno danas," *Književne novine,* January 6 (on the attitude of the editors of *Književne novine* towards current literary and artistic problems).

Pavlović, Miodrag. "Popodne u jednom dobu. Razgovor o dva filma i jednom pesniku," *Svedočanstva,* no. 6 (on Lautréamont's "Les chants de Maldoror").

Mišić, Zoran. "Još jedno popodne sa Maldororom," *Svedočanstva,* no. 7 (in response to M. Pavlović's "Popodne u jednom dobu").

Vučo, Aleksandar. "Jedna panorama mlade lirike" (introduction), *Svedočanstva,* August 23.

Djilas, Milovan. "Vučovi 'dokazi' slobode," *Književne novine,* September 14 (in response to A. Vučo's introduction to "Jedna panorama mlade lirike").

Bihalji-Merin, Oto. "Razgovori na Bledskom jezeru," *Književnost,* no. 6 (thoughts on the development of our new literature).

Davičo, Oskar. "Razgovori ovde," *Književne novine,* September 28 (in response to Oto Bihalji-Merin's "Razgovori na Bledskom jezeru").

Drenovac, Bora. "U susret neizbežnoj borbi," *Književne novine,* no. 64.

Barković, Josip. "Očigledan dokaz Bore Drenovca," *Krugovi,* no. 6 (in response to B. Drenovac's article "U susret neizbežnoj borbi").

Pavletić, Vlatko. "Umjetnost i sloboda," *Krugovi,* no. 1.

———. "Bumerang—kritika i uzurpatori javnog mišljenja," *Krugovi,* no. 1.

———. "Diskusija i anketa *Krugova,*" *Krugovi,* no. 2 (on the relationship between literature and the public).

"Zašto je pubika ravnodušna," (inquiry), *Krugovi,* no. 3.

Rotković, Radoslav. "Zašto je publika ravnodušna," *Krugovi,* no. 3 (a reply to the inquiry).

———. "Umjetnost i umješnost (jedan novi prilog uz stari članak Marka Ristića)," *Krugovi,* no. 6.

"O časopisu *Krugovi,*" *Medjutim,* no. 2.

E. S. "Automatizam i nadrealizam," *Krugovi,* no. 2.

Desnica, Vladan. "Zapisi o umjetnosti, *Krugovi*, no. 5, 6, 7.
Kranjec, Miško. "Poezija odmaknjenosti," (I–III), *Ljubljanski dnevnik*, July 5–8.
———. "Kam pelja ta pot" (I–VII), *Ljubljanski dnevnik*, January 3–10.
Ziherl, Boris. "O omladinskom časopisu *Beseda*," *Književne novine*, February 2 (on M. Kranjec's article "Kam pelje ta pot").
Vidmar, Josip. "Edvard Kocbek: 'Strah in pogum'," *Novi svet*, no. 1, reprinted in *Književne novine*, February 2.
Vipotnik, Janez. "K novi Kocbekovi knjigi," *Borec*, no. 1 (on E. Kocbek's book *Strah in pogum*).
Ziherl, Boris. "Še enkrat okrog *Besede*," *Ljudska pravica*, January 26.
Kos, Janko. "O sodobnih problemih v literarni kritiki," *Novi svet*, no. 7–8 (on the collection of critiques of Josip Vidmar).
Mitrev, Dimitar. "Za 'molčenjeto' na kritika za recenzatskata 'aktivnost' i za *Goce*," *Sovremenost*, no. 3 (on V. Markovski's play *Goce*).
Bogićević, Miodrag. "Neki problemi poezije mladih," *Omladinska riječ*, April 20 (a look at the literary evenings of student-writers at the University of Sarajevo).

1953

POETRY

Davičo, Oskar. *Čovekov čovek* (poem), Nopok, Belgrade.
Pavlović, Miodrag. *Stub sećanja*, Nopok, Belgrade.
Popa, Vasko. *Kora*, Nopok, Belgrade (Branko Prize).
Cesarić, Dobriša. *Osvijetljeni put* (Prize of the Yugoslav Writers' Union).
Popović, Vladimir. *Lirske minijature*, Zora, Zagreb (Prize of the Croatian Writers' Society).
Franičević-Pločar, Jure. *Stope na kamenu*, Zagreb (Prize of the Croatian Writers' Society).
Miličević, Pavletić, Novak. *Pjesme*, Zora, Zagreb.
Ković, Zlobec, Menart, Pavček. *Pesmi štirih*, SKZ, Ljubljana.
Koneski, Blaže. *Pesni*, Kočo Racin, Skopje (Prize of the Macedonian Writers' Society).
Todorovski, Gane. *Trevožni zvuci*, Kočo Racin, Skopje, (November 13 Prize).
Ivanovski, Srbo. *Sredbi i razdelbi*, Kočo Racin, Skopje (Prize of the Macedonian Writers' Society).

PROSE

Krleža, Miroslav. *Sabrana djela* (I–XXXVI), Zora, Zagreb.
Petrović, Rasko. *Ljudi govore* (story), Nopok, Belgrade.
Lalić, Mihailo. *Zlo proljeće* (novel), Nopok, Belgrade (Prize of the Yugo-slav Writers' Union).
Isaković, Antonije. *Velika deca* (stories), Nopok, Belgrade (Zmaj Prize).
Radović, Dušan. *Kapetan Džon Piplfoks* (radio-play), published 1964, Prosveta, Belgrade.
Marinković, Ranko. *Ruke* (short stories), Kultura, Zagreb (Prize of the Yugoslav Writers' Union).
————. *Pod balkonima* (short stories), Prosveta, Belgrade.
Šegedin, Petar. *Mrtvo more* (short stories), Kultura, Zagreb (Prize of the City of Zagreb).
Jelić, Vojin. *Andjeli lijepo pjevaju* (novel), Zora, Zagreb.
Kosmač, Ciril. *Pomladni dan* (story), Prešernova družba, Ljubljana.
Sijarić, Ćamil. *Ram-Bulja* (tales), Svjetlost, Sarajevo (Prize of the Bos-nian-Hercegovinian Writers' Society).

CRITIQUES AND ESSAYS

Krleža, Miroslav. "O Erazmu Roterdamskom" (essay), Zora, Zagreb.
————. *Critiques*, Matica hrvatska, Zagreb.
Ristić, Marko. "Predgovor za nekoliko nenapisanir romana i dnevnik tog predgovora" (1935), Prosveta, Belgrade.
Mišić, Zoran. *Reč i vreme* (essays), Nopok, Belgrade.
Jeličić, Živko. *Lica i autori* (essays), Kultura, Zagreb (Prize of the Croa-tian Writers' Society).

COLLECTIONS AND ANTHOLOGIES

Antologija novije srpske lirike (9th edition), compiled by Bogdan Popo-vić, SKZ, Belgrade.
Antologija starije srpske poezije (edited by Mladen Leskovac), Matica srpska, Novi Sad (Prize of the Serbian Writers' Union).

TRANSLATIONS OF WORKS BY YUGOSLAV AUTHORS

Andrić, Ivo. *Na Drini ćuprija*, Berlin, Zurich.

TRANSLATIONS OF WORKS BY FOREIGN AUTHORS

Mayakovski, Vladimir. *Oblak v shtanah*, Omladina, Belgrade.
Yesenyin, Sergei. *Poems*, Nopok, Belgrade.

García Lorca, Federico. *El Romancero gitano (?)*, Prosveta, Belgrade.
Hemingway, Ernest. *The Sun Also Rises*, Nopok, Belgrade.
————. *The Snows of Kilimanjaro*, Nopok, Belgrade.
Kafka, Franz. *Der Prozess*, Nopok, Belgrade.
Faulkner, William. *Intruder in the Dust*, Nopok, Belgrade.
Mann, Thomas. *Lotte in Weimar*, Nopok, Belgrade.
Mayakovski, Vladimir. *Banya*, Zora, Zagreb.
Steinbeck, John. *Flight* (short story), Cankarjeva založba, Ljubljana.
Faulkner, William. *Light in August*, Bratstvo-jedinstvo, Novi Sad.
Moravia, Alberto. *Il Conformista*, Bratstvo-jedinstvo, Novi Sad.

NEW JOURNALS AND PERIODICALS

Nova misao. Monthly; editor-in-chief Skender Kulenović; Belgrade, 1953–54 (ceased publication with no. 1, 1954).
Vidici. Literary and cultural journal; editors Vuk Filipović and Miloš Ilić; Belgrade, 1953–.
Naša sodobnost. Editors Boris Ziherl and Ferdo Kozak; Ljubljana, 1953– (in 1962 name changed to *Sodobnost*).
Susreti. Literary and cultural journal; editor-in-chief Radonja Vešović; Cetinje, 1952–63 (as of no. 9–10, 1963, *Susreti* merged with the journal *Stvaranje*).

LITERARY PRIZES

Yugoslav Writers' Union Prize for an author's life work; established 1953 as the highest national literary award.
1st award given to Miroslav Krleža in 1952.

DECEASED

Etbin Kristan, Anica Savić-Rebac, Marko Car.

ARTICLES AND POLEMICS

Davičo, Oskar. "Neotpori na dnevnom redu (I–V)," *Nova misao*, no. 1, 2, 4, 5, 7.
Feler, Miroslav. "Pismo Oskaru Daviču," *Nova misao*, no. 5 (in response to Davičo's article "Neotpori na dnevnom redu").
Kardelj, Edvard. 'O slobodi naužnog i umetničkog stvaranja," *Letopis Matice srpske*, vol. 371.
Djilas, Milovan. "Poetski roman Oskara Daviča," *Nova misao*, no. 1.
Bulatović, Božo. "Jedan loš kritičar, jedna čudna knjiga i jedan suviše

pohvalan sud o njoj," *Susreti*, no. 4 (on P. Džadžić's review of "Nedeljni dan pod okupacijom" and M. Djilas's "O romanu, 'Pesma' Oskara Daviča").

Dončević, Ivan. "O prvomajskim nagradama Saveza književnika Jugoslavije," *Borba*, May 8 (on the prize awarded to Vladan Desnica for his short stories *Olupina na suncu*).

Bogdanović, Milan. "Povodom izjave Ivana Dončevića o prvomajskim književnim nagradama," *Borba*, May 10.

Kulenović, Skender. "Eli Finci kao književni kritičar," *Nova misao*, no. 2, 3.

Majstorović, Stevan. "Jedna stara pojava u časopisu 'Nova misao'," NIN, March 15 (in response to Skender Kulenović's article "Eli Finci kao književni kritičar").

Franičević, Marin. "O slobodi stvaranja i tendenciji i još o nečem," *Vjesnik NF Hrvatske*, January 1.

——. "Malo buke, malo prašine ijoš o nečem," *Vjesnik NFH*, January 11 (a continuation of the article "O slobodi stvaranja, tendenciji, i još o nečem," and on Radoslava Rotković's article in *Studentski list*, December 5.

Pavletić, Vlatko. "Kritika kritike," *Krugovi*, no. 3.

Barković, Josip. "Zakašnjela mudrost Vladana Desnice," *Krugovi*, no. 1 (on V. Desnica's article "Zapisi o umjetnosti").

——. "Kako *Medjutim* pravi sebi reklamu," *Krugovi*, no. 7 (in response to "O časopisu 'Krugovi'," published in *Medjutim*, no. 1, 2).

Habazin, Andjelko. "Frulaštvo i saksofonizam," *Krugovi*, no. 9.

Miličević, Nikola. "Medju-team Šoljan-Slamnig," *Krugovi*, no. 8 (on the continuation of the article "O 'Krugovima'" in *Medjutim*, no. 2).

Gamulin, Grga. "Dva pojma modernog," *Naprijed*, November 6.

Ziherl, Boris. "Nekaj opomb o naši kritiki, *Naša sodobnost*, no. 7–8.

Vidmar, Josip. "O estetskih kriteriji," *Naša sodobnost*, no. 7–8.

Kermauner, Taras. "O estetskih in esteticističkih kriteriji, literarne kritike," *Naša sodobnost*, no. 7–8

——. 'O estetskih in esteticističkih kriteriji," *Naša sodobnost*, no. 9–10.

Kos, Janko. "Boris Ziherl in naša kritika," *Beseda*, no. 9.

——. "Kaj je z marksizmon v slovenski literarni kritiki," *Beseda*, no. 10.

Kermauner, Taras. "O dveh prevladujoćih tipih v sodobni slovenski kritiki," *Beseda*, no. 6.

Paternu, Boris. "Generalno čišćenje pojmova ali literarno rokovnjaštvo,"

Beseda, no. 7–8 (in response to T. Kermauner's article "O dveh prevladujočih tipih v sodobni slovenski kritiki").

Kos, Janko. "Prispevek k splošnemu čiśćenju pojmov o kritiki," *Beseda,* no. 7–8 (in response to B. Paternu's article "Generalno čiśćenje pojmova ali literarno rokovnjaštvo").

Kermauner, Taras. "Poezija in slovenski psevdomarksizem," *Beseda,* no. 9.

Solev, Dimitar. "Na marginite od 'Seloto' na Janevski," *Mlada literatura,* no. 3–4.

Šopov, Aco. "Mesto odgovor. Borba na mnenija ili . . . politikantski aluzii," *Sovremenost,* no. 3 (review of the weekly supplement *Razgledi* and the newspaper *Nova Makedonija*).

Kisić, Čedo. "Estetika," *Borba,* August 18 (on the publication of Miroslav Feler's book *Criticisms*).

1954

POETRY

Gradnik, Alojz. *Raspa v vetru.*

Matić, Dušan. *Bagdala,* Prosveta, Belgrade.

Radičević, Branko V. *Zemlja,* Mladost, Sarajevo.

Radović, Dušan. *Poštovana deco,* Mlado pokolenje, Belgrade.

Todorović, Gordana. *Gimnazijski trenutak,* Nopok, Belgrade (Branko Prize).

Hristić, Jovan. *Dnevnik o Ulisu,* Nopok, Belgrade.

Lukić, Velimir. *Poziv godine,* Nopok, Belgrade.

Vrkljan, Irena. *Krik je samo tišina,* Nopok, Belgrade.

Ujević, Tin. *Žedan kamen na studencu,* Društvo književnika Hrvatske, Zagreb.

Mihalić, Slavko. *Komorna muzika,* Lykos, Zagreb.

Ivšić, Radovan. *Tanke 1940–54,* private edition, Zagreb.

Markovski, Venko. *Nad plamnati bezdni,* author's edition, Skopje.

Dizdar, Mak. *Plivačica,* Veselin Masleša, Sarajevo.

Humo, Hamza. *Izabrane pjesme,* Svjetlost, Sarajevo.

PROSE

Andrić, Ivo. *Prokleta avlija* (story), Matica srpska, Novi Sad (Prize of Yugoslav Writers' Union).

Ćosić, Dobrica. *Koreni* (novel), Prosveta, Belgrade (NIN Award).

Vučo, Aleksandar. *Raspust* (novel), Nopok, Belgrade (Prize of the Yugoslav Writers' Union).

Konstantinović, Radomir. *Daj nam danas* (novel), Nopok, Belgrade (Prize of the Serbian Writers' Association).

Kaleb, Vjekoslav. *Bijeli kamen* (novel), Kultura, Zagreb (Prize of the City of Zagreb).

―――――. *Divota prašine* (novel), Mladost, Zagreb (Prize of the Yugoslav Writers' Union and the Yugoslav Publishers' Association).

Šinko, Ervin. *Optimisti* (novel).

Desnica, Vladan. *Proljeća Ivana Galeba* (novel), Svjetlost, Sarajevo (Zmaj Award).

Vidas, Fedor. *Popodne kad sam sretan* (short stories).

Matković, Marijan. *Na kraju puta* (play), JAZU, vol. 301, Zagreb (Prize of the Croatian Writers' Society).

Potrč, Ivan. *Na kmetih* (novel), SKZ, Ljubljana (Prešern award).

Župančič, Beno. *Veter in cesta* (stories), SKZ, Ljubljana (Prize of the Slovenian Writers' Society).

Kovačić, Hing, Bohanec. *Novele treh*, Obzorja, Maribor (Prize of the Slovenian Writers' Society).

Janevski, Slavko. *Klovnovi i lug'e* (short stories), Kočo Racin, Skopje (November 13 Prize).

Djurović, Dušan. *Ždrijelo* (stories), Naraodna prosvjeta, Sarajevo (Prize of the Bosnian-Hercegovinian Writers' Association).

CRITIQUES AND ESSAYS

Gligorić, Velibor. *Srpski realisti*, Prosveta Belgrade (Zmaj award).

Ristić, Marko. "Tri mrtva pesnika," JAZU, vol. 301, Zagreb (Prize of the Yugoslav Writers' Union).

Barac, Antun. *Jugoslavenska književnost, Povijest književnosti*, Matica hrvatska, Zagreb.

Vidmar, Josip. *Meditacije*, Državna založba Slovenije, Ljubljana (Prize of the Yugoslav Writers' Union).

Mitrev, Dimitar. *Vapčarov* (essays), Kočo Racin, Skopje (Prize of the Macedonian Writers' Society).

TRANSLATIONS OF WORKS BY YUGOSLAV AUTHORS

Andrić, Ivo. *Na Drini ćuprija*, Stuttgart.

TRANSLATIONS OF WORKS BY FOREIGN AUTHORS

Gide, André. *Paludes*, Prosveta, Belgrade.

Wolfe, Thomas. *Look Homeward, Angel* (I–II), Nolit, Belgrade.
Faulkner, William. *Knight's Gambit*, Prosveta, Belgrade.
Hemingway, Ernest. *To Have and Have Not*, Omladina, Belgrade.
Moravia, Alberto. *Gli Indiferenti*, Nopok, Belgrade.

NEW LITERARY JOURNALS AND PERIODICALS

Crveno jeste. Literary periodical; editor-in-chief Galib Sulejmani; Belgrade, 1954 (one issue only).
Razgledi. Art, culture, science and topics of general interest; editor Vlado Maleski; Skopje, 1954 (in 1958 changed from a newspaper to a periodical, with Kole Čašule as editor).
Mogućnosti. Periodical for literature, art and cultural issues; editor-in-chief Živko Jeličić; Split, 1954–.

PROBLEMS OF LITERARY LANGUAGE

The Novi Sad agreement on a literary Serbo-Croatian language, Novi Sad, December 10.

CONGRESSES AND PLENARY MEETINGS OF
LITERARY ASSOCIATIONS

Extraordinary plenum of the Yugoslav Writers' Union, Belgrade, November 10–13.
Reports by:
Miroslav Krleža: "O tendenciji"
Boro Pavlović: "O savremenom i modernom u književnosti"
Ervin Šinko: "O nekim zajedničkim karakteristikama raznih programskih estetika i odnosu prema umjetničkom stvaralaštvu"
Slobodan Novak: "O savremenom i modernom u književnosti"
Josip Vidmar: "Realizam i fantastika"
Janko Kos: "O marksističkoj estetici i o marksističkoj literarnoj kritici"

LITERARY PRIZES

Highest Yugoslav literary award for the author's life work: Veljko Petrović

DECEASED

Risto Ratković, Rihard Katalinić-Jeretov.

ARTICLES AND POLEMICS

Rehar, Voja. "Ideologizacija vizuelnog sveta," *Književne novine*, June 17.

238   CONTEMPORARY YUGOSLAV LITERATURE

Perović, Puniša. "Uredništvu 'Književnih novina'," *Književne novine*, June 24 (in response to V. Reha's article "Ideologizacija vizuelnog sveta").

Rehar, Voja. "Odgovor Puniši Peroviću," *Književne novine*, July 15.

Mladenović, Tanasije. "*Otkrovenja* Oskara Daviča," *Književne novine*, February 11 (on Oscar Davičo's book *Čovekov čovek*).

Mihajlović, Borislav. "Neznanje ili falsifikat Tanasija Mladenovića," *Književne novine*, February 16.

Mladenović, Tanasije. "U odgovor Mihajloviću-Mihizu," *Književne novine*, February 16.

Kermauner, Taras. "Opredeljevanje lepote in estetska zveda," *Beseda*, no. 1.

Kos, Janko. "Definicija umetnosti in neumetnosti," *Beseda*, no. 1.

———. "Metamorfoze," *Beseda*, no. 8–10.

Mitrev, Dimitar. "Literatura vo. 1953 (I–II)," *Razgledi*, no. 1, 2.

Martinovski, Cvetko. "Staro novo . . . ipak staro," *Sovremenost*, no. 4.

———. "Razgled na dva broja *Razgleda*," *Sovremenost*, no. 4.

Pendovski, Branko. "Marginalii," *Razgledi*, May 6 (on certain literary questions raised by C. Martinovski's articles "Staro novo . . . ipak staro" and "Razgled na dva broja 'Razgleda'").

———. "Realizam i novo. Negacija i negacija. Konjokradci i stavokradci," *Razgledi*, no. 12 (in response to C. Martinovski's article "Razgled na dva broja 'Razgleda'").

Djurčinov, Milan. "Marginalii na tema: novo," *Mlada literatura*, no. 2.

Popovski, Ante. "Lutanja ili pretenzii," *Sovremenost*, no. 6 (in response to Branko Pendovski's "Marginalija"), *Razgledi*, no. 12.

Solev, Dimitar. "Slučaj ili pojava," *Razgledi*, no. 19 (polemic on modern poetry written in response to A. Popovski's article "Lutanja ili pretenzii").

Djurčinov, Milan. "Navednat nad eden lirski tekst," *Razgledi*, no. 12 (a letter to Srbo Ivanovski on his new short story).

Kisić, Čedo. "Savremena umjetnost i problem estetskog sistema," *Oslobodenje*, August 13 (polemic with Žarko Vidović).

1955

POETRY

Maksimović, Desanka. *Miris zemlje* (selection), Prosveta, Belgrade (Zmaj Award).

Ristić, Marko. *Nox microcosmica (1923–1953)*, Nolit, Belgrade.

Blagojević, Desimir. *Dolazak medj cvrčke*, Nolit, Belgrade.

Raičković, Stevan. *Balada o predvečerju*, Nolit, Belgrade (Prize of the Serbian Writers' Association).

Čiplić, Bogdan. *Paorske balade*, Matica srpska, Novi Sad.

Ugrinov, Pavle. *Bačka zapevka* (poem), Matica srpska, Novi Sad (Branko Prize).

Lalić, Ivan V. *Bivši dječak*, Lykos, Zagreb.

Krklec, Gustav. *Žubor života* (selection), Prosveta, Belgrade (Prize of the Croatian Writers' Society).

Parun, Vesna. *Crna maslina*, Društvo književnika Hrvatske, Zagreb (Prize of the City of Zagreb).

Kaštelan, Jure. *Biti ili ne*, Mladost, Zagreb (Prize of the Croatian Writers' Society).

Vučetić, Šime, *Ljubav i čovek*, Zora, Zagreb (Prize of the Croatian Writers' Society).

Tomičić, Zlatko. *Četvrtoga ne razumijem*, Društvo književnika Hrvatske, Zagreb.

Madjer, Miroslav. *Mislim na suncu*, Društvo književnika Hrvatske, Zagreb.

Šopov, Aco. *Slej se so tišinata*, Kočo Racin, Skopje (Kočo Racin award).

Koneski, Blaže. *Vezilka*, Kultura, Skopje (Prize of the Yugoslav Writers' Union).

Vešović, Radonja. *Gajtan vode u dolini*, Narodna knjiga, Cetinje.

Perović, Sreten. *Mramorno pleme*, Narodna knjiga, Cetinje.

PROSE

Petrović, Rastko. *Burleska gospodina Peruna, boga groma* (novel), Rad, Belgrade.

Lalić, Mihailo. *Raskid* (novel), Narodna knjiga, Cetinje (Prize of the Serbian Writers' Association).

Božić, Mirko. *Neisplakani* (novel), Zora, Zagreb (*NIN* Award).

Simić, Novak. *Braća i kumiri* (novel), Kultura, Zagreb (Prize of the Yugoslav Writers' Union).

Desnica, Vladan. *Proljeće u Badrovcu* (stories), Prosveta, Belgrade.

Novak, Slobodan. *Izgubljeni zavičaj* (short stories), Pododbor MH, Split.

Kuzmanović, Vojislav. *Petar na pijesku* (short stories), Zora, Zagreb.

Kozak, Ferdo. *Popotoval sem u domovino*, Državna založba Slovenije, Ljubljana (Prešern award).

Koneski, Blaže. *Lozje* (short stories), Kočo Racin, Skopje (November 13 award).

Pendovski, Branko. *Igra* (short stories), Kultura, Skopje.

Ivanov, Blagoja. *Sedum umiranja* (short novel), Kultura, Skopje.

CRITIQUES AND ESSAYS

Izvanredni kongres Saveza književnika Jugoslavije, Savez književnika Jugoslavije, Belgrade.

Šegedin, Petar. *Eseji*, Kultura, Zagreb.

Simić, Stanislav. *Jezik i pjesnik* (essays), DKH, Zagreb.

Hergešić, Ivo. *Književni portreti, 1–3* (essays), Lykos, Zagreb.

Pavletić, Vlatko. *Sudbina automata* (critiques); DKH, Zagreb.

Šinko, Ervin. *Roman jednog romana* (notes from a Moscow diary), 1935–47), Zora, Zagreb.

Spasov, Aleksandar. *Patišta kon zborot* (critiques and reflections), Kultura, Skopje.

COLLECTIONS AND ANTHOLOGIES

Antologija srpske proze, I–II (edited by Velibor Gligorić), Nolit, Belgrade.

Posleratna srpska poezija (1945–55), compiled by Predrag Palavestra; Omladina, Belgrade.

Četrdesetorica — pregled mlade hrvatske lirike (compiled by Cesarić, Tadijanović and Vučetić), Zora, Zagreb.

TRANSLATIONS OF WORKS BY FOREIGN AUTHORS

Shaw, George Bernard. *The Adventures of the Black Girl in Her Search for God*, Prosveta, Belgrade.

Joyce, James. *Dubliners*, Državna založba Slovenije, Ljubljana.

Gide, André. *Voyage au Congo*, Mladinska knjiga, Ljubljana.

Mann, Thomas. *Doktor Faustus*, Svjetlost, Sarajevo.

Hemingway, Ernest. *The Old Man and the Sea*, DZS, Ljubljana.

NEW LITERARY JOURNALS AND PERIODICALS

Delo. Literary monthly; editor-in-chief Antonije Isaković; Belgrade, 1955.

Savremenik. Monthly; editor-in-chief Velibor Gligorić; Belgrade, 1955–.

Polja. Literary and cultural monthly; editor-in-chief Florika Štefan; Novi Sad, 1955–.

Korijen. Literary and cultural periodical; editor-in-chief Stjepan Boban; Banja Luka, 1955–. (Since 1960, published under the title *Putevi*.)

Rukovet. Periodical for literature, art and social problems; editor-in-chief Lazar Merković; Subotica, 1955–.

LITERARY CONGRESSES AND PLENARY MEETINGS

Fourth Congress of the Yugoslav Writers' Union, September 15–17.
Reports:
Milan Bogdanović: "Opšti osvrt na razvojne linije naše književnosti"
Dimitar Mitrev: "Deset godina slobodne makedonske književnosti"
Marijan Matković: "Deset godina jugoslovenske dramske književnosti"
Mira Alečković: "Deset godina jugoslovenske literature za decu"
Živko Jeličić: "O hrvatskoj prozi"
Novak Simić: "O suvremenoj hrvatskoj lirici"

LITERARY PRIZES

Highest Yugoslav literary award for the author's life work: Viktor Car-Emin

DECEASED

Stanislav Vinaver, Antun Barac, Augustin Tin Ujević, Mihovil Kombol, Milan Marjanović, Radoslav Petkovski, Isak Samokovlija.

ARTICLES AND POLEMICS

Ristić, Marko. "O modernom i modernizmu, opet (I–III)," *Delo*, nos. 1, 2, 5.

Lerik, Ivan. "O modernističkoj umetnosti" (pamphlet), Zrenjanin, p. 57.

Matić, Dušan. "Tragedija zbirke pesama (I–II)," *Delo*, nos. 1, and 2.

Bogdanović, Milan. "Književnost i politika," *Savremenik*, nos. 7–8.

Džadžić, Petar. "Savremena jugoslovenska književnost" (in Italian), *Il ponte*, nos. 8–9.

Prilike (Review of the first ten issues of *Delo*); participants: Stojan Ćelić, Dobrica Ćosić, Oskar Davičo, Petar Džadžić, Antonije Isaković, Sveta Lukić, Zoran Mišić, Vasko Popa, Miodrag P. Protić, Aleksandar Vučo, *Delo*, no. 10.

Lukić, Sveta. "Još jedna reč o popularnosti, jasnosti i razumljivosti kao estetičkom kriterijumu," *Delo*, no. 8.

Alimpić, Dobrivoje. "Neke karakteristike naše 'moderne' poezije," *Književnost i jezik u školi*, no. 4.

Rudolf, Branko. "Forma in družba," *Naši razgledi*, no. 2 (on the contemporary aesthetic crisis).

Dokler, Janez. "Umetnost je ukročeno življenje," *Obzornik*, no. 1.

Stardelov, Gorgi. "Umetnost i intuicija (I–II)," *Razgledi*, nos. 2, 3 (on Bretonian surrealism).

Hadži Vasilev, Mito. "Marksistička estetika ili eklekticizam," *Sovremenost*, no. 5 (in response to Gorgi Stardelov's article).

Solev, Dimitar. "Kom 'Vapcarov' od Dimitar Mitrev," *Razgledi*, no. 8.

Abadžiev, Georgi. "Po povod 'Vapčarov' od Dimitar Mitrev," *Sovremenost*, no. 1.

Djurčinov, Milan. "Edna neodgovorna analogija ad hoc," *Razgledi*, no. 22 (on the October issue of *Mlada literatura*).

——. "Temi i razgovori za lug'eto," (Slavko Janevski's *Klovnovi i lug'e*), *Razgledi*, no. 4.

Kuljan, Spase. "Apologija na skepsata," *Razgledi*, no. 6 (on Venka Markovski's poem "Nad plamnati bezdni").

Markovski, Venko. "Stremenot na lovskot," *Razgledi*, no. 7 (in response to "Apologija na skepsata").

Kuljan, Spase. "Neostvaren stremež na Venko Markovski," *Razgledi*, no. 8 (polemic with V. Markovski).

"Beleška na redakcijata kon polemika (V. Markovski-S. Kuljan)," *Razgledi*, no. 8.

Todorovski, "Zašto istupiv od 'Sovremenost,'" *Razgledi*, no. 8 (the writer's motives for leaving the editorial board of *Sovremenost*).

Spasov, Aleksandar. "Prostorot na edna poezija," *Razgledi*, nos. 5, 6 (marginal notes on Blaže Koneski's poems *Pesme*).

Stardelov, Gorgi. "Literatura i izraz," *Ragzledi*, no. 7.

1956

POETRY

Popa, Vasko. *Nepočin polje*, Matica srpska, Novi Sad (Zmaj Award).

Blagojević, Desimir. *Tri kantate*, Nolit, Belgrade (Prize of the Serbian Writers' Association).

Ujević, Tin. *Pobješnjela krava*, Lykos, Zagreb.

Cesarić, Dobriša. *Goli časovi*, Matica srpska, Novi Sad.

Mihalić, Slavko. *Put u nepostojanje*, Lykos, Zagreb (Prize of the Croatian Writers' Society).

Tadijanović, Dragutin. *Blagdan žetve* (collected poems), Zora Seljačka sloga, Zagreb.

Popović, Vladimir. *Povelja sna i jave* (selected poems), Prosveta, Belgrade (Prize of the City of Zagreb).

Gotovac, Vlado. *Pjesme od uvijek*, Lykos, Zagreb.

Tomičić, Zlatko. *Dosegnuti ja* (selected poems), Lykos, Zagreb.

Krmpotić, Vesna. *Poezija*, DKH, Zagreb.

Vipotnik, Cene. *Drevo na samem*, Slovenski knjižni zavod, Ljubljana (Prize of the Yugoslav Writers' Union and Prešern Award).

Ković, Kajetan. *Prezgodnji dan*, Primorska založba Lipa, Koper (Prize of the Slovenian Writers' Society).

Matevski, Mateja. *Doždovi*, Kultura, Skopje (Prize of the Macedonian Writers' Society).

Todorovski, Gane. *Spokoen čekor*, Kultura, Skopje.

Ivanovski, Srbo. *Beli krinovi*, Kultura, Skopje.

Tahmiščić, Husein. *Budna vrteška*, Narodna prosvjeta, Sarajevo.

PROSE

Davičo, Oskar. *Beton i svici* (novel), Prosveta, Belgrade (NIN award).

Konstantinović, Radomir. *Mišolovka* (novel), Kosmos, Belgrade.

Ćopić, Branko. *Doživljaji Nikoletine Bursaća*, Svjetlost, Sarajevo (Belgrade October Award).

Koš, Erih. *Veliki Mak*, Matica srpska, Novi Sad (Prize of the Yugoslav Writers' Union).

Bulatović, Miodrag. *Djavoli dolaze* (short stories), Nolit, Belgrade (Prize of the Serbian Writers' Society).

Obrenović-Lebović, *Nebeski odred* (play), Pozorišni život, Belgrade.

Ćosić, Bora. *Kuća lopova* (novel), Nolit, Belgrade.

Marinković, Ranko. *Glorija* (play), IBI, Zagreb (Prize of the City of Zagreb).

Kolar, Slavko. *Svoga tela gospodar* (play), ZDK, Zagreb.

Dončević, Ivan. *Mirotvorci* (novel), Kultura, Zagreb (Prize of the Yugoslav Writers' Union).

Jelić, Vojin. *Nebo nema obala* (novel), Kultura, Zagreb (Prize of the Croatian Writers' Society).

Kozak, Juš. *Balada o ulici v neenakih kiticah* (novel), Državna založba Slovenije, Ljubljana.

Ribić, Ivan. *Dolina mira* (scenario and account).

Janevski, Slavko. *Dve Marii* (novel), Kočo Racin, Skopje (Prize of the Macedonian Writers' Society).

Solev, Dimitar. *Okopneti snegovi* (stories), Kultura, Skopje.

Asanović, Sreten. *Dugi trenuci* (stories), Narodna knjiga, Cetinje (Prize of the Montenegrin Writers' Association).

CRITIQUES AND ESSAYS

Krleža, Miroslav. *Davni dani (zapisi 1914–1921)*, Zora, Zagreb.

Sekulić, Isidora. *Govor i jezik — kulturna smotra naroda*, Prosveta, Belgrade (Prize of the Yugoslav Writers' Union).

Matić, Dušan. *Anina balska haljina* (essays), SKZ, Belgrade (Prize of the Serbian Writers' Association).

Ristić, Marko. *Ljudi u nevremenu* (essays and articles), Kultura, Zagreb.

Mitrev, Dimitar. *Kriterium i dogma* (essays), Kočo Racin, Skopje (Kočo Racin award).

Krklec, Gustav. *Pisma Martina Lipnjaka iz provincije*, JBJ, Zagreb.

Mihajlović-Mihiz, Borislav. *Od istog čitaoca*, Nolit, Belgrade.

COLLECTIONS AND ANTHOLOGIES

Srpski pesnici izmedju dva rata (edited by Borislav Mihajlović-Mihiz), Nolit, Belgrade.

Antologija novije hrvatske lirike (edited by Mihovil Kombol), Nolit, Belgrade.

Antologija srpske poezije (edited by Zoran Mišić), Matica srpska, Novi Sad.

TRANSLATIONS OF WORKS BY YUGOSLAV AUTHORS

Andrić, Ivo. *Na Drini ćuprija*, Paris, Moscow, Warsaw.
    Travnička hronika, Paris (2 editions), Budapest.

Ćosić, Dobrica. *Daleko je sunce*, Bratislava, Prague, Moscow.
    Koreni, Sofia.

TRANSLATIONS OF WORKS BY FOREIGN AUTHORS

Anthology of World Poetry (edited by Jeličic and Krklec), Kultura, Zagreb.

Suvremena engleska poezija (Contemporary English Poetry), (edited by Šoljan and Slamnig), Lykos, Zagreb.

Baudelaire, Charles. *Les Fleurs du Mal*, Prosveta, Belgrade.

Mallarmé, Rimbaud, Valéry. *Poems*, Lykos, Zagreb.

Steinbeck, John. *East of Eden*, Kultura, Zagreb.

Camus, Albert. *La Peste*, Kočo Racin, Skopje.

Hemingway, Ernest. *Across the River and into the Trees,* Minerva, Subotica.

Moravia, Alberto. *La Romana,* Minerva, Subotica.

LITERARY PRIZES

The Yugoslav Writers' Union and the Publishers Association Award for the author's life work: Ivo Andrić.

ARTICLES AND POLEMICS

Lukić, Sveta. "Estetika," *Delo,* no. 1–2.

Habazin, Andjelko. "Atomsko doba—atomska estetika," *Mogučnosti,* no. 3 (polemic with Sveta Lukić).

Kos, Janko. "Umetnost i klasna baza," *Delo,* no. 8–9.

Mišić, Zoran. "Za jedinstveni jugoslovenski kriterijum," *Delo,* no. 7.

Kos, Erih. "O jedinstvenom jugoslovenskom kriteriju," *Savremenik,* no. 11.

Šega, Drago. "Kriterijum i stvarnost," *Naša stvarnost,* no. 10.

Mišić, Zoran. "Oko jedinstvenog jugoslovenskog kriterijuma," *Delo,* no. 12.

S. Z. "Afera Džadžić i kompanija," (on Džadžić's article in *Il ponte*), *Savremenik,* no. 3.

Isaković, Antonije. "S. Z.", *Delo,* no. 5.

Džadžić, Petar. "Ipak komentar," *Delo,* no. 7.

Ristić, Marko. "Izjava Marka Ristića," *Delo,* no. 7.

Vidmar, Josip. "Iz dnevnika," *Delo,* no. 5.

Ziherl, Boris. "Umetnost i idejnost," *Savremenik,* nos. 7–8, 9, 10, 11, 12 (polemic with J. Vidmar).

Solev, Dimitar. "Vreme i izraz," *Delo,* no. 1–2.

———. "Vistini kako paradoksi skice za eden pogled na rekapitulacija," *Razgledi,* no. 7 (a ten year survey of Macedonian literary life).

———. "Kreativnost i karakter," *Razgledi,* no. 1.

Spasov, Aleksandar. "Vrednosti i kriteriumi, *Razgledi,* no. 1.

Stardelov, Gorgi. "Za kritikata bez dokazi," *Sovremenost,* no. 1–2.

Bogićević, Miodrag. "Nacionalno i univerzalno u literaturi," *Odjek,* December 12.

Leovac, Slavko. "Zanosi života i književnosti," *Omladinska riječ,* December 14 (on Bosnian-Hercegovinian poetry).

———. "Strasti i ženerozitet," *Zivot,* no. 9 (on contemporary criticism).

Kisić, Čedo. "Čemu brutalna negacija," *Oslobodenje,* November 25 (on Sead Fetahagić's letter to the editor of *Oslobodjenje* and his statement on literary life in Sarajevo in *Vjesnik u Srijedu*).

1957

POETRY

Dedinac, Milan. *Od nemila do nedraga (1921–1956)* Nolit, Belgrade (Belgrade October Prize).

Miljković, Branko. *Uzalud je budim*, Omladina, Belgrade.

Krnjević, Vuk. *Zaboravljanje kučnog reda*, Omladina, Belgrade.

Radović, Borislav. *Poetičnosti*, Prosveta, Belgrade (Branko Award).

Kolundžija, Dragan. *Zatvorenik u ruži*, Nolit, Belgrade.

Danojlić, Milovan. *Urodjenički psalmi*, Nolit, Belgrade.

Golob, Zvonimir. *Afrika*, Lykos, Zagreb.

Kaštelan, Jure. *Malo kamena i puno snova* (poems), Lykos, Zagreb (Zagreb May Prize).

Parun, Vesna. *Vidrama vjerna*, Zora, Zagreb.

Pupačić, Josip. *Cvijet izvan sebe*, Zora, Zagreb (Zagreb May Prize).

Vrkljan, Irena. *Paralele*, Lykos, Zagreb.

Slaviček, Milivoj. *Daleka pokrajina*, Lykos, Zagreb (City of Zagreb Prize).

Ivančan, Dubravko. *Slobodna noć*, Lykos, Zagreb.

Šopov, Aco. *Vetrot nosi ubavo vreme* (poems), Kočo Racin, Skopje (Prize of the Macedonian Writers' Society).

Perović, Sreten. *Spisak* (Prize of the Montenegrin Writers' Association).

PROSE

Lalić, Mihailo. *Lelejska gora* (novel), Nolit, Belgrade (Prize of the Serbian Writers' Association).

Vučo, Aleksandar. *Mrtve javke* (novel), Kultura, Zagreb (NIN Award).

Matić, Dušan. *Kocka je bačena* (novel), Prosveta, Belgrade.

Ćopić, Branko. *Gluvi barut* (novel), Prosveta, Belgrade.

Obrenović, Aleksandar. *Varijacije* (play) (Prize of the Tribune of the Young in Novi Sad, and the Prix Italia, 1958).

Lukić, Sveta. *Razlozi* (prose), Nolit, Belgrade.

Božić, Mirko. *Ljuljačka u tužnoj vrbi* (play), Nolit, Belgrade.

Desnica, Vladan. *Proljeća Ivana Galeba* (novel), Svjetlost, Sarajevo (Zmaj Award).

Kaleb, Vjekoslav. *Samrtni zvuci* (short stories), Svjetlost, Sarajevo (Zagreb May Prize).

Franičević-Pločar, Jure. *Raspukline* (novel), Zora, Zagreb (Prize of the Croatian Writers' Society).

Prica, Čedo. *Nekoga moraš voljeti* (novel), Kultura, Zagreb (*Mladost* Award).

Šoljan, Antun. *Specijalni izaslanici* (short stories), DKH, Zagreb (Prize of the Croatian Writers' Society).

Drušković, Drago (Rok Arih). *Zato* (stories), Cankarjeva založba, Ljubljana (Prize of the Slovenian Writers' Society).

Hing, Andrej. *Usodni rob* (short stories), Obzorja, Maribor.

Zupančić, Beno. *Sedmina* (novel), Slovenska matica, Ljubljana (Prešern and *Mladost* awards).

Solev, Dimitar. *Pod usvitenost* (novel), Kultura, Skopje (Prize of the Macedonian Writers' Society).

Oljača, Mladen. *Molitva za moju braću* (novel), Narodna prosvjeta, Sarajevo (Prize of the Serbian Writers' Association).

Trifković, Risto. *Na terasi* (stories), Džepna knjiga, Sarajevo (Prize of the Bosnian-Hercegovinian Writers' Association).

CRITIQUES AND ESSAYS

Ziherl, Boris. "Umetnost i idejnost," (essay), Kultura, Belgrade.

Džadžić, Petar. "Ivo Andrić" (essay), Nolit, Belgrade (Award of the Tribune of the Young).

Ziherl, Boris. *Književnost in družba*, Cankarjeva založba, Ljubljana (Prešern Award).

Gavrilović, Zoran. *Kritika i kritičari (I)*, Rad, Belgrade.

Šinko, Ervin. *Falanga antikrista i drugi komentari*, Zora, Zagreb (Zagreb May Prize).

Desnica, Vladan. "Priča o tipičnome (o pojmovima 'tipa' i 'tipičnoga' i njihovoj neshodnosti na području estetike)," Univerzum, Zagreb.

Begić, Midhat. *Raskršća* (essays), Svjetlost, Sarajevo (Prize of the City of Sarajevo).

Hristić, Jovan. *Poezija i kritika poezije*, Matica srpska, Novi Sad.

Boškovski, Jovan. *Oplemeneta igra* (theater reviews), Kočo Racin, Skopje.

COLLECTIONS AND ANTHOLOGIES

Jugoslovenska lirika moderna (arranged by Petar Lasta), Školska knjiga, Zagreb.

Antologija hrvatskih eseja (edited by Ivo Frangeš), Nolit, Belgrade.

Vrata vremena (poslijeratni jugoslovenski pjesnici). Edited by Lalić and Pupačić; Lykos, Zagreb.

248   CONTEMPORARY YUGOSLAV LITERATURE

TRANSLATIONS OF WORKS BY YUGOSLAV AUTHORS

Andrić, Ivo. *Izbor*, Moscow.

———. *Na Drini ćuprija*, Kiev.

Ćosić, Dobrica. *Daleko je sunce*, Warsaw, Budapest, Bucharest, Rome, Berlin.

———. *Koreni*, Prague, Warsaw.

Čopić, Branko. *Prolom*, Sofia.

———. *Doživljaji Nikoletine Bursača*, Kiev.

Minderović, Čedomir. *Oblaci nad Tarom*, Peking.

Božić, Mirko. *Neisplakani*, Sofia.

Marinković, Ranko. *Glorija*, Prague.

Kaleb, Vjekoslav. *Divota prašine*, Warsaw.

TRANSLATIONS OF WORKS BY FOREIGN AUTHORS

Antologija savremene engleske poezije (edited by Brkić and Pavlović), Nolit, Belgrade. (Anthology of contemporary English poetry).

Mayakovski, Vladimir. *Vladimir Ilyich Lenin* (poem), Mladost, Zagreb.

———. *Poem*, Cankarjeva založba, Ljubljana.

Yesenin, Sergei. Poems, Kočo Racin, Skopje.

Mann, Thomas. *Buddenbrooks*, Državna založba Slovenije, Ljubljana.

Wolfe, Thomas. *Look Homeward, Angel*, Cankarjeva založba, Ljubljana.

Gide, André. *Voyage au Congo*, Kultura, Skopje.

Lukacs, Georg. *Probläme des Realismus*, Svjetlost, Sarajevo.

NEW LITERARY JOURNALS AND PERIODICALS

Literatura. Literary and cultural periodical; editor-in-chief Mirko Božić; Zagreb, 1957–59 (ceased publication with issue no. 3, 1959).

Revija 57. Literary and cultural review; editors, Veno Taufer and Vital Klabus; Ljubljana, 1957–58 (ceased publication with issue no. 4, 1958).

Izraz. Periodical of literature and artistic criticism; editor-in-chief Midhat Begić; Sarajevo, 1957–.

LITERARY PRIZES

The Yugoslav Writers' Union and the Yugoslav Publishers' Association Award for the author's life work: Juš Kozak.

DECEASED

Mile Pavlović-Krpa, Julije Benešić, Drago Žerve, Ferdo Kozak, Emil Petrović.

ARTICLES AND POLEMICS

Jeremić, Dragan, M. "Teze o 'neosimbolizmu'," *Polja*, no. 2.

Velmar-Janković, Svetlana. "Subjektivne varijacije o generaciji i vremenu," *Delo*, no. 12.

Iskušenje poezije (an examination of poetic creativity); participants: Stevan Raičković, Milan Dedinac, Jovan Hristić, Oskar Davičo, Gane Todorovski, Gordana Todorović, Svetozar Brkić, Velimir Lukić, Vasko Popa, Bora Pavlović, Vesna Krmpotić, Kajetan Kovič, Borislav Radović, Ciril Zlobec, Ivan V. Lalić, Milovan Danojlić, Tomislav Sabljak, Dragan Kolundžija, Mirjana Stefanović, Dane Zajc, Irena Vrkljan, Branko Miljković, Vesna Parun, Zvonimir Golob and Sveta Lukić (conclusion); *Delo*, no. 1.

Discussion on Criticism; participants: Velibor Gligorić, Božo Milačić, Radojica Tautović, Živan Milisavac, Dimitar Mitrev, Slavko Leovac, Vlatko Pavletić, Marijan Jurković, Dragan M. Jeremić, Ivan Lerik; *Savremenik*, no. 5–6.

Anketa: Šta je moderno i gdje ga vidite? (Inquiry on modernism). Participants: Pavle Stefanović, Jakov Gotovac, Dragan M. Jeremić, Šime Vučetić, Jovan Hristić, Fadil Hadžić, Čedo Prica, Milivoj Slaviček, Vlatko Pavletić, Jean Cassou, Karlo Ostojić, Ivan Foht, Boro Pavlović, Lazar Trifunović, Zlatko Tomičić; Elio Vittorini, Guiseppe Petronio, Dragiša Živković, Henri Lefebvre, Oskar Davičo; Isidora Sekulić, Boris Ziherl; Midhat Begić; *Izraz*, no. 3, no. 4, no. 5, no. 6, no. 7–8, no. 10.

Ziherl, Boris. "Još jednom o nesporazumima i razmimoilaženjima," *Savremenik*, no. 2, 3.

Vidmar, Josip. "Nesporazumi oko idejnosti," *Delo*, nos. 7, 12 (same article appeared in *Naša sodobnost*, nos. 10, 11, 12).

Rudolf, Branko. "Obrobne opaske ke estetki 'modernega'," *Naša sodobnost*, no. 10.

Hadži Vasilev, Mito. "Filozofiranje 'pod zvezdite nebesni,'" *Sovremenost*, no. 2 (on Abdulah Sarčević's article).

Pavlović, Pavao Vuk. "O ishodištu estetike," *Zbornik zagrebacke klasične gimnazije*, Zagreb.

Bogičević, Miodrag. "Velika isčekivanja," *Izraz*, no. 5 (variations on our contemporary literature).

Leovac, Slavko. "Mit i poezija," *Savremenik*, no. 1.

Posavac, Zlatko. "Umjetnost kao društveni fenomen," *Naše teme*, no. 3.

250 CONTEMPORARY YUGOSLAV LITERATURE

1958

POETRY

Raičković, Stevan. *Kasno leto,* Nolit, Belgrade (Belgrade October Prize).
Mladenović, Tanasije. *Pod pepelom zvezda* (poems), Nolit, Belgrade.
Kostić, Dušan. *Zaboravljeni snjegovi* (poems), Nolit, Belgrade.
Radičević, Branko V. *Večita pešadija,* Nolit, Belgrade.
Lalić, Ivan V. *Velika vrata mora* (poems), Nolit, Belgrade.
Šnajder, Djuro. *Ljubavnici u tudjim očima* (poems), Naprijed, Zagreb.
Bor, Matej. *Sled naših senc* (Prize of the Slovenian Writers' Society).
Zajc, Dane. *Požgana trava,* author's edition, Ljubljana.
Vipotnik, Cene. *Dvadeset bratov,* Mladinska knjiga, Ljubljana.
Zlobec, Ciril. *Ljubezen,* Obzoria, Maribor (Prežihov award).
Popovski, Ante. *Vardar* (poems), Kočo Racin, Skopje.

PROSE

Andrić, Ivo. *Izabrana dela (I–IV),* Prosveta, Belgrade and Svjetlost, Sarajevo.
Davičo, Oskar. *Radni naslov beskraja* (novel), Nolit, Belgrade (Belgrade October Prize).
Sekulić, Isidora. *Kronika palanačkog groblja,* SKZ, Belgrade.
Ćopić, Branko. *Ne tuguj, bronzana stražo* (novel), Svjetlost, Sarajevo (NIN Award).
Bulatović, Miodrag. *Vuk i zvono* (stories), Zora, Zagreb (Prize of the Serbian Writers' Association).
Crnjanski, Miloš. *Konak* (play), Minerva, Subotica.
Olujić, Grozdana. *Izlet u nebo* (novel), Narodna prosvjeta, Sarajevo.
Marković, Marijan. *Vašar snova* (play), Sterijino pozorje, Novi Sad (Sterijino pozorje prize).
———. *Heraklo* (play), (Zagreb May Prize).
Smole, Dominik. *Crni dnevi in beli dan* (novel), Obzorja, Maribor.
Rozman, Smiljan. *Nekdo* (novel), Obzorja, Maribor (Prežihov award).

CRITIQUES AND ESSAYS

Pavlović, Miodrag. *Rokovi poezije* (essays), SKZ, Belgrade.
Vučetić, Šime. *Krležino književno djelo* (essay), Svjetlost, Sarajevo (Zagreb May Prize).
Hadži Vasilev, Mito. *Odraz-izraz,* Kočo Racin, Skopje.

Mitrev, Dimitar. *Minato i literatura*, Institut za nacionalnu istoriju, Skopje.
Bandić, Miloš. *Vreme romana*, Prosveta, Belgrade.

COLLECTIONS AND ANTHOLOGIES

Antologija srpske književne kritike (compiled by Zoran Mišić), Nolit,
  Belgrade.
Antologija novije kajkavske lirike (edited by Nikola Pavić), Lykos, Zagreb.
Antologija hrvatskih pjesama u prozi (edited by Tadijanović, Tomičić),
  Matica hrvatska, Zagreb.
Hrvatski književni kritičari, I–II (selection and commentaries by Vlatko
  Pavletić), Matica hrvatska, Zagreb.
Antologija hrvatske drame, I–II (edited by Marijan Matković), Nolit,
  Belgrade.

TRANSLATIONS OF WORKS BY YUGOSLAV AUTHORS

Andrić, Ivo. *Na Drini ćuprija*, Budapest.
———. *Travnička hronika*, London.
———. *Gospodjica*, East Berlin.
Krleža, Miroslav. *Izabrana dela*, Moscow.
Davićo, Oskar. *Pesma*, East Berlin, Warsaw.
———. *Beton i svici*, Budapest.
Ćopić, Branko. *Doživljaji Nikoletine Bursaća*, Sofia, Prague, Moscow.
———. *Prolom*, Warsaw.
Ćosić, Dobrica. *Koreni*, Berlin, Budapest.
Kostić, Dušan. *Gluva pećina*, Sofia.
Marinković, Ranko. *Glorija*, Moscow.
———. *Ruke*, Warsaw.
Isaković, Antonije. *Velika deca*, Prague.

TRANSLATIONS OF WORKS BY FOREIGN AUTHORS

Brecht, Bertholt. *Kalendergeschichten*, Matica srpska, Novi Sad.
García Lorca, Federico. Poems, Cankarjeva založba, Ljubljana.
Sartre, Jean-Paul. *Le Mur*, Epoha, Zagreb.
Camus, Albert. *La Chute*, Mladost, Zagreb.
Mann, Thomas. *Bekentnisse des Hochstaplers Felix Krull*, Cankarjeva
  založba, Ljubljana.
Mayakovski, Vladimir. *Klop*, Zora, Zagreb.
Steinbeck, John. *East of Eden*, Cankarjeva založba, Ljubljana.
Moravia, Alberto. *LaCiociara* (novel), Otokar Keršovani, Rijeka.

————. *Racconti Romani*, Budućnost, Novi Sad.

————. *Il Disprezzo*, DZS, Ljubljana.

LITERARY CONGRESSES AND PLENARY MEETINGS

Fifth Congress of the Yugoslav Writers' Union, Belgrade, November 25–28.
Reports:
Vidmar, Josip. "O značaju programa Saveza komunista Jugoslavije za književnike i književnost."

LITERARY FESTIVALS

Second Yugoslav Poetry Festival, Rijeka, May 31–June 5.

LITERARY PRIZES

Highest Yugoslav literary award for the author's life work: Milan Bogdanović.

DECEASED

Isidora Sekulić, Tugomir Alaupović, Lili Novi.

ARTICLES AND POLEMICS

Vidmar, Josip. "Estetički nesporazumi," *Delo*, no. 1.

————. 'U začaranom krugo," *Delo*, no. 6, 7.

Gamulin, Grga. "Problemi avangarde," *Savremenik*, no. 4.

Makavejev, Dušan. "Umetnost treba cimnuti," *Delo*, no. 3.

"Odgovori jugoslovenskih pisaca na anketu časopisa *Les temps modernes*"; contributors: Marko Ristić, Josip Vidmar, Dobrica Ćosić; *Delo*, no. 11.

Tautović, Radojica. "U ime čitaoca," *Savremenik*, no. 7 (on the problems of the relationship between the critic and the public).

Kaleb, Vjekoslav. "Formalizam kao 'prodor u novo'," *Vjesnik*, October 26.

Vidović, Žarko. "Sloboda stvaranja," *Oslobodjenje*, October 10 and 11.

1959

POETRY

Krleža, Miroslav. *Simfonije* (selected works), Zora, Zagreb.

Crnjanski, Miloš. *Itaka i komentari*, Prosveta, Belgrade.

Matić, Dušan. *Budjenje materije*, Matica srpska, Novi Sad (Serbian 7th of July Award).

Davičo, Oskar. *Kairos*, Nolit, Belgrade (Zmaj Award).

Šćepanović, B. and Miljković, B. *Smrću protiv smrti*, Mlado pokolenje, Belgrade.

Minderović, Čedomir. *Potonula džunka*, Lykos, Zagreb.

Danojlić, Milovan. *Kako spavaju tramvaji* (children's poems), Mlado pokolenje, Belgrade (Mladost prize).

Parun, Vesna. *Koralj vraćen moru*, Lykos, Zagreb.

Čudina, Marija. *Nestvarne djevojčice*, Mladost, Zagreb.

Slaviček, Milivoj. *Modro veče*, Zora, Zagreb.

Vodnik, Anton. *Glas tišine*, Mohorjeva družba, Celje (prize of the Society of Slovenian Writers).

Strniša, Gregor. *Mozaiki*, Lipa, Koper.

Urošević, Vlada. *Eden drug grad*, Kultura, Skopje (Mladost Award).

PROSE

Krleža, Miroslav. *Aretej* (play), published in 1963, Zora, Zagreb (city of Zagreb prize).

Njeguš, Roksanda. *Kidanje* (novel), Kosmos, Belgrade.

Bulatović, Miodrag. *Crveni petao leti prema nebu* (novel), Naprijed, Zagreb.

Marinković, Ranko. *Poniženje Sokrata* (short stories), Naprijed, Zagreb.

Kavčić, Vladimir. *Ne vraćaj se sam* (novel), Državna založba Slovenije, Ljubljana (Prize of the Slovenian Writers' Society).

Mihelić, Mira. *April* (novel), Državna založba Slovenije, Ljubljana (Prize of the Slovenian Writers' Society).

Vuković, Čedo. *Mrtvo duboko* (novel), Grafički zavod, Titograd.

CRITIQUES AND ESSAYS

Frangeš, Ivo. *Stilističke studije*, Naprijed, Zagreb.

Foht, Ivan. "Istina i biće umjetnosti," Svjetlost, Sarajevo.

Bogičević, Miodrag. "Razgovor sa čitaocem," Svjetlost, Sarajevo.

COLLECTIONS AND ANTHOLOGIES

Jugoslovenska revolucionarna poezija (arranged by Dizdar, Franičević, Minderović, Šopov, and Zlobec), Svjetlost, Sarajevo and Kočo Racin, Skopje.

Poezija bunta i otpora (arranged by Gavrilović, Kulenović and Raičković), Prosveta, Belgrade.

Hrvatski pjesnici izmedju dva rata (selected by Nikola Miličević), Školska knjiga, Zagreb.

TRANSLATIONS OF WORKS BY YUGOSLAV AUTHORS

Andrić, Ivo. *Na Drini ćuprija*, London, New York, Munich.

――――. *Travnička hronika*, Berlin.

Ćopić, Branko. *Prolom*, Moscow.

DaviČo, Oskar. *Pesma*, London.

Božić, Mirko. *Kurlani*, Moscow.

Oljača, Mladen. *Molitva za moju braću*, Warsaw.

TRANSLATIONS OF WORKS BY FOREIGN AUTHORS

Anthology of Modern Spanish Poetry (edited by Nikola Miličević), Lykos, Zagreb.

Sartre, Jean-Paul. *Les chemins de la liberté*, Nolit, Belgrade.

Kafka, Franz. *Amerika*, Mlado pokolenje, Belgrade.

Wolfe, Thomas. *The Web and the Rock*, Nolit, Belgrade.

Moravia, Alberto. *La Mascherata*, Minerva, Subotica.

――――. *Raconti Romani*, Lipa, Koper.

Beckett, Samuel. *Molloy*, Kosmos, Belgrade.

――――. *Endgame*, Znanstvena knjižara, Zagreb.

Mann, Thomas. *Der Zauberberg*, Cankarjeva založba, Ljubljana.

Hemingway, Ernest. *A Farewell to Arms*, Kultura, Skopje.

NEW LITERARY JOURNALS AND PERIODICALS

Književnik, Cultural, artistic and literary monthly; editor-in-chief Josip Pupačić; Zagreb, 1959–61 (new series).

LITERARY FESTIVALS

Third Yugoslav Poetry Festival, Niš-Ohrid Superhighway, July 3–9.

DECEASED

Borivoje Jevtić, Vladimir Kovačić, Lojz Krajger, Pavel Golija, Boris Bojadžijski.

ARTICLES AND POLEMICS

Lukić, Sveta. "Socijalistički realizam," *Delo*, no. 1.

Pavletic, Vlatko. "U čemu je suština," *Književne novine*, September 11.

Koljević, Svetozar. "Moral želje kod modernih romansijera," *Književnost*, no. 2.

Begić, Midhat. "Na stepenicama izmedju stvarnosti i apstrakcije," *Izraz*, no. 7–8.

Foht, Ivan. "Umjetnost i partijnost," *Pregled*, no. 9.

Marković, Mihailo. "Značenje umetničkih simbola," *Književne novine*, December 4.

Jeremić, Dragan M. "Estetički fragmenti," *Savremenik*, no. 10.

Rudolf, Branko. "O poteh v abstraktno umetnost in o realizmu," *Večer*, no. 15.

Kos, Janko. "Poetska tema," *Izraz*, no. 11–12.

Hadzi Vasilev, Mito. "O ždanovizmu, idejnosti, tendencioznosti i nekim drugim pitanjima," *Savremenik*, no. 7.

1960

POETRY

Davičo, Oskar. *Tropi* (poems), Lykos, Zagreb.

Miljković, Branko. *Vatra i ništa*, Prosveta, Belgrade (Belgrade October Prize).

Cesarić, Dobriša. *Izabrane pjesme*, Matica hrvatska, Zagreb (Zmaj award).

Tomičić, Zlatko. *Budni Faun* (poems), Pododbor Matice hrvatske, Vinkovci.

Sabljak, Tomislav. *Situacije* (poems), Lykos, Zagreb.

Glumac, B., Majdak, Z., Majetić, A. *Pjesme*, Lykos, Zagreb.

Horvatić, Dubravko. *Groznica*, private edition, Zagreb.

Todorovski, Gane. *Božilak*, Kočo Racin, Skopje (Kočo Racin Award).

Andreevski, Petre M. *Jazli*, Kočo Racin, Skopje.

Dizdar, Mak. *Okrutnosti kruga*, Veselin Masleša, Sarajevo (Prize of the Bosnian-Hercegovinian Writers' Association).

Krnjević, Vuk. *Dva brata uboga*, Svjetlost, Sarajevo (Prize of the Bosnian-Hercegovinian Writers' Association).

PROSE

Petrović, Veljko. *Sabrana dela* (I–VIII), Matica srpska, Novi Sad (1954–1960).

Andrić, Ivo. *Lica* (short stories), Mladost, Zagreb.

Lalić, Mihailo. *Hajka* (novel), Nolit, Belgrade (Belgrade October Prize).

Konstantinović, Radomir. *Izlazak* (novel), SKZ, Belgrade (NIN Award).

Nikolić, Nebojša. *M-sje Žozef*, radio-play (Prix Italia, 1961).

Jeličić, Živko. *Mlaka koža* (novel), Mladost, Zagreb.

Prica, Čedo. *Svijet viden na kraju* (novel), Naprijed, Zagreb.

Barković, Josip. *Zeleni dječak* (children's stories), Matica hrvatska, Zagreb.

Kreft, Bratko. *Balada o poročniku in Marjutki*, Obzorja, Maribor.

Momirovski, Tome. *Grešna nedela* (novel), Kočo Racin, Skopje (13th of November Prize).

Solev, Dimitar. *Po rekata in sproti nea* (short stories), Kočo Racin, Skopje (Kočo Racin award).

Fetahagić, Sead. *Četvrtak poslije petka* (short stories), Svjetlost, Sarajevo (Mladost award).

CRITIQUES AND ESSAYS

Vučetić, Šime. *Hrvatska književnost 1914–1941* (a study), Lykos, Zagreb.

Pavletić, Vlatko. *Trenutak sadašnjosti* (critiques and articles), NJP, Zagreb.

Leovac, Slavko, *Mit i poezija*, Svjetlost, Sarajevo (Sarajevo 6th of April Prize).

COLLECTIONS AND ANTHOLOGIES

Hrvatska književna kritika (selected by Šime Vučetić).

Posleratna srpska pripovetka (compiled by Petar Džadžić), Progres, Novi Sad.

Voz djetinjstva (anthology of children's poetry), edited by Borislav Pavić; Svjetlost, Sarajevo.

Povoeni makedonski poeti (compiled by Dimitar Mitrev), Kočo Racin, Skopje.

Povoeni makedonski prozaisti (compiled by Gorgi Stardelov), Kočo Racin, Skopje.

PROBLEMS OF LITERARY LANGUAGE

Pravopis srpskohrvatskog književnog jezika (by the commission for standard orthography: Aleksić, Balić, Jonke, Stévanović, and Vuković), Belgrade, Zagreb.

Koneski, Gosev. *Makedonski pravopis sa pravopisen rečnik*, Državno knigoizdatelstvo na Makedonija, Skopje (11th of October Prize).

TRANSLATIONS OF WORKS BY YUGOSLAV AUTHORS

Ćopić, Branko. *Prolom*, Prague.

———. *Doživljaji Nikoletine Bursaća*, Berlin.

Maksimović, Desanka. *Miris zemlje*, Moscow.

Desnica, Vladan. *Prolječa Ivana Galeba*, Warsaw.
Božič, Mirko. *Kurlani*, Warsaw.
Potrč, Ivan. *Zločin*, Budapest.
Popa, Vasko. *Izbor*, Cracow.
Bulatović, Miodrag. *Crveni petao leti prema nebu*, Stockholm, Milan, Munich.

TRANSLATIONS OF WORKS BY FOREIGN AUTHORS

Anthology of Contemporary French Poetry (compiled by Božo Kukolja), Lykos, Zagreb.
Miller, Arthur. *The Crucible*, Mlado pokolenja, Belgrade.
Sartre, Jean-Paul. *Les morts sans sepulture*, Državna založba Slovenije, Ljubljana.
Moravia, Alberto. (*Gli Indifferenti*), Obzorja, Maribor.
Lukacs, Georg. *Die Zerstörung der Vernunft*, Cankarjeva založba, Ljubljana.
Hemingway, Ernest. *The Old Man and the Sea*, Kultura, Skopje.
    A Farewell to Arms, Obzorja, Maribor.
Steinbeck, John. *Short Stories*, Kočo Racin, Skopje.

NEW LITERARY JOURNALS AND PERIODICALS

Telegram. Yugoslav weekly; editor-in-chief Fadil Hadžić, Zagreb, 1960–.
Perspektive. Monthly for cultural and social problems; editor-in-chief Dominik Smole; Ljubljana, 1963–64 (ceased publication with no. 37, 1963–64).

LITERARY PRIZES

Highest National Award for the author's life work: Josip Vidmar.

DECEASED

Sima Pandurović, Milan Čurčin, Stanislav Šimić, Nikola Pavić.

ARTICLES AND POLEMICS

Konstantinović, Rade. "Oklevetana dogma," *Delo*, no. 1.
Ćosić, Bora. "Naš smeh — Napredak komičnog ikustva," *Delo*, no. 12.
Lukić, Sveta. "Todoru Pavlovu — o kriterijumima," *Delo*, no. 1 (polemic with Todor Pavlov on socialist realism and Yugoslav literature).
Hristić, Jovan. "Kratak spis o jeziku," *Delo*, no. 12.
Razgovor o kritici; participants: Sveta Lukić, Dušan Matić, Oskar Davičo,

Petar Džadžić, Aleksandar Vučo, Muharem Pervić, Milosav Mirković; *Delo*, no. 6.

Mitrev, Dimitar. "Za problemot na realizmot i modernizmot," *Trudovi*, no. 1–2.

Popović, Bruno. "Pjevanje i življenje," *Književna tribina*, April 29.

Kangrga, Milan. "Marksizam i estetika," *Naše teme*, no. 2.

Čopić, Špelca. "Misli o abstraktni umetnosti," *Naša sodobnost*, no. 1.

Rudolf, Branko. "Glose o izrazu realizem," *Naša sodobnost*, no. 1.

Bulajić, Stevan. "Malogradjanin i umjetnost," *Svijet*, April 5.

Stardelov, Gorgi. "Marksizmot i estetikata," *Kulturen život*, no. 8.

Kos, Janko. "Družbeno-ideološka struktura in progresivnost današnje književnosti," *Perspektive*, no. 3.

1961

POETRY

Lukić, Velimir. *Čudesni predeo*, Nolit, Belgrade.

Mihalić, Slavko. *Godišnja doba*, Lykos, Zagreb (Prize of the City of Zagreb).

Udović, Jože. *Ogledalo sanj*, Cankarjeva založba, Ljubljana.

Smole, Dominik. *Antigona* (verse play), Državna založba Slovenije, Ljubljana (VI Sterijino pozorje award).

Zajc, Dane. *Jezik is zemlje*, Cankarjeva založba, Ljubljana.

Pavlovski, Radovan. *Suša svadba i selidbi*, Kočo Racin, Skopje (Mladost award).

Krnjević, Vuk. *Pejzaži mrtvih*, Veselin Masleša, Sarajevo.

PROSE

Petrović, Rastko. *Dan šesti* (novel), Nolit, Belgrade.

Ćosić, Dobrica. *Deobe (I–III)* (novel), Prosveta, Belgrade (7th of July Prize of Serbia).

Stefanović, Mirjana. *Odlomci izmišljenog dnevnika*, Matica srpska, Novi Sad.

Šoljan, Antun. *Izdajice* (novel), Zora, Zagreb.

Novak, Slobodan. *Tvrdi grad* (short stories), Zora, Zagreb (Zagreb May Award).

Bor, Matej. *Daljave* (novel), Cankarjeva založba, Ljubljana (Prešern award).

Kralj, Vladimir. *Mož, ki je strigel z ušesi* (short stories), Mladinska knjiga, Ljubljana.

Hing, Andrej. *Planota* (short stories), Cankarjeva založba, Ljubljana.

Abadžijev, Georgi. *Pustina* (novel), Kočo Racin, Skopje (11th of October Prize).

Georgijevski, Taško. *Zidovi* (novel), Skopje (11th of October Prize).

CRITIQUES AND ESSAYS

Andrić, Ivo. "Zapisi o Goji" (essay), Matica srpska, Novi Sad.

Krleža, Miroslav. *Knjiga eseja* (selection), SKZ, Belgrade.

Makedonska književnost (compiled by Blaže Koneski), SKZ, Belgrade.

Uvod u književnost (edited by Petre, Škreb), Znanje, Zagreb.

Milačic, Dušan. *Stendahl* (monograph), Rad, Belgrade (Belgrade October Prize).

Matić, Dušan. *Na tapet dana* (essays), Matica srpska, Novi Sad.

Tahmišćić, Husein. *Ponovo osvojen grad* (essays), Svjetlost, Sarajevo.

COLLECTIONS AND ANTHOLOGIES

Panorama savremene bosansko-hercegovačke poezije (selected by R. Trifković), Udruženje Književnika Bosne-Hercegovine, Sarajevo.

Antologija savramene makedonske poezije i proze (compiled by A. Spasov, M. Djurčinov and D. Solev), Nolit, Belgrade.

Antologija slovenačke poezije, I–II (selected by C. Vipotnik, M. Šega, and J. Kastelanec), Nolit, Belgrade.

Antologija slovenačke proze, I–II (selected by Bojan Štih and Milan Šega), Nolit, Belgrade.

Crvena zora vremena (anthology of revolutionary Yugoslav poetry), edited by Blažo Šćepanović; Kulturno-prosvetno veće Jugoslavije, Belgrade.

Lirika upora (selected by Mitja Mejak), Cankarjeva založba, Ljubljana.

Antologija savremene poezije za decu, Mlado pokolenje, Belgrade.

Borba i literatura (edited by Mitrev and Spasov), Kultura, Skopje.

TRANSLATIONS OF WORKS BY YUGOSLAV AUTHORS

Ćopić, Branko. *Doživljaji Nikoletine Bursaća*, Berlin.

Župančić, Oton. *Izbor stihova pod naslovom, Probuždenie*, Moscow.

Maksimović, Desanka. *Prolećni sastanak*, Moscow.

Ćosić, Dobrica. *Daleko je sunce*, Copenhagen.

Lalić, Mihailo. *Svadba*, Bratislava.

Marinković, Ranko. *Ruke*, Stuttgart.

Bulatović, Miodrag. *Crveni petao leti prema nebu*, Barcelona, Milan.

TRANSLATIONS OF WORKS BY FOREIGN AUTHORS

Steinbeck, John. *The Pastures of Heaven*, Mlado pokolenje, Belgrade.

Baudelaire, Charles. *Les Fleurs du Mal*, Matica hrvatska, Zagreb.

Kafka, Franz. *Das Schloss*, Prosveta, Belgrade.

Shaw, George Bernard. *Candida*, Rad, Belgrade.

Breton, André. *Manifeste du surréalisme*, Bagdala, Kruševac.

Kafka, Franz. Essay, Mladinska knjiga, Ljubljana.

Lukacs, Georg. *Probläme des Realismus*, Cankarjeva založba, Ljubljana.

Camus, Albert. *Le Mythe de Sisyphe*, Veselin Masleša, Sarajevo.

Steinbeck, John. *East of Eden*, Svjetlost, Sarajevo.

Moravia, Alberto. *La Noia*, Otokar Keršovani, Rijeka.

―――. *Racconti Romani*, Kočo Racin, Skopje.

NEW LITERARY JOURNALS AND PERIODICALS

Danas. Review of culture, art and social problems; editor Stevan Majsto-rović; Belgrade, 1961–63 (ceased publication with no. 46, 1963).

LITERARY CONGRESSES AND PLENARY MEETINGS

6th Congress of the Yugoslav Writers' Union, Sarajevo, September 16–18. Reports:

Franičević-Pločar, Jure. "Uloga jugoslovenske književnosti, u našoj revoluciji i uticaj revolucije na našu književnost."

Ramić, Rizo; Janevski, Slavko; Vuković, Čedo; Mejak, Mitja; Ćosić, Dobrica. "Kraći osvrti na ljude i dogadjaje iz jugoslovenske revolucije."

LITERARY PRIZES

Nobel Prize for Literature: Ivo Andrić.

DECEASED

Dušan Nikolajević, Branko Miljković, Josip Kosor, Herbert Grin, Marko Marković.

ARTICLES AND POLEMICS

Ristić, Marko. "Dnevnik," *Danas*, nos. 1, 2, 3, 4, 5, 11 and 12.

Konstantinović, Rade. "O umnom i bezumnom" (letter to Marko Ristić), *Danas*, no. 12.

Ristić, Marko. "Pismo," *Danas*, no. 13.

"Diskusija o kriterijumima za ocenjivanje vrednosti umetničkog dela," participants: Ivan Foht, Dragan M. Jeremić, Miodrag B. Protić, Eleonora Mičunović, Milan Ranković; *Gledišta*, no. 4.

"Naše književne teme" (discussion), participants: Muharem Pervić, Oskar Davičo, Dragan M. Jeremić, Dušan Matić, Dobrica Ćosić, Sveta Lukić, Eli Finci, Aleksandar Vučo, Milosav Mirković, Milan Vlajčić, Petar Džadžić; *Delo*, no. 12.

Mikecin, Vjekoslav. "Estetička pitanja i pitanja o estetici," *Naše teme*, no. 11.

Šoljan, Antun. "Književnost i publika; Indikacije problema u sociološkom pristupu književnom djelu," *Književnik*, no. 1.

Gotovac, Vlado. "Umjetnost se suprotstavlja nhilizmu," *Telegram*, April 21.

Special issue devoted to the program and policies of *Književnik*; compiled by members of the group including: Duško Car, Vlado Gotovac, Stanko Jurisa, Vesna Krmpotić, Ivan Kušan, Tomislav Ladan, Slobodan Novak, Ivan Slamnig, Antun Šoljan; *Književnik*, no. 29.

Foht, Ivan. "Tegobe teorije odraza," *Izraz*, no. 2.

1962

POETRY

Lalić, Ivan V. *Vreme, vatre, vrtovi*, Matica srpska, Novi Sad (Zmaj award).

Matić, Dušan. *Laža i paralaža noći*, Nolit, Belgrade.

Lukić, Velimir. *Okamenjeno more* (verse play), Prosveta, Belgrade (Belgrade October Prize).

Mrkonjić, Zvonimir. *Gdje ste*, Pododbor Matice hrvatske, Split.

Ganza, Mate. *Pjesme strpljenja*, Matica hrvatska, Split (*Mladost* award).

Urošević, Vlada. *Nevidelica*, Kultura, Skopje.

Djuzel, Bogomil. *Medovina*, Kočo Racin, Skopje.

Andreevski, Petre M. *I na nebo i na zemja*, Kočo Racin, Skopje.

Boškovski, Petar. *Suvodolica*, Nolit, Belgrade.

Kralj, Milo. *Smrt umire prva*, Obod, Cetinje.

Krakar, Lojze. *Cvet pelina*, Cankarjeva založba, Ljubljana (Prešern award).

PROSE

Kozak, Juš. *Izbrano delo* (I–IV), Državna založba Slovenije, Ljubljana.

Krleža, Miroslav. *Banket u Blitvi* (vol. III), (novel), Forum, Zagreb.

——. *Zastave* (novel), Forum, Zagreb (Njegoš award).

Lalić, Mihailo. *Lelejska gora* (novel, two versions), Nolit, Belgrade (Nolit award).

Isaković, Antonije. *Paprat i vatra* (short stories), Nolit, Belgrade (7th of July Award of Serbia).

Koš, Erih. *Vrapci Van Pia* (novel), Nolit, Belgrade.

Kovač, Mirko. *Gubilište* (novel), Polja, Novi Sad.

Hristić, Jovan. *Orest-Čiste ruke* (play), Progres, Novi Sad (Sterijino Pozorije Award).

Horvat, Joža. *Mačak pod šlemom* (novel), Naprijed, Zagreb (Zagreb May Award).

Kozak, Primož. *Afera* (play), Državna založba Slovenije, Ljubljana.

Zlobec, Ciril. *Moška leta našega otroštva* (novel), Borec, Ljubljana (Kajuh award).

Drakul, Simon. *Belato dolina* (novel), Kočo Racin, Skopje.

Selimović, Meša. *Tudja zemlja* (novel), Veselin Masleša, Sarajevo.

CRITIQUES AND ESSAYS

Ladan, Tomislav. *Zoon graphicon* (essays and critiques), Veselin Masleša, Sarajevo.

Boško, Božidar. *Na raspotjih časa* (essays and articles), Obzorja, Maribor.

COLLECTIONS AND ANTHOLOGIES

Novija jugoslovenska poezija (compiled by Popović, Vučetić, Petre and Mitrev), Naprijed, Zagreb.

Lirika Crne Gore 1918–1962 (compiled by Vuković and Djonović), Obod, Cetinje.

Pesme gorske i ponosne (the poetry of Yugoslav Shiptars); edited by Esad Mekuli; Nolit, Belgrade.

TRANSLATIONS OF WORKS BY YUGOSLAV AUTHORS

Andrić, Ivo. *Na Drini ćuprija*, Stockholm, Munich, Berlin, Frankfurt, Helsinki, Istanbul, Athens, Teheran, Bucharest, Lisbon, Milan (9th edition).

Ćopić, Branko. *Prolom*, Budapest.

Vučo, Aleksandar, *Raspust*, Berlin.

Šegedin, Petar. *Djeca božja*, Vienna.

Oljača, Mladen. *Molitva za moju braću*, Munich.

Koš, Erih. *Veliki Mak*, New York.

Bulatović, Miodrag. *Crveni petao leti prema nebu*, Milan, New York, London, Oslo.

―――. *Djavoli dolaze*, Munich.

TRANSLATIONS OF WORKS BY FOREIGN AUTHORS

Wolfe, Thomas. Short stories, Nolit, Belgrade.

Kafka, Franz. *Der Prozess*, Cankarjeva založba, Ljubljana.

Camus, Albert. Short Stories, Državna založba Slovenije, Ljubljana.

Sartre, Jean-Paul. *Les Séquestrés d'Altona*, Kočo Racin, Skopje.

Miller, Arthur. *The Misfits*, Mladost, Zagreb.

Steinbeck, John. *Of Mice and Men, The Red Pony, Cannery Row*, Znanje, Zagreb.

Kafka, Franz. *Der Prozess*, Kočo Racin, Skopje.

DECEASED

Stevan Jakovljević, Milan Tokin, Branko Gavela, Franc Finžgar.

ARTICLES AND POLEMICS

Pervić, Muharem. "Angažovana književnost epohe," *Politika*, April 29.

Gluščević, Zoran. "Angažovana ili neangažovana literatura," *Knjizevne novine*, June 1.

Pervić, Muharem. "Kako se sve postaje ždanovac," *Delo*, no. 7.

Hristić, Jovan. "Angažovana umetnost," *Danas*, May 9.

Majstorović, Stevan. "Neangažovana angažovanost," *Danas*, May 9.

Konstantinović, Rade. "Pohvala putovanja," *Danas*, November 7.

Tautović, Radojica. "Um i umetnost," *Književne novine*, October 5.

Pirjevec, Dušan. "Slovenstvo, jugoslovenstvo i socijalizam," *Delo*, no. 1.

Ćosić, Dobrica. "Nacija, integracija, socijalizam," *Delo*, no. 2.

Kozak, Primož. "Nacija ili društvo," *Delo*, no. 3.

Pirjevec, Dušan. "Odgovor D. Ćosiću," *Delo*, no. 3.

Ćosić, Dobrica. "Čitaocima," *Delo*, no. 5.

Klabus, Vital. "Slovenska književnost 1961," *Perspektive*, nos. 15, 16, 20.

Kos, Janko, "Funkcije in disfunkcije slovenske literarne zgodovine," *Perspektive*, no. 18.

Peratoner, Ervin. "Imamo li marksističku kritiku," *Naše teme*, no. 6.

Petrović, Svetozar. "Marksisti i kritika," *Naše teme*, no. 9 (polemic with E. Peratoner).

Car, Duško. "Hrvatska književnost u protekloj godini," *Delo*, no. 2.

Glumac, Branislav. "O 'protekloj godini' Duška Cara," *Delo*, no. 8–9.

Car, Duško. 'U pohvalu mudroslovlju," *Delo*, no. 6.

Vaupotić, Miroslav. "Još jednom o 'hrvatskoj književnosti u protekloj godini'," *Delo*, no. 8–9.

1963

POETRY

Pavlović, Miodrag. *Mleko iskoni*, Prosveta, Belgrade.

Raičković, Stevan. *Kamerna uspavanka*, Prosveta, Belgrade (Zmaj award and 7th of July Award of Serbia).

———. *Pesme*, SKZ, Belgrade.

Hristić, Jovan. *Aleksandrijska škola*, Prosveta, Belgrade.

Kocbek, Edvard. *Groza*, Slovenska matica, Ljubljana.

Taufer, Veno. *Jetnik prostosti*, Cankarjeva založba, Ljubljana.

Strniša, Gregor. *Odisej*, Cankarjeva založba, Ljubljana.

Šopov, Aco. *Nebidnina*, Kočo Racin, Skopje.

Matevski, Mateja. *Ramnodenica*, Kultura, Skopje.

Djuzel, Bogomil. *Alhemijska ruža*, Kultura, Skopje.

Vešović, Radonja. *Krčag na vjetru*, Prosveta, Belgrade.

PROSE

Andrić, Ivo. *Sabrana dela (I–X)*, Prosveta, Belgrade. Mladost, Zagreb. Državna založba Slovenije, Ljubljana. Svjetlost, Sarajevo.

Krleža, Miroslav. *Sabrana djela (I–XXI)*, Zora, Zagreb.

Mihajlović, Borislav. *Banović Strahinja* (play), Prosveta, Belgrade(Sterijino pozorje 1st prize).

Davičo, Oskar. *Gladi* (novel), Nolit, Belgrade (NIN — critics' award).

———. *Ćutnje* (novel), Nolit, Belgrade.

Pavlović, Živojin. *Krivudava reka* (stories), Nolit, Belgrade.

Drainac, Rade. *Crni dani* (notes), Kosmos, Belgrade.

Bulatović Vib, Vlada. *Budilnik* (satire), Nolit, Belgrade.

Majetić, Alojz. *Čangi* (novel), Progres, Novi Sad.

Zajc, Dane. *Otroka reke* (verse play), Cankarjeva založba, Ljubljana.

Čingo, Živko. *Paskvelija* (short stories), Kultura, Skopje.

Božić, Petar. *Izven* (novel), DZS, Ljubljana.

CRITIQUES AND ESSAYS

Vinaver, Stanislav. *Nadgramatika* (selected essays), Prosveta, Belgrade,

Vidmar, Josip. *Za i protiv* (essays, translated from the Slovenian), Nolit, Belgrade.

Petrović, Svetozar. *Kritika i djelo*, Zora, Zagreb.

COLLECTIONS AND ANTHOLOGIES

Hrvatski pjesnici izmedju dva svjetska rata (edited by Vlatko Pavletić), Nolit, Belgrade.

TRANSLATIONS OF WORKS BY YUGOSLAV AUTHORS

Ćosić, Dobrica. *Daleko je sunce*, Prague.

Lalić, Mihailo. *Hajka*, Warsaw.

Crnjanski, Miloš. *Seobe*, Warsaw, Vienna, Munich, Basel.

Maksimović, Desanka. *Miris zemlje*, Sofia.

Desnica, Vladan. *Zimsko ljetovanje*, Warsaw.

Kaleb, Vjekoslav. *Divota prašine*, Bratislava.

Koš, Erih. *Veliki Mak*, Moscow.

Šegedin, Petar. *Djeca božja*, Paris.

Bulatović, Miodrag. *Crveni petao leti prema nebu*, Paris, Amsterdam.

TRANSLATIONS OF WORKS BY FOREIGN AUTHORS

Sholokhov, Mikhail. *Sobranie Sochinenii*, Kultura, Belgrade.

Proust, Marcel. *A la recherche du temps perdu*, Državna založba Slovenije, Ljubljana.

Steinbeck, John. *Travels with Charley*, DZS, Ljubljana.

Sartre, Jean-Paul. *Les Jeux sont faits*, Obzorja, Maribor.

Moravia, Alberto. *La Ciociara*, Prešernova družba, Ljubljana.

NEW LITERARY JOURNALS AND PERIODICALS

Kolo. Periodical of the *Matica Hrvatska* for literature, art and culture, founded 1842. New series, editor-in-chief Vlatko Pavletić, Zagreb.

DECEASED

Georgi Abadžijev, Fran Albreht, Danko Andjelinović, Viktor Car Emin, Josip Pavičić, Djerdj Sabo, Stanko Tomašić, Bogomir Magajna.

ARTICLES AND POLEMICS

Stojanović, Svetozar. "Teze o našoj satiri," *Politika*, September 15.

Majstorović, Stevan. "Poslednji broj," *Danas*, February 27 (on the cessation of publication of *Danas*).

Lukić, Sveta. "Socijalistički estetizam," *Politika*, April 28.

Supek, Rudi. "Sloboda i polideterminizam u kritici kulture," *Delo*, no. 12.

Djurković, Dejan. "Proces," *Delo*, no. 12 (on the banning of the film *Grad*).

Sutlić, Vanja. "Svjetovno-povijesne pretpostavke čiste umjetnosti," *Naše teme*, no. 6.

Popović, Bruno. "Trenutak pjesme i stvarnosti života," *Forum*, no. 9.

Ristić, Marko. "12 C," *Forum*, no. 12.

Oljača, Mladen. "Zar se zaista ne razlikujemo," *Književne novine*, April 5 (viewpoint of our literary discussions).

Božović, Božidar. "Razlike ali kakve," *Književne novine*, April 19 (in response to M. Oljača's article "Zar se zaista ne razlikujemo").

Mladenović, Tanasije. "Pravo na kritiku i pravo biti kritikovan," *Književne novine*, May 5.

Kos, Janko. "Sodobna slovenska lirika," *Perspektive*, no. 29, 30, 31.

Petrić, Vladimir. "Gde se stiču prošlost i sadašnjost," *Književne novine*, November 29.

―――. "Ka obličju tradicije ili na jezgru njenom?," *Književne novine*, December 27.

"Godina zrelih ostvarenja," *Književne novine*, December 27 (a number of critics writing on the literary situation in 1963).

1964

POETRY

Maksimović, Desanka. *Tražim pomilovanje*, Matica srpska, Novi Sad.

Radović, Borislav. *Maina*, Nolit, Belgrade.

Mladenović, Tanasije. *Vetar vremena* (selected poems), Prosveta, Belgrade.

Dragojević, Danijel. *U tvom stvarnom tijelu*, Naprijed, Zagreb.

Krnjević, Vuk. *Prividjenja gospodina Proteja*, Prosveta, Belgrade

Petrović, Branislav. *Gradilište*, Prosveta, Belgrade.

Pavček, Tone. *Ujeti ocean*, Lipa, Koper (Prešern award).

Zlobec, Ciril. *Najina oaza*, Lipa, Koper (Prešern award).

PROSE

Ćopić, Branko. *Sabrana dela (I–XII)*, Prosveta, Belgrade, Svjetlost, Sarajevo.

―――. *Osma ofanziva* (novel), Prosveta, Belgrade.

Davičo, Oskar. *Tajne* (novel), Nolit, Belgrade (Nolit award).

Koš, Erih. *Imena* (novel), Branko Djonović, Belgrade.

Pavlović, Miodrag. *Igre bezimenih* (plays), Prosveta, Belgrade (October Prize).

David, Filip. *Bunar u tamnoj šumi* (short stories), Prosveta, Belgrade (Mladost award).

Čolaković, Rodoljub. *Kazivanje o jednom pokoljenju*, Naprijed, Zagreb.

Kozak, Juš. *Pavlihova kronika* (novel), Slovenska matica, Ljubljana.

Rozman, Smiljan. *Druščina* (novel), Obzorja, Maribor (Prešern Award).

Kovačić, Lojze. *Ključi mesta* (short stories), Državna založba Slovenije, Ljubljana.

Šegedin, Petar. *Orfej u maloj bašti* (short stories), Svjetlost, Sarajevo (AVNOJ and *Vjesnik* awards).

Ivanov, Blagoja. *Crveno rondo* (short stories), Kočo Racin, Skopje.

Janevski, Slavko. *I bol i bes* (novel), Kočo Racin, Skopje (11th of October Prize).

Jovanovski, Meto. *Zemja i tegoba* (novel), Kultura, Skopje.

Andreevski, Petre M. *Sedmiot den* (stories), Kultura, Skopje.

Solev, Dimitar. *Kratkata prolet na Mono Samonikov* (novel), Kultura, Skopje (11th of October Prize).

CRITIQUES AND ESSAYS

Ćosić, Dobrica. *Akcija* (notes and articles), Prosveta, Belgrade.

Bihalji-Merin, Oto. *Graditelji moderne misli u književnosti i umetnosti*, Prosveta, Belgrade.

Ristić, Marko. *Hacer tiempo* (essays), Prosveta, Belgrade.

Milošević, Nikola. *Antropološki eseji*, Nolit, Belgrade (Nolit award).

Gluščević, Zoran. *Putevi humaniteta*, Prosveta, Belgrade.

Hristić, Jovan. *Poezija i filozofija*, Matica srpska, Novi Sad.

Palavestra, Predrag, *Književnost Mlade Bosne*, Veselin Masleša, Sarajevo.

Škreb-Flaker. *Stilovi i razdoblja*, Naprijed, Zagreb.

Ladan, Tomislav. *Razmišljanja* (essays), Naprijed, Zagreb (Zagreb May Award).

COLLECTIONS AND ANTHOLOGIES

Krležin zbornik (edited by Frangeš and Flaker), Naprijed, Zagreb.

Antologija srpskog pesništva od 13–20, veka (compiled by Miodrag Pavlović), SKZ, Belgrade.

Srpska i hrvatska poezija XX veka (compiled by P. Palavestra), Savremena škola, Belgrade.

TRANSLATIONS OF WORKS BY YUGOSLAV AUTHORS

Ćopić, Branko. *Prolom*, Berlin.

Marinković, Ranko. *Ruke*, Stockholm.

Bulatović, Miodrag. *Crveni petao leti prema nebu*, Tel Aviv, Bratislava, Amsterdam, Warsaw, Paris.

Smole, Dominik. *Antigona*, Bratislava.

Šopov, Aco. *Izbor stihova*, Moscow.

TRANSLATIONS OF WORKS BY FOREIGN AUTHORS

O'Neill, Eugene. *Long Day's Journey into Night*, Rad, Belgrade.

Savremeni ruski pisci, I–IV (Aleksandar Flaker), Naprijed, Zagreb (Zagreb award).

Steinbeck, John. *The Red Pony*, Obzorja, Maribor.

Hemingway, Ernest. *The Sun Also Rises*, Obzorja, Maribor.

Sartre, Jean-Paul. *La Nausée*, Cankarjeva založba, Ljubljana.

Miller, Arthur. *The Crucible*, Mladinska knjiga, Ljubljana.

Gide, André. *Les Faux monnayeurs*, Državna založba Slovenije, Ljubljana.

Wolfe, Thomas. *You Can't Go Home Again* (I–II), Progres, Novi Sad.

———. *Of Time and the River* (I–II), Državna založba Slovenije, Ljubljana.

Camus, Albert. *L'Étranger*, Kultura, Skopje.

Faulkner, William. *Intruder in the Dust*, Kočo Racin, Skopje.

Sartre, Jean-Paul. *L'Existentialisme est un humananisme*, Veselin Masleša, Sarajevo.

LITERARY CONGRESSES AND PLENARY MEETINGS

7th Congress of Yugoslav Writers' Union, Titograd, September 24–26 (discussion of the topic "The Worker and His Place in Our Society").

DECEASED

Milan Bogdanović, Juš Kozak, Slavko Kolar, Petar Slijepćević, Jože Pahor.

ARTICLES AND POLEMICS

Simpozji o kritici. (Symposium on Criticism). Participants: Brune Popović, Jovan Hristić, Vjeran Župa, Sveta Lukić, Taras Kermauner, Tomislav Ladan, Pavle Zorić, Miroslav Egerić, *Razlog*, no. 4.

Selimović, Meša. "Životna i umjetnička činjenica," *Izraz*, no. 1.

Ćosić, Dobrica. "Predlozi za razgovor o smislu i razlozima angažovanja danas, ili kako vršiti 'poziv čoveka', kako stvarati danas" (lecture to the students and faculty of the University of Belgrade, sponsored by *Javnost*, April 9, 1964), *Gledišta*, no. 5.

"O 'Predlozima za razgovor o smislu i razlozima angažovanja danas' Dobrice Ćosića," *Gledišta*, no. 6–7; discussants: Svetozar Stojanović, Nikola Milošević, Mladen Čaldarević, Nikša Stipčevic, Raša Popov, Marko Ristić, Miloš Stambolić, Milojko Drulović, Sveta Lukić, Oskar Davičo, Žika Berisavljević, Ljuba Tadić, Jagoš Djuretić, Kosara Pavlović, Dobrica Ćosić.

Jeremić, Dragan M. "Filozofske koncepcije savremene jugoslovenske književnosti," *Izraz*, no. 2.

"Kritičari o književnoj situaciji 1964 godine," *Književne novine*, December 25.

Šolar, Milivoj. "Moderni roman i moderna znanost," *Razlog*, no. 8.

Mirić, Milan. "Pisac i društvo," *Razlog*, no. 7 (on the discussions held at the 7th Congress of the Yugoslav Writers' Union).

Cvitan, Dalibor. "Suvremena hrvatska poezija," *Forum*, no. 11.

1965

POETRY

Dedinac, Milan. *Poziv na putovanje* (selected poems), Prosveta, Belgrade.

Bećković, Matija. *Tako je govorio Matija*, Prosveta, Belgrade.

Krmpotić, Vesna. *Jama bića*, Nolit, Belgrade.

Djuzel, Bogomil. *Mironosnici*, Kultura, Skopje.

Perović, Sreten. *Prepoznavanje vremena*, Grafički zavod, Titograd.

PROSE

Marinković, Ranko. *Kiklop* (novel), Prosveta, Belgrade(NIN, Zmaj and Goran awards).

Kiš, Danilo. *Bašta, pepeo* (novel), Prosveta, Belgrade.

Pekić, Borislav. *Vreme čuda* (story), Prosveta, Belgrade.

Smiljanić, Radomir, *Martinov izlazak* (novel), Otokar Keršovani, Rijeka (1st Prize of *Telegram*).

Bulatović Vib, Vlada. *Menjačnica ideala* (satire), Kultura, Belgrade.

Lukić, Velimir. *Farse*, Prosveta, Belgrade.

Majdak, Zvonimir. *Mladić* (novel), Mladost, Zagreb.

Urošević, Vlada. *Vkusot na praskite* (stories), Kultura, Skopje.

Pendovski, Branko. *Skali* (novel), Kultura, Skopje.

CRITIQUES AND ESSAYS

Ćosić, Dobrica. *Akcija*, Prosveta, Belgrade.

Jeremić, Dragan. *Prsti nevernog Tome* (essays), Nolit, Belgrade.

Džadžić, Petar. *Branko Miljković ili neukrotiva reč*, Prosveta, Belgrade (Belgrade October Prize).

Milošević, Nikola. *Negativni junak* (essays), Vuk Karadžić, Belgrade.

Šoljan, Antun. *Trogodišnja kronika poezije hrvatske i srpske*, Naprijed, Zagreb.

Mejak, Mitja. *Književna kronika 1962–1965*, Obzorja, Maribor (Prešern award).

COLLECTIONS AND ANTHOLOGIES

Panorama hrvatske književnosti XX stoljeća (compiled by V. Pavletić), Stvarnost, Zagreb.

TRANSLATIONS OF WORKS BY YUGOSLAV AUTHORS

Ćosić, Dobrica. *Daleko je sunce*, Helsinki.

Lalić, Mihailo. *Lelejska gora*, Bratislava, Prague, Sofia, New York.

Koš, Erih. *Veliki Mak*, Hamburg.

Kaleb, Vjekoslav. *Divota prašine*, Berlin.

Oljača, Mladen. *Molitva za moju braću*, Milan, Paris.

Bulatović, Miodrag. *Heroj na magarcu*, Munich, Paris.

TRANSLATIONS OF WORKS BY FOREIGN AUTHORS

Proust, Marcel. *A la recherche du temps perdu* (I–VIII), Zora, Zagreb.

Gide, André. *Les Caves du Vatican*, Cankarjeva založba, Ljubljana.

Breton, André. Poems, Bagdala, Kruševac.

Steinbeck, John. *Cannery Row*, Mladinska knjiga, Ljubljana.

Moravia, Alberto. *L'Amor Coniugale*, DKZ, Ljubljana.

Hemingway, Ernest. *To Have and Have Not*, Obzorja, Maribor.

CONGRESSES AND PLENARY MEETINGS

Extraordinary Congress of the Yugoslav Writers' Union, Belgrade, December 21–22, 1965 (20th anniversary of the union). Discussion of the topic: the writer, his work and society and the introduction of the new statutes of the Writers' Union.

DECEASED

Anton Vodnik, Stale Popov.

ARTICLES AND POLEMICS

Vlahović, Veljko. "Stvaralac i društvo," *Književne novine*, July 24 (from a speech given July 8).

Mihajlov, Mihajlo. "Ljeto moskovsko 1964 (I–II)," *Delo*, no. 1, 2.

"Objašnjenje redakcije," *Delo*, no. 3 (on the banning of the February issue of *Delo* because of the publication of M. Mihajlov's article).

Bogićević, Miodrag. "Mistika jednog hroničara," *Komunist*, February 11 (on Mihajlo Mihajlov's "Ljeto moskovsko 1964").

"Čudno letovanje Mihajla Mihajlova," *NIN*, February 28.

Lukić, Sveta. "Tokovi i struje u našoj današnjoj literaturi," *Delo*, no. 8–9.

"Tokovi i struje u savremenoj jugoslovenskoj literaturi" (discussion by the editorial board of *Delo*); participants: Miloš I. Bandić, Petar Džadžić, Miroslav Egerić, Zoran Gluščević, Vuk Krnjević, Sveta Lukić, Dušan Matić, Milosav Mirković, Miodrag Pavlović, Muharem Pervić, Raša Popov, Slobodan Selenić, Živorad Stojković, Aleksandar Vučo, Božo Vukadinović; *Delo*, no. 11.

Lukić, Sveta. "Naše književne raspre (I–III)," *Borba*, June 27, July 4 and 11.

Gotovac, Vlado. "Pjesništvo i čovjekovo podneblje," *Razlog*, no. 7–8.

Diskusija na temu "Dilemite na pisatelot pred socijalističkata stvarnost"; participants: Milan Djurčinov, Slobodan Micković, Tome Momirovski, Meto Jovanovski, Vasilj Iljoski, Boško Smanovski, Petre Andreevski, Petar Sirilov, Ante Popovski, Aco Šopov, Gorgi Stardelov; *Sovremenost*, no. 4.

Stardelov, Gorgi. "Povik za edna nova literarna konfrontacija – nacrt za edna kritika na našiot literaturen panartizam," *Sovremenost*, no. 3.

Solev, Dimitar, "Situacija 1965," *Razgledi*, no. 1.

———. "Kritika vo nedoumica," *Razgledi*, no. 6.

Mitrev, Dimitar. "Pomeg'u situaciji i realizacii," *Sovremenost*, no. 9 (polemic with D. Solev).

Ćosić, Dobrica. "Naš društveni i književni trenutak," *Delo*, no. 7.

Damnjanović, Milan. "'Sociološki ekvivalent' umetničke vrednosti," *Književne novine*, April 3.

"Protiv kabadahiluka," *Književne novine*, May 15 (on Oskar Davičo's interview in *Jedinstvo*, May 1, 1965).

"Izjava upravnog odbora Srpske književne zadruge," *Književne novine*, June 12 (on Oskar Davičo's interview in *Jedinstvo*).

Lukić, Velimir. "Lako je nama koji smo na vlasti, a teško Oskaru koji nije," *Književne novine*, May 29 (on O. Davičo's interview).

Ristić, Marko. "O jednoj antologiji opet," *Forum*, no. 3 (on M. Pavlović's anthology of Serbian poetry).

Golob, Zvonimir. "Mogućnosti i granice kritike," *Forum*, no. 1–2.

Gotovac, Vlado. "O napadima na 'Razlog'," *Razlog*, no. 38–40 (on *Večernji lists*'s, *VUS*'s and *Telegram*'s attacks on *Razlog*).

Župa, Vjeran. "Pjesnik i sloboda," *Razlog*, no. 35 (on the poetry of Branko Miljković).

————. "Kako je Ladan očitao lekciju Sartru," *Razlog*, no. 37 (on T. Ladan's interview in *Odjek*, August 1).

Palavestra, Predrag. "Ko je tražio djavola," *Književne novine*, November 27 (in connection with the discussion on trends and currents in contemporary Yugoslav literature in *Delo*).

Zorić, Pavle. "Teroristička književnost," *Književne novine*, December 11 (on the appearance of new groups and on the impatience of literary circles).

GLOSSARY
OF LITERARY TERMS

društvo — society
država — the state
državni — state (adj.)
estetika — aesthetics
Hrvatska — Croatia, Croatian
izabran, -a, -o — selected
izdanje — edition
knjiga — book
književni, -a, -o — literary
književnik — writer
književnost — literature
kritičar — critic
kritika — critique, criticism
Madjar — member of the Hungarian
  minority of Voyvodina
mlad, -a, -o — young
nadrealizam — surrealism
naš, -a, -e — our
nov, -a, -o — new
novine — newspaper
pesma — poem
pesnik — poet
pisac — author
poezija — poetry
priča — story
proza — prose
publika — public
roman — novel
savez — association, union

savremen, -a, -o — contemporary
Šiptar — member of the Albanian
  minority in Yugoslavia
škola — school
Slovenska — Slovenian
Srpska — Serbian
teorija — theory
star, -a, -o — old
umetnost, umjetnost — art
vreme — time

PERIODICALS

Beseda — The Word
Borba — The Struggle
Delo — Opus
Književne novine — Literary Gazette
Krugovi — Circles
Mladost — Youth
Nova misao — New Thought
Pečat — Seal
Perspektive — Perspectives
Politika — Politics
Razgledi — Views
Savremenik — Contemporary Man
Sovremenost — The Contemporary
  Scene
Svedočanstva — Testimonies, Proofs
Tribina Mladih — Forum of the
  Young

INDEX